Rebel at Large  **W9-BNS-143**

DATE DUE

SEP 11 2012	

LIBRARY OF CONGRESS CATALOGUING-IN-PUBLICATION DATA

Van Buskirk, Philip (Philip Clayton), 1833–1903.
    Rebel at large : the diary of Confederate deserter Philip Van
Buskirk / edited and with an introduction by B. R. Burg.
        p.   cm.
    Includes bibliographical references and index.

    ISBN 978-0-7864-4293-5
    softcover : 50# alkaline paper ∞

    1. Van Buskirk, Philip C. (Philip Clayton), 1833–1903 —
Diaries.   2. Soldiers — Confederate States of America — Diaries.
3. Military deserters — Confederate States of America — Diaries.
4. United States — History — Civil War, 1861–1865 — Personal
narratives, Confederate.   5. Confederate States of America.
Army. Virginia Infantry Regiment, 13th — Biography.
6. Prisoners of war — United States — Diaries.   7. United States —
History — Civil War, 1861–1865 — Prisoners and prisons.
8. United States — History — Civil War, 1861–1865 — Social
aspects.   9. Civil-military relations — United States — History —
19th century.   I. Burg, B. R. (Barry Richard), 1938–
II. Title.
E605.V29   2009
973.7'82 — dc22   2009023846

British Library cataloguing data are available

Cover images ©2009 Photos.com; ©2009 Shutterstock.

Manufactured in the United States of America

McFarland & Company, Inc., Publishers
    Box 611, Jefferson, North Carolina 28640
        www.mcfarlandpub.com

For Judy Marie Shelton-Burg

Acknowledgments

In undertaking any historical editing project, one relies of necessity on the skills and knowledge of mentors, colleagues, and friends. Mentioning their names on an acknowledgments page hardly seems thanks enough for their contributions. Still, it is often the only way most of them can be repaid for their assistance and encouragement. My most profound debts are owed to Lyman H. Butterfield and Mark Friedlaender, two of America's premier documentary editors. The year I spent under their tutelage at *The Adams Papers* was one of the most extraordinary and inspiring of my life.

My next debt is to John R. Frisch, who first told me of the existence of Philip Van Buskirk's diary. He allowed me to borrow his copy of the earliest surviving volume to find out if it was of any interest to me. Obviously it was. Others who have helped along the way are Dorothy Rapp, who provided information on the West Point career of Philip's father; Thomas Reider and Elizabeth L. Plummer, both of the Ohio Historical Society; and Greg Carroll at the West Virginia Division of Archives and History. Steve Cunningham of the West Virginia Book Company also deserves my gratitude. He lent a hand solving a particularly knotty problem. Civil War specialists who have given freely of their time and advice are Brooks Simpson and Peter Lysy.

Grants for travel and microfilming were provided by the National Endowment for the Humanities and Arizona State University. Other institutions that have been generous in their support of my work with Van Buskirk and his diary are the Marine Historical Center, the National Archives, Georgetown University, and the United States Naval Academy. The staff of the University of Washington's Allen Library have been particularly supportive over the years, providing me first with hospitality and advice, and later with film and photographs to speed my work. Robert D.

Acknowledgments

Monroe allowed me to use his partial typescript of a missing diary volume covering Van Buskirk's participation in Commodore Matthew C. Perry's first voyage to Japan. Karyl Winn and Janet Ness made my stay at the University of Washington pleasant and fruitful. Beth Luey, Carla Rickerson, and James Stack provided vital assistance when needed to get the publication of the diary underway. An NEH/ASHP seminar at Washington State University, under the direction of Susan Kilgore, helped me refine my techniques for electronic searching. The Interlibrary Loan Service of Hayden Library at Arizona State University labored long and hard for me. Without their support, I could never have completed this project.

The last to whom I would like to give thanks, of course, is Philip C. Van Buskirk. We have been companions for some time now, and I would like him to know how much I have enjoyed looking over his shoulder as he recorded his life. I hope he would approve of my editing his wartime diary.

Contents

chronicle he kept.[1] It was donated to the University of Washington in Seattle, along with the other volumes of the diary, by his heirs shortly after his death.[2]

The initial volume of the Civil War diary that Van Buskirk kept from early 1861 to the spring of 1862 cannot now be located. It was taken from him when he was captured by Union forces in May of 1862, and never returned despite his best efforts to retrieve it. At one point he tried to resurrect the missing entries from January of 1861 to the spring of 1862 — and to include events remembered from June to December of 1862 as well — on blank pages in the back of an earlier volume. He worked largely from memory although there is some indication he may have had an itinerary to help him with dates and locations. In any case, he put little effort into the project. Many pages in the reconstitution are headed with the names of months, but are entirely blank. It is obvious even for the months where entries were made that there was much he did not recall.[3] The few, half-hearted scribbles that resulted from the attempt to recreate the first volume and to record imperfectly remembered events for the second half of 1862 are here included in a short section immediately preceding the 1863–1865 entries.

The surviving volume of the diary that covers the period from 1863 to the end of 1865 was copied by Van Buskirk in 1890 from pocket-sized notebooks containing the original entries.[4] The copy was then professionally bound for preservation and protection, and the notebooks were discarded. It is likely that the 1890 version is an exceedingly accurate rendition of his 1863–1865 notebooks. Material he copied into other volumes from newspapers and government documents can be correlated with the original sources in numerous cases, and the comparisons reveal him to be a meticulous and scrupulously accurate copyist.[5]

Van Buskirk frequently exercised creative license in his penmanship. He used different forms and styles as it suited him for major and minor headings. No attempt has been made to imitate these variations in the printed edition of the diary. The diary's erratic capitalization has been modernized, and some changes to the punctuation and paragraphing have been made in the interest of clarity or to compensate for the unavoidable differences in appearance between manuscript and print format. Slips of the pen have been silently corrected. The names of ships and titles of books have been italicized, although it was Van Buskirk's habit to enclose them in quotation marks. All other italics as well as underscores and crossed-

out words are those he included in the diary text. Entries written verti-
cally from top to bottom down the page, perpendicular to the horizontal
text and sometimes directly over it, are reproduced immediately after the
text next to or over which they were written. It was Van Buskirk's regular
practice to compile lists of people he met and places he stayed overnight
along with summaries of his monthly entries, graphs charting his moods,
and some of his activities. These lists, summaries, and graphs duplicate
material in the regular diary entries and are not included in the printed
version of the diary. The layouts of several personal letters reproduced in
the diary have been slightly altered for clarity and convenience. Citations
to the diary are usually by volume number and entry date. Undated items
are cited by volume number and by brief descriptions of their locations
within the volumes in which they are contained.

Introduction

Philip C. Van Buskirk described his life each day as he lived it, and was rarely inclined to reflect or reminisce. Still, enough bits and pieces of information about his ancestry and childhood are scattered throughout the dozens of his diary volumes to produce a fragmented narrative of his family history and early life.[1] William Van Buskirk, Philip's father, entered West Point in 1819, but left two years later for unknown reasons.[2] The son was once told that the elder Van Buskirk was expelled along with dozens of his classmates for attempting to blow up a faculty member who struck one of their number, but nothing in the academy's archives suggest he was dismissed, nor is there evidence a large number of students were expelled in 1821 or 1822.[3] The only record of William's departure is his resignation from West Point on December 31, 1821. Some time later, the former cadet married Ora Moore, a childhood friend. Their first son, Philip, was born on March 4, 1833, at Charles Town, Virginia.

William Van Buskirk eventually entered the legal profession. The son later claimed his father was a respected member of the bar, but added that this was not a universally accepted opinion. Despite the note of caution, lawyer Van Buskirk was an able man. He was elected to the Maryland legislature in Annapolis, and while there he served on several committees, was once nominated to be colonel of the Fiftieth Regiment of Maryland militia, and ultimately became Maryland's secretary of state.

Things seemed to be going well for the Van Buskirks in the 1840s, but behind the imposing facade of their large, three-story house on Green Street not far from the state capital there were difficulties. The relationship between the father and his small son was often hostile. Late in 1844, Philip ran away from home following a dispute over his pet squirrel. He fled westward, working as a toll gatherer, a cook's helper on a river steamer, and at several other menial jobs. His sojourn ended in Cumberland, Maryland, where the family had lived before moving to Annapolis. There, 150 miles from home, the louse-infested runaway survived the winter of 1844-1845 at a wagoners' inn. It was at the inn that young Van Buskirk, scarcely ten or eleven years old, had his first sexual experience. He later wrote in his diary that a local "loafer" offered him a penny to come to a nearby barn and help him with an unnamed task. There, where the two were hidden away, the man induced the boy to masturbate him. At the time, young Van Buskirk had no idea what the entire business was about. He and the loafer did not repeat the encounter, and the boy went away from the experience puzzled rather than enlightened. As he explained, it never occurred to him to do "it" upon himself.

There is no information on his return home to Annapolis in the spring, but by March he was enrolled at Georgetown College in Washington, D.C. The school's records show a payment of $150 for his tuition, and later another two dollars was paid for music tutoring. At the time of Van Buskirk's enrollment, the college was hardly more than a preparatory school. Only about twenty-five percent of the less-than-two-hundred-member student body were enrolled in the advanced classes. The boys in the junior division were exposed to a standard curriculum, which included instruction in religion, the classics, mathematics, poetry, rhetoric, and several additional subjects. Van Buskirk paid $2.50 for a Latin dictionary and $1.25 for his geography text and a Bible. The remainder of his books were all under half a dollar. The smallest outlay was for a catechism. It cost 6¼ cents. The schoolbooks he listed by name were *Vivi Roma* and *Historia Sacra*. The others were recorded only by subjects and purchase prices. The daily routine at Georgetown, as might be expected at a Jesuit school, ran with military precision. Mass, classes, prayers, and meals adhered to a tight schedule. Student sojourns into Washington were forbidden without faculty chaperones, and all outgoing and incoming mail, even that from family and friends, was censored.

While at Georgetown, Van Buskirk required a good deal of apparel to keep himself socially acceptable. The college ledger shows that he purchased numerous wardrobe items during his tenure, including boots, suspenders, socks, a jacket, gloves, and caps. He also bought toiletries and postage stamps for his letters home. Still, while adequately garbed and provided for, he made do with less than many of the students. He complained that his funds were too limited to allow him to purchase circus and concert tickets, nor was he able to buy a leghorn hat or a frock coat like those worn by many of his school fellows. Although young Philip was suitably accoutered, the college's records indicate something was amiss. He was listed as the son of William Van Buskirk, but the entry contained the additional information that he was the ward of a Dr. Samuel Semmes. In fact the family was plagued by financial difficulties despite its apparent prosperity, which explains why Philip's $150 tuition was paid by Semmes rather than his father.[4]

Philip frittered away an entire year at Georgetown, getting on well enough with other students, but rarely attending to his books. Meanwhile, William Van Buskirk, by this time hopelessly in debt, went to the courthouse in Annapolis in June of 1845, placed the butt of a muzzle-loading rifle on the floor and used its ramrod to trip the trigger, firing a ball between his eyes and into his brain. A note addressed to Dr. Semmes was found in the dead man's hat. It instructed him to inform the family of the suicide.

When Philip withdrew from Georgetown the next year, Semmes paid his outstanding charges. He later enrolled at St. John's College in Annapolis, but was no more attentive to his studies there than he had been at Georgetown. He and a close friend earned the distinction of being at the bottom of their class.

In the journals he kept over the years Van Buskirk rarely harkened back to his childhood, but the few recollections he set down were consistently negative. He recorded the names of three boys who bullied him in 1843 many years after the incident took place. A fellow student, a nephew of President James K. Polk, once stuffed his own boots with paper to make himself taller and gain a place ahead of Van Buskirk in a school line. Four decades later he was still angry enough over being humiliated in such a fashion to write about it. Family members scarcely fared better in the diary than the lads who bested him. From time to time he wrote of the suicide, brooded over whether someday he would be able to retire his father's debts, and lamented that the elder Van Buskirk was a cold, distant man who was kind to others but showed no affection to his son. Philip claimed he was very much an unloved child. He hardly knew his brother, who rated no more than a single mention in the diary. William Eckert Van Buskirk was much younger than Philip and died as a child. The one family member who earned Philip's genuine ire was his mother. He blamed her for forcing his father into suicide, and wrote disparagingly of her perverse character and unsuitability as a parent. The complaints against her were most often of a general sort, but the diary does include an incident highlighting her ineptitude. According to Van Buskirk, somewhere around the time he was ten or twelve, his mother made what he characterized as an "indecent" remark about his brother. He did not record the comment, but said it provoked the first libidinous thought he ever experienced. Later he decided whatever she had said was not harmful. It was only because of his sensitive nature that he was offended.[5]

Ora Van Buskirk's financial situation deteriorated further after her husband's suicide, and her son was exhibiting no more academic aptitude at St. Johns' than he had shown at Georgetown. She decided something must be done to mitigate both of these misfortunes. She journeyed to Washington, D.C., with Philip, and on June 1, 1846, enlisted him for an eight-year term of service as a drummer boy in the United States Marines.

The newly-minted Marine was first read the regulations on mutiny and desertion, then assigned to the corps' headquarters barracks at the intersection of Eighth and I streets, SE, in Washington, where he was quartered in a large room set aside for music boys. Marine Corps records describe the recruit as having gray eyes, fair hair, and a light complexion. No one wrote down his height, which makes it impossible to discover his pay grade. Youngsters were placed into three different classifications on the basis of age, height and qualifications, and paid accordingly. The rates ranged from five to seven dollars per month. No matter what category boys were assigned, their disposable income was far less than their official salaries. They were allowed to send money home, but the sum rarely amounted to more than one dollar per month. Another dollar was deducted and put into a savings plan. The accumulated funds were then returned to their owners at the end of their enlistments or when they reached their majority. The schoolmaster received a dollar per month from each of his charges, and seventy-five cents was deducted for the washerwoman. This meant young recruits who actually sent a monthly dollar to their families had between $1.25 and $3.25 of disposable income. The money the boys retained was customarily spent on beer and sweets.[6]

During Philip's six months of training, while he lived with the other student drummers and fifers, he shared with them the fear and loneliness that only children can know when first separated from their parents. He also learned much about the ways of the world while assigned to the music room, and was appalled by what he described as the depravity of his comrades. Although he had once engaged in masturbation when a runaway in

Cumberland, Maryland, that single experience hardly prepared him for what he observed in the Marine Corps. Some of the boys masturbated openly and the others learned from their example, but all of the instruction did not come from peers. For a short time a battalion of volunteers for the Mexican War was quartered with the young musicians, and one of them, a man identified only as "Rio Grande," held forth to a rapt audience of juveniles about sexual matters generally and about *"doing it for yourself."* Not only did Rio Grande provide information to the boys, he instructed them on technique. Van Buskirk was disgusted by what he called the demonstrations of "self-abuse," and did not become a regular masturbator while he trained to be a drummer.

After his instruction was complete, young Philip was assigned a regular round of duties, beating drum calls and doing guard duty. In the summer of 1847, a year after enlisting, he received his first assignment at sea on board the forty-four-gun U.S.S. *Cumberland,* then about to sail off to the war against Mexico. Most of the fighting was over by November of 1847 when the ship anchored off Vera Cruz to become part of the United States Navy's coastal blockading force. The days passed slowly for the musician during that winter and through the spring of 1848. He beat drum calls, chatted with other sailors and Marines, wrote in the diary he had begun keeping, went ashore from time to time, and once managed to commit an unspecified breach of regulations that almost earned him a flogging.

In June of 1848, the United States Senate ratified the Treaty of Guadalupe Hidalgo ending the war, the *Cumberland* returned home, and Philip Van Buskirk was assigned to the Pensacola Navy Yard, a major supply base for American ships operating in the Caribbean. While at the navy yard, Van Buskirk began to masturbate frequently. The causes of what he styled as "self-abuse" might have been the result of his physical maturation and the greater degree of privacy available to him, but the rampant sexuality of his environment was probably a contributing factor. He described his fellow Marines at Pensacola as "abandoned" characters who engaged in the grossest of conversations. He reproached himself for masturbating, but despite his efforts to stop, his indulgences grew more and more frequent, along with his spermatorrhea — as nocturnal emission was generally known in the nineteenth century. According to leading medical authorities, the root cause of spermatorrhea was masturbation, and it was an epidemic among America's young men. Those afflicted experienced not only nocturnal emission, but suffered from listlessness, sterility, assorted pains, acne, poor posture, sagging jaws, hollow eyes, troubled gait, penile flaccidity, and an additional host of symptoms.[7] Desperate to restrain himself, overwhelmed with guilt, and frantically hoping to find a cure, Van Buskirk began poring over the substantial literature available on his sickness. The first of the works he read, a tract entitled *Self-Preservation*, did not diminish his urges but imbued him more deeply with notions of the sin and destructiveness of the "solitary vice." Other readings terrorized him with the certain results of his now firmly established habit. Alfred Stillé's *Elements of General Pathology* taught him that masturbation would cause twitching, involuntary ejaculation, and a permanently shrunken penis. From Anthelme Balthasar Richerand's *Elements of Physiology* he learned of the shepherd who, after a course of activity that involved over a dozen masturbations per day, fell into convulsions and began to emit blood rather than semen. The pages that he ripped out from a borrowed copy of Dr. William Young's *Pocket Aesculapius* before returning it to its owner provided warnings equally dire. "Physicians of all ages," according to the passage Van Buskirk copied from Young into his diary, "have been unanimously of the opinion that the loss of one ounce of this fluid (semen), by the unnatural act of self-pollution, or nocturnal emissions, weakens the system more completely than the abstraction of forty ounces of blood." Other books Van Buskirk read were L. D. Fleming's *Self-Pollution: The Cause of Youthful Decay* and Leopold Deslandes' *Manhood: The Cause and Cure of Premature Decline with Directions for Its Perfect Restoration*. The drummer wrote with eloquence when he expounded on the solitary vice in the pages of his diary. His usual daily entries were as bland as might be expected from any young man devoid of literary talent. But when he cataloged the evils of masturbation, he wrote with passion. It was not merely the subject that sent his prose soaring. His diary notations were paraphrased from the melodramatic, anti-masturbatory tracts he read in the hope of curing his addiction. Amid the flow of baroque rhetoric, Van Buskirk made it clear he knew what fate awaited him. Every learned author provided a litany of what would befall masturbators. They would suffer from symptoms that ranged from acne and blindness to spermatorrhea and death at a young age. The only solution was to stop, but it was difficult to do at a place like Pensacola, where the enlisted men at the post were a nasty, degraded lot wallowing in dissipation.[8]

The officers were even worse in Van Buskirk's opinion than the men they commanded, and they apparently reciprocated his feelings. After only a short time at his new assignment he acquired a reputation among his superiors as a rascally fellow, and his antics earned him a six-week stay in the brig. While confined, the drummer plotted revenge. He would desert, he decided, and in the process be rid of military discipline as well as the debts he had contracted over the preceding few months. On July 11, 1849, he was ordered to carry the navy yard mail into the town of Pensacola. He never returned. With several dollars in savings, a dollar donated by a friend who knew of his plan, and a purloined fifty cents, he absconded from the United States Marine Corps.

Van Buskirk wandered about the southern states for the next year and a half. He worked as a casual laborer, was once fired for incompetence from the post of clerk at a military academy, swindled boarding house keepers out of their rent, cheated a wagoner of his fare, and left a debt for new clothes, cigars, and a cigar case to a small group of people who were unfortunate enough to have set him up in business as a tobacconist. By March of 1851, he was in western Virginia with his mother, who had somehow managed to acquire a small farm near Charles Town. His tasks included tending pigs and chickens, planting vegetables, and helping Isaac, his mother's ancient slave, with the chores.

The month after his return to Virginia, Van Buskirk traveled to Washington, D.C., to obtain a discharge from the Marine Corps. Before he departed, his mother gave him a sum of money. It is unclear whether it was to help obtain the discharge, to make purchases for the farm, or for some other use. The money never went for its intended purpose. Van Buskirk squandered it in the city, and rather than face his mother's rage, he reenlisted in the Marines. On June 18, 1851, he and fifer William McFarland boarded the U.S.S. *Plymouth*, a massively-armed sloop of war then making ready to join the navy's East India Squadron operating off the China coast.[9]

Shortly after arriving in Hong Kong, the ship was dispatched to Shanghai at the request of United States commissioner Humphrey Marshall to protect American mercantile interests from anti-foreign elements. The fears of Westerners in China were exaggerated, although not entirely baseless, but Van Buskirk evidently had little concern for whatever dangers might await foreigners in the city. Instead, he reveled in the role of tourist. Unlike his fellow sailors and Marines who spent their brief periods ashore in riotous excess, drunk and whoring about, Van Buskirk took in the sights. He wandered city lanes and country roads, visiting temples, mosques, cemeteries, festivals or musical performances, and generally absorbing the exotic ambience. In Shanghai he made the acquaintance of local leaders of the Taiping rebels, visited their homes, donned their regalia from time to time for his meanderings, and stole small items of military gear from his ship to give them as gifts. Cribbing percussion caps from the *Plymouth* was justified, he probably reasoned, because he knew of a lieutenant from the U.S.S. *Saratoga* who was pilfering caps from his ship and providing them to the Tiapings in far larger quantities than a mere drummer could carry off. He once took a Chinese acquaintance's pistol on board the *Plymouth* to have the ship's armorer repair it for the owner. The Chinese he knew reciprocated with tea and sweets, and by sharing an occasional opium pipe with him.

Although Van Buskirk enjoyed the hospitality of ranking Tiapings, his greatest pleasure in wandering about Shanghai and its environs was meeting with small children, whose acquaintance he procured not with gear pilfered from his ship but with sweets and fruit he bestowed upon them.[10] It was a pattern of behavior well-established by 1854. He could at will assemble a gaggle of children in any Asian port by distributing treats. He frequently wrote of how their purity improved his own spirits. There is no indication at this stage of his life, his late teens, that his partiality toward the little boys and girls he gathered around him was any more than avuncular, but this was about to change. In due course his interests became more focused on handsome lads, usually those who served on board United States Navy ships. He expressed no particular preferences for eye or hair color, but from the physical perfection of those he selected for his attentions Van Buskirk divined purity of character. The explications he read on masturbation and genuine manhood had been clear. Evil and ugliness were intertwined in the physiognomy of onanists. Their volcanic, acne-ridden faces, their shaking hands, and their shambling, shuffling steps signaled their descent into perdition. His loves all were handsome, and thus radiated purity.[11]

Van Buskirk's first serious infatuation was with one of his fellow Marines, a lad named George Schultz, who also served with the East India Squadron. In 1852 George was on board the *Saratoga*, a ship that was often in port with the *Plymouth*. The diarist wrote frequently of the youngster, and once recorded how he dressed himself in the best of borrowed clothing for a meeting with him. A description of Schultz in the diary left no doubt Van Buskirk was smitten. George was a "genius of a young boy of twelve summers, good build, and size not exceeding four feet." He plied him with mandarin oranges and small items of clothing in return for Schultz's sitting on his lap or promising to learn to read and write. Someday, he mused, he would plant a magnificent orchard and name one of the trees after Schultz. Van Buskirk was also attracted to the *Saratoga*'s fifer, whom he identified only as Mintz, but there was no doubt which of the two musicians he preferred. Mintz, after all, lacked the boyish innocence of Schultz. He was bright and well-built, but he was five years older and six inches taller than Van Buskirk. He also had a wife. There is no evidence either of the *Saratoga*'s musicians felt any attraction to the *Plymouth*'s drummer. In fact, from the diary entries it appears neither of them cared for his company. Still, despite their conspicuous disinterest, Van Buskirk's infatuation did not slacken. Schultz was his first abiding love in the years he served on the China coast.[12]

Although he focused his attention on George Schultz in the early 1850s, Schultz was not the only boy who appeared often in the drummer's thoughts and on his diary pages. Van Buskirk wrote from time to time of an old chum named Roderick Masson and several other lads he met during his days as a schoolboy or during his wanderings after deserting from Pensacola. There is no indication any of these relationships included a physical component. Anguished entries in the diary during his service with the East India Squadron make it clear that those to whom Van Buskirk offered his love never reciprocated his feelings. Most often they found him a tedious and disgusting fellow, hardly worthy of their friendship let alone any sort of more abiding relationship. It was a situation that would encounter throughout his life.[13]

The infatuation with George Schultz did not outlast 1852. Not only were Van Buskirk's feelings continually discouraged by the object of his love, but he soon discovered there were other attractions. The East India Squadron's ships carried a gaggle of boys, a good number of whom were handsome enough to catch the drummer's eye. Over the next two years he went through a string of temporary infatuations. One transitory love object was a fifer on another ship. A second was identified only as Caravallo, a Portuguese boy who spoke no English. When young James Keenan attracted his attention, he gave him enough money for cakes and oranges in the morning and evening for a time. He dreamed often of the two music boys on board the U.S.S. *Macedonian*, Jared Mundell and William Dagenhart, a pair whose friendship he actively sought. Befriending them was an expensive process. He once ordered boxes with engraved plates for the two from a Chinese artisan. Mundell's cost $2.00 and Dagenhart's $1.50, a considerable sum for a Marine musician. He then filled their boxes with gifts — knives, pencils, coins, silk handkerchiefs, mirrors, and other small items. The boxes were sewn into canvas bags and sent to them on board the *Macedonian*. Van Buskirk did not limit himself entirely to ship's boys. While wandering ashore in Shanghai in the late spring of 1854, he passed a French guardhouse where a comely lad asked him in for a drink of wine.[14] While there, another boy at the post attracted the American's attention, and he invited him to visit the *Plymouth*. The meeting was set for the next Tuesday, and Van Buskirk went to work, feverishly polishing his rudimentary French language skills. He also expended considerable energy on his teeth, brushing them with soap and charcoal, hoping to give them a sparkle equal to that of his guest's. The drummer then assembled a splendid supper for the boy, but it was all for naught. He never appeared, and so, disappointed as usual, Van Buskirk shared the fare with another friend from the squadron.[15]

The unnamed French friend was only one of a string of lads pursued by Van Buskirk. Often his purpose in cultivating them was to effect their moral reformation. Fifteen-year-old George Base, of the U.S. Str. *Mississippi*, was one of the boys he set out to guide spiritually. If the rumors were true, Base was as corrupt as any youngster in the navy. Van Buskirk's Catholic education taught him how to move forward with his project. He went on board the steamer with two books he was sure would improve the rumored reprobate's character. The first was a history of Rome and the other a pamphlet setting out the evils of masturbation. Base returned the books in short order with a note containing an obvious lie. He claimed to have read both volumes the night before. The boy from the *Mississippi* was obviously interested in cultivating Van Buskirk, realizing that he could be easily manipulated. He asked for more books, preferably novels of the sort he customarily read. Van Buskirk did not respond to his request, and did not record his reasons for abandoning Base so quickly. In most circumstances he would have continued his servile attempts to gain acceptance. Perhaps the lad was deficient in the physical beauties usual in those who attracted him, or the drummer may have decided that he was beyond reformation.

Another of Van Buskirk's challenges in trying to elevate the moral tone of the ships' boys came in the person of George Coleman, whom he nicknamed the "Imp." If ever anyone existed beyond the bounds of redemption, it was the Imp, according to the multiple diary entries that referred to him. His father had sent him to sea in the hope he would be reformed, but shipboard life had no such effect. Although young, he had mastered all the navy's vices. He drank, smoked, swore, stole, and engaged in sodomy with the chaplain's boy and with one of the officers' Chinese servants. The Imp also disrupted the relationship between the drummer and another boy, George W. Reever. At one point he moved into the cozy nest under the boom cover created by the two with a single overcoat and a ditty bag that they shared as a pillow. Reever and the Imp soon fell into the practice of mutual masturbation, much to Van Buskirk's horror.

Coleman also undercut another of the drummer's reformation projects, his attempts to dissuade a young mizzentopman, Andrew Milne, from masturbating. In Milne's case, the monitory course consisted of moral instruction buttressed with stories of the dire physical consequences sure to befall practitioners of the solitary vice. Milne had little patience with the proffered instruction. He lied to Van Buskirk, saying he had never masturbated except once, and added an admission sure to distress the diarist. He confessed to having done it with numerous shipmates. Van Buskirk estimated Milne had gone "chaw for chaw," as mutual masturbation was called in navy parlance, at least seven times.[16] The connection between the drummer and his reluctant student was noticed by at least one of the *Plymouth*'s crew. A quartermaster chided Van Buskirk for sleeping with the boy on deck. Evidently piqued by the comments, he recorded the entire dialogue.

> QUARTERMASTER: Well! You lays alongside o' boys now o' nights, do you? ... Why ain't you ashamed of yourself to have a boy alongside you all night?
> VAN BUSKIRK: Not exactly, considering who the boy is, and that nothing bad results from our sleeping together.
> Q: Who the boy is! Why that boy would _ _ _ _ a jackass [this and subsequent four-letter omissions in the quotation are Van Buskirk's].
> V: I don't care if he would _ _ _ _ a jackass. I know he don't _ _ _ _ me. Every night passed with me by the boy is a night spent in innocence — when he sleeps with me, he is out of harm's way, and if he didn't sleep with me he'd certainly sleep with somebody else, and in that case bad consequences might indeed result.
> Q: Oh Hell! Now do you mean to say that you sleeps alongside o' boys o' nights and don't do nothing?

> V: Well, you might as well drop the subject — I see you are a little more
> interested than you ought to be — You are jealous.[17]

In due course, Milne became the companion of a lieutenant. Such blatant
and unrepentant activity led to the abandonment of efforts to save the boy
Van Buskirk now claimed looked like a girl, and to whom he referred as
"Miss Milne" or the "little slut."

The drummer was very likely becoming accustomed to rejection after
his experiences with Base, Reever, and Milne. In any case, there was no
need to brood long over his failures with them. By the time he abandoned
Milne, he had already endured the experience of dealing with profound
and overwhelming grief. He had earlier been enamored of Alexander
Scroggy, a boy from the U.S.S. *Vandalia*, since he first saw him in November of 1853. Scroggy was fourteen years old and from Philadelphia according to a diary entry that also contained a string of terms that described
him as dignified, decent, symmetrical, graceful, intelligent, handsome, and
with a clear, translucent skin. There is no indication that twenty-year-old
Van Buskirk ever actually met Scroggy, but he thought of him constantly
and dreamed of him with some frequency. When word came in June that
the boy had died, Van Buskirk fell into deep depression. He inquired into
the circumstances of Scroggy's death, and learned that he had succumbed
to a fever. One of the *Vandalia*'s crewmen also told him of making a brass
plate and nailing it to his coffin. The plate read "A. R. Scroggy, Aged 15."
Van Buskirk preserved the inscription in a diary entry made on June 22,
1854, but recording it in no way assuaged his grief. He sought consola-
tion in religion, but found only a limited measure of comfort in prayer
and devotions. He wanted to believe Scroggy was in Heaven, but he knew
that after time at sea he might have fallen victim to the vices that lurked
on board ship and earned himself a place in Hell. For a time he bordered
his diary pages in black as proof of his unabated distress. By November
he tried another tack to staunch his grief. He began writing a letter to
Scroggy's mother and asked a sailor known for his poetic abilities to write
a commemorative verse to enclose with it. When he received the poem he
was happy with it, but uncharacteristically did not inscribe it into the
diary. It is not certain whether the letter and the poem were ever sent.[18]

Most of Van Buskirk's infatuations waxed and waned as circumstances
dictated, then after a time they faded into mere memories. The exception
to this was his love for two brothers from the squadron's flagship, the

U.S.S. *Susquehanna*. They were John W. and James E. Hibbs. The earliest reference to them is in an entry of September of 1852. He wrote that he loved them both, and that they were moral boys. When the *Plymouth* and the *Susquehanna* were anchored near each other at Macao he wrote to them regularly. The brothers let him know at one point that they planned to visit him on October 3rd. On receiving the news he was mad with excitement and anxiety. But like the French lad, they did not appear on the appointed day. His hopes dashed, Van Buskirk sank into despondency. Desperate to see his young loves, and failing to get explicit permission to go to their ship, he lay in wait, and when the next boat from the *Plymouth* pulled for the *Susquehanna* he leapt on board. When he arrived, he found the elder of the boys unwilling to deal with him. He spent the afternoon with the younger brother, James — referred to throughout the diary by his middle name, Emery. An evening boat took the dejected drummer back to the *Plymouth*.[19]

Despite the humiliation handed to him by the pair, Van Buskirk was an indefatigable suitor. Several days later he managed another visit to the flagship to track down the boys. Much to his dismay, he found John suffering from the residual effects of a drinking bout ashore the previous evening in the company of a marine sergeant. Always anxious to improve his young loves, Van Buskirk managed to extract a promise from him never to get drunk again, a promise easily made by anyone suffering the miseries of overindulgence. He spent the afternoon with the two brothers, the coldness of his previous visit forgotten. Most of their conversation consisted of gossip about shipboard vice. Music boys had a taste for scandal, he later wrote, and they had few qualms about spreading vicious tales about one another.[20]

The courtship of John Hibbs moved forward in the usual fashion during the autumn of 1852. Although unable to visit the *Susquehanna* during the closing months of the year, Van Buskirk kept in touch with a stream of notes telling him of his love and advising him to abstain from alcohol. Gifts sent with the notes included rings, a penknife, pictures, books, brass buttons, and a jar of jelly. The jelly had earlier been purchased for another beautiful navy lad, John Pons, but he rejected it along with the oranges and bananas Van Buskirk tried to give him. Not one to waste such comestibles, Van Buskirk regifted the jelly to Hibbs, then he, a boatswain's mate, and fellow *Plymouth* musician, William McFarland, ate the fruit.[21]

The cavalier treatment he endured from John and Emery was not the most painful aspect of his attempts to curry favor with them. Their beauty attracted other suitors, and Van Buskirk was aghast at the thought that some member of the *Susquehana*'s crew or some other man from the East India Squadron might secure their affections and lead them into vice. He suspected McFarland had designs on John Hibbs since he admitted having dreamt of him on occasion. Time provided no respite for the drummer during 1852 and 1853. He became distraught over the news that John, the "little idol" of his soul, had taken a younger boy named Hodge as a lover. When a crewman from the *Susquehanna* told him Emery was somehow involved in the romance the pain intensified. The more he learned, the more his torment grew, especially after he heard a shipmate refer to "that fellow who ***** Hibbs" [Van Buskirk's stars]. On another occasion he heard of a lad in the squadron who wore a ring inscribed with the name "J. W. Hibbs." Over a period of months additional tales of the Hibbs brothers' homoerotic involvements agitated Van Buskirk beyond endurance. In desperation he again turned to prayer, but for a second time he found it provided him little solace. After failing to obtain divine relief he decided he must abandon John and Emery, but found that impossible to do. When he learned of the death of the boys' mother he rimmed his diary pages in black and set himself on a course of four weeks mourning for her. Such private efforts, he knew, would have little effect on his relationship with the Hibbs brothers, so he sought to console them. He found them on shore, in a Shanghai tavern, drinking with men from their ship only a week after receiving the sad news. They were bearing up remarkably well, he decided, dealing with their grief like "little philosophers."[22]

The end of Van Buskirk's agony and infatuation came when the *Plymouth* sailed for home in 1854. With no more opportunities to write, visit, or send gifts to John and Emery, they disappeared from the pages of his diary. When his path crossed with theirs in Washington, D.C., a year later the flame was gone. He mentioned the meeting in a brief note, but without the passion he had used earlier when writing of them. In fact, he no longer needed to rekindle his old feelings for the two. There were at the Marine Corps Headquarters where he was stationed a new and virtually unlimited number of young and beautiful boys living in the music room, including his old love, George Schultz, who one evening brought him some pears.[23]

It was while serving with the *Plymouth* during her assignment at Shanghai that Van Buskirk was first subjected to enemy fire, after having spent eight peaceable years in the Marines. As a member of an Anglo-American force assaulting a Chinese fort on April 4, 1854, the drummer charged forward with the first rank of attackers. When one of his companions fell mortally wounded, he abandoned his drum, picked up the dead man's musket, and continued the charge. After the front line of Marines was broken by fire from the fort, he retreated with his comrades, and took up a position away from the tenanted walls. Having failed to secure ammunition from the corpse of the man whose musket he had appropriated, he was forced to beg rounds from other Marines to shoot at the enemy. He never actually saw a Chinese soldier at any of the embrasures, but he fired from time to time anyway, hoping one of his shots might hit an unseen foe. The engagement, later named the Battle of Muddy Flat, went on for several hours before a British force was able to capture the fort from the opposite side. There were few souvenirs of the battle for the Americans, only a small number of flags thrown down to them by the victorious Britons. This upset Van Buskirk very little. It was a memorable day for him, despite the insignificance of the skirmish, the loss of one Marine and the wounding of three more. He gloried in his first taste of combat, and reflected afterward that he knew at last that he would not bolt and run in fear from an armed and dangerous enemy.[24]

While serving on board the *Plymouth*, whether in port or at sea, Van Buskirk had ample time for leisure. He wrote in his diary, attended the many theatricals produced by the squadron's sailors, and read. Books of every description were widely available to American mariners in the nineteenth-century navy. Most of the larger warships carried their own libraries, but even smaller vessels had ample stocks of books, newspapers, and periodicals. The reading material consisted largely of religious works donated by various missionary groups and lurid fiction of the sort prized by the ill-educated men who served before the mast.[25] Unlike most of his associates, the drummer usually read for self-improvement rather than for pleasure. He was acutely conscious of his status as the scion of a distinguished though ruined family. The low station he occupied as a Marine musician weighed heavily upon him, but he knew there was no one to come to his rescue. If he were to attain the eminence to which birth and education entitled him, he would have to do it on his own. The only way to gain the status he craved was by reading books to improve his character and enhance his qualifications for what he envisioned as the first step upward, an appointment as a naval purser. From there, he dreamed of rising to the rank of admiral, returning to Maryland to reclaim his father's seat in the legislature, and perhaps some day advancing to the United States House of Representatives or the Senate. As part of the program for advancement, he read widely in books designed to improve his marksmanship, help him understand infantry tactics, make him adept at swordsmanship, and impart any other skills that might be useful for promotion. Inspiration was provided by encouraging works like George Craik's *Pursuit of Knowledge under Difficulties* and Horace Mann's *A Few Thoughts for a Young Man*.[26] So certain was he of success that he studied not only to attain it but to enjoy it when it was secured. Once ensconced on some lofty social plain, he reasoned, it would be essential to have mastered the skills described in the anonymously written *The Art of Good Behavior; and Letter Writer on Love, Courtship, and Marriage: A Complete Guide for Ladies and Gentlemen, particularly Those Who Have not Enjoyed the Advantages of Fashionable Life*.[27]

Not all of the young Marine's reading was devoted directly to self-improvement. He knew he needed a well-rounded education to succeed. His literary tastes were deliberately eclectic, and included history, travel tales, biographies, and an assortment of serious novels. He even recorded looking through at least one piece of pornography, a work entitled *Silas Shovewell*.[28]

Van Buskirk did not entirely neglect God in his search for self-improvement. He occasionally read the Bible, and from time to time browsed religious works, but found dealing with theological concepts difficult. At least one book, Dr. Archibald Alexander's *Brief Compendium of Biblical Truth*, severely taxed his comprehension.[29] He offered up prayers when convenient, but rarely kept to the schedules of devotion he regularly prescribed for himself. Even in his quest for divine blessings, he did not forget his determination to improve. At one point he decided it would be spiritually beneficial to learn French.

Rumors began circulating through the *Plymouth*'s crew in early 1853 of a planned expedition to Japan, but it was not until March, when Commodore Matthew C. Perry arrived to replace John Aulick as squadron commander of the American flotilla stationed in the Far East, that Van Buskirk gave any indication of enthusiasm for the project. On April 7, he wrote:

ARRIVAL OF COMMODORE PERRY; The U.S. Steamer *Mississippi*, bearing the broad pennant of *Matthew C. Perry, Commander-in-Chief of the U.S. Squadron in the Seas of China and Japan*, arrived in the [Hong Kong] harbor shortly before sundown. After being saluted by the *Ply-*

mouth and *Saratoga*, the great commodore anchored very near us and
fired seven guns. Everything teems with excitement.[30]

The next day the rumors were officially confirmed, and Van Buskirk was
ecstatic. "The long projected *expedition to Japan* is no hoax," he wrote
excitedly,[31] though his enthusiasm was surely tempered when he heard that
Perry carried orders from Secretary of the Navy John P. Kennedy requiring all journals, diaries, notebooks, and the like kept by officers and men
during the expedition be turned over to the United States government at
the conclusion of the mission. Several officers suspended their journal
keeping as a result of the order, but Van Buskirk was not to take so dras-
tic an action. Instead he discontinued making entries in his bulky diary
volume, and began something he called "Journal of the Cruise," a smaller
book, small enough, presumably, to be concealed from the officers of the
Plymouth.

Since he was already known among his shipmates as a compulsive
diarist, Van Buskirk was uncertain how successful it would be to transfer
his daily observations to a volume easily hidden. An officer of the ship
reminded him at one point that his diary would have to be surrendered
after the return from Japan. He tried to counter this distressing news by
claiming that the order applied only to officers. This clearly was not the
case. It was addressed to "all officers and other persons attached to the vessels under [Perry's] command." Still, despite the unambiguous wording,
he persisted in subjecting it to his own interpretation. He explained his
view to Edward C. Doran, the *Plymouth*'s purser, hoping to have his claim
reinforced by someone with at least a modicum of authority. Doran was
not willing to oblige the young Marine, explaining that the word "all" in
the order referred to everyone sailing with the expedition.

In early July 1853, the two side-wheel steamers and two sloops that
made up Perry's small flotilla reached Japan. Van Buskirk wrote little about
the activities of the expedition in the small notebook that he substituted
for his diary. If he were aware of what was transpiring on official levels, he
chose not to comment on it. He was one of the party that went ashore
with Commodore Perry to present a letter from the president of the United
States to a representative of the emperor of Japan, but he preserved nothing of what he observed of the historic occasion.[32] In typical fashion, he
wrote only of what impinged directly upon him. His diary page for the
day was filled with a lament over a lost drumstick and the clever way he

fashioned a replacement for it from a strip of bamboo. The next addition to his record was made after the fleet of four ships sailed from Japan, bound for Hong Kong.

The *Plymouth* was scheduled to return to the United States in 1854, and so did not accompany Commodore Perry on his second expedition to Japan. On the homeward voyage Van Buskirk spent considerable time contemplating the future, but no matter what course of action he chose, embarking on the new and successful life he planned required him to create a new man. He had his hair trimmed, rubbed it with oil, combed it, brushed it to a high gloss, then resolved to make personal grooming one of his regular habits. Once ashore in America, he purchased an entirely new wardrobe, but before he officially became a civilian, he was ordered to Washington, D.C. The Marine Corps, desperately short of recruits, informed him when he arrived at headquarters that they planned to reinstate the years-old charges of desertion against him if he did not reenlist. In return for committing himself to another four years of service, he would be allowed thirty days leave before reporting for duty at his next post.

Whatever thoughts he had about the threat combined with a job offer went unrecorded. On January 16, 1855, he was discharged from the United States Marines. On the same day he reenlisted, then set out for home. Van Buskirk did not use the thirty days he had been allotted. After a short time, he was back in Washington with the Marines. He wrote nothing of the visit with his mother or his other relatives, and give no reason for his early return from leave.

Life as a headquarters Marine was as leisurely an affair as serving on board ship. Four months after resuming his duties, he was promoted from drummer to corporal. His new assignment consisted largely of directing the activities of fourteen privates. He also drilled as many as two dozen men in the rudiments of marching and the manual of arms. From time to time he served as acting sergeant, lieutenant, or captain during close-order drill. On sundry occasions he was part of funeral processions, ran errands for officers, served as a hospital steward, and once helped put out a fire. Earlier in his career, Van Buskirk had managed to find trouble wherever he was posted, and he managed to do so again at headquarters barracks, repeatedly violating the chain of command, performing guard duty in an unsatisfactory manner, and regularly antagonizing superiors as well as subordinates.

In 1856, he received orders for the U.S.S. *Portsmouth*, scheduled to join the East India Squadron. Her mission was the same as that of the *Plymouth* five years before: to protect American commercial and diplomatic installations in China. The situation by 1856 was far more precarious than it had been half a decade earlier. It appeared likely the Chinese intended to block access to Canton, and if they did the lives of Westerners would likely be in danger. Plans were drawn up by concerned nations to destroy the series of forts that controlled the Pearl River, the only water route from Hong Kong and Macao to Canton. When the assault on the forts began, Van Buskirk, freshly promoted to sergeant, prided himself on being among the vanguard. He admonished himself to keep a level head in the fight, but the battle to take the forts tested neither him nor his comrades in arms. Although the Marines suffered numerous casualties when they moved forward to dislodge the Chinese, the bloody hand-to-hand combat anticipated by some did not take place. The defenders retreated from their positions as the attackers advanced, and many of them were shot as they fled.

In typical fashion, Sergeant Van Buskirk wrote of what he observed nearby rather than describing broader events. The hatred his fellow Marines held for the Chinese appalled him. He wrote of the brutality suffered by the people of villages that came under their control, and of the use of Chinese for long-range target practice. One of the American officers on board the *Plymouth*, Commander Andrew H. Foote, ordered a halt to the vicious mayhem, but his efforts had no effect on men so far from the ship and away from his direct control.

It was about this time that Van Buskirk temporarily lost his enthusiasm for meticulous diary keeping. He gave no reason for his change of habit, but while on board the *Portsmouth* he began summarizing whole months in a few paragraphs rather than making his laborious and detailed daily entries. As a result of the new practice, a good deal of his life is lost for the period from 1856 to 1857, and nothing survives of the intricacies of his loves and the concomitant suffering he surely endured. His promotion to sergeant probably had no bearing on the decision to switch to an abbreviated manner of diary keeping. He had little more to do in his new and elevated post than he had to do as a drummer or corporal. The days passed with reading, studying, and relaxing in the manner to which he had become accustomed as a Marine.

Although Van Buskirk was in high spirits during the operation against the Pearl River forts in October and November of 1856, most of the time on the *Portsmouth* he was in ill health. He was plagued by corns and a draining ear, but these were minor matters, cured with the passage of time and assorted medicines. Far more serious was the dysentery he contracted at about the time he was ashore assaulting the forts. The disease began with cramps and loose bowels, and he became desperately ill. With the onset of bloody defecation, his weight decreased and he endured extreme pain. He was placed on a regimen of brandy, tincture of opium, and morphine, but these brought no relief. At one time he appeared so gaunt that his commanding officer loaned him two dollars to buy extra rations from the ship's cooks in the hope that the additional nourishment would assist in returning him to health. The severity of the dysentery decreased from time to time, but it always returned in full force, bringing with it severe cramps, pain, and bloody stools. In March of 1857, he was transferred from the *Portsmouth* to a hospital on shore. There he improved to some degree, but he did not recover his health entirely. He eventually returned to the ship and was allowed to perform light duty, but the navy's physicians decided he should be ordered back to America. Van Buskirk was not immediately sent home, although there is no indication of the reasons he remained on board the *Portsmouth* as it cruised between Japan and Macao. He evidently felt better near the end of the year, but by then the navy decided to follow the earlier recommendation of the doctors. He was transferred to the U.S.S. *Levant* on December 6, 1857. The next day the ship sailed for the United States.

The ailing sergeant spent several weeks in the Boston naval hospital after his return in April of 1858, but the ministrations of physicians were no more effective in America than they had been in the Far East. The only way to restore his health, he decided, was through his own efforts, and to do this, he first needed to discover the source of his affliction. He began a detailed record of his food intake, the weather, abdominal cramps, and bowel movements in hopes that correlating the four factors would reveal the cause or causes of the disease. Throughout the diary in the latter half of 1858, interspersed among the pages of entries, are rows and columns filled with data he thought necessary to discover a cure. Notations describing stools in detail (color, texture, blood content, volume, configuration, and frequency) appear along with climatological observations, dietary information, and a record of where he spent each day, on ship or ashore.

Compounding Van Buskirk's misery from the dysentery were the agonies he endured over his continuing spermatorrhea. He knew from the books and pamphlets he read that the disease resulted from masturbation, but many eminent physicians whose works the ill and depressed Marine also read maintained that some foods stimulated nocturnal emission while others reduced its frequency. So he began a careful record of nocturnal emissions, just as he did with his stools, and tried to correlate both with his diet. He discovered, of course, that contrary to prevailing medical opinion there was simply no correlation between what he ate and his spermatorrhea.

His last effort at seeking out a cure came with the purchase of *Boyhood's Perils and Manhood's Curse* by Dr. Seth Pancoast. It surely disappointed him, for the treatments it contained were no different than those in other works he had read. The only additional remedy it offered beyond what he already knew of was to sleep with the head in a northerly direction to maintain the body's polarity and balance out electric and nervous energies. In due course he gave away his copy of Pancoast, and mused sadly about suffering from his boyhood sins.[33]

In June of 1858, Van Buskirk was back in Washington, but did not take up residence at either the musicians' room of the Marine Corps Headquarters barracks or the Washington Navy Yard. He ate and slept at the house of Mrs. Elizabeth Schultz, just behind the headquarters barracks on Eighth and I streets. Mrs. Schultz was the mother of his old love, George Schultz, with whom he had been smitten half a dozen years earlier. The fact that George was living at home probably had some influence on his decision. The two of them shared a bed, a not uncommon occurrence in nineteenth-century America, and Van Buskirk experienced the rebirth of his old feelings. "The more I came to know George," he wrote, "the more I loved him.[34]

Within weeks after Van Buskirk moved into the Schultz home, George was ordered to sea. He left Washington, D.C., at the end of June. Soon after, his younger brother, John, returned from a cruise on board the U.S.S. *Constitution* and settled into the vacant half of the shared bed. John had never had much appeal for Van Buskirk, and the new arrangement was not to his liking. The younger brother evidently tossed much or talked in his sleep making the nights difficult for his bunkmate. The older Schultz was back home within a week, having deserted his ship, but his reunion with Van Buskirk was short lived. He was taken into custody for desertion, tossed in the guardroom for a time, then ordered to the U.S.S. *Sabine*. Philip and George said their farewells and kissed goodbye at the railroad station, then Schultz caught a train to join his ship in New York, where it was berthed. Van Buskirk was disturbed over his friend not so much because of the parting but because the young man had strayed so far from the pure and innocent lad he once idealized.[35] He poured out his disappointment in one of his most poignant diary entries:

> Sailors say that on board of a man-of-war a good looking boy may have three men in his keeping, to wit: a fancy-man, a fighting man, and a damned fool. The last named is kept only for the purpose of being drawn upon to supply the wants of the other three. He is so fond of the boy that he can refuse him nothing. The boy's smile is happiness, his frown misery.... I am inclined to think — I mean there is almost evidence enough to compel me to believe that George all along has only regarded me in the light of a "damned fool" whom it was profitable to retain by the use of extra arts, pretended affection, and profound hypocrisy.[36]

The only thing that sustained Van Buskirk during these discouraging days in the spring and early summer of 1858 as he battled dysentery, spermatorrhea, and depression over George Schultz was his hope for advancement. Through a distant relative, he sought to obtain a commission in the Marine Corps. One of Van Buskirk's aunts was married to a James E. Boyd of Mill Creek, Virginia. Boyd's sister was the wife of a Virginia congressman, Charles James Faulkner. An interview was scheduled for Sergeant Van Buskirk with the man he hoped would be his patron. Boyd was quite energetic in helping his nephew, providing hospitality for him for several days, arranging the meeting with Faulkner, and driving him to the congressman's house in his buggy. Before the visit, Van Buskirk sank into one of his periodic bouts of depression. He worried that his interlocutor would uncover the defects in his character and education. If that were to happen, he despaired of all hope of becoming a lieutenant. Still, in his usual fashion, he resolved firmly to himself to be an exemplary officer if given the chance. Faulkner seemed interested in helping, but explained to his distant relative-by-marriage that the commissions were few, there were many who sought them, and a number of applicants had powerful family connections. Faulkner also provided the discouraging information that since Van Buskirk had served as an enlisted man, obtaining a lieutenancy for him would be particularly difficult. The information was not new to Van Buskirk. Years earlier he had read a pamphlet by John S. Devlin, who claimed arrogant and elitist officers had destroyed his career in the Corps because he had prior service as an enlisted man. The situation had not changed over the years. In 1858 the Marine Corps continued to look askance at officers who came up from the ranks, Faulkner explained.

Van Buskirk had several more interviews with the congressman that gave him a small measure of encouragement. He was also promised a chance to meet the president. After months of trying Faulkner was unable to secure the hoped-for commission, but he did make good on his promise. He presented Van Buskirk to President James Buchannan on December 16th. The meeting was duly noted in the diary, but there was no additional comment.

Van Buskirk was disheartened by the inability of his kinsman to advance his career, but he continued his quest. He wrote letters to the secretary of the navy and to Senator James M. Mason of Virginia. Both men responded with notes of encouragement, but neither offered to assist him.[37]

With his dreams of becoming an officer unfulfilled and his four-year term of service coming to an end in January of 1859, Van Buskirk decided to reenlist. There were no other alternatives. He had failed to become an officer, there was no help available to him from any quarter, he was deeply in debt, and he needed the $51 reenlistment bounty to help pay his creditors. The first difficulty he encountered after his decision to remain in the Corps was at the medical examination. He was still defecating six or seven times per day, and his stools were thin and bloody. The examining physician pronounced him physically unfit and rejected him for service. His first disability pension payment of $3.25 was to be paid in February. Van Buskirk was aghast at this turn of events. He wrote in his diary, with only slight exaggeration, that the pension would not even cover his laundry expenses let alone enable him to retire debts of over $100.[38]

As the recipient of an inadequate government pension, he set out to find work. In February, he journeyed to Annapolis to seek a job as a watchman at the United States Naval Academy. It was the policy at the school to hire former sailors and Marines whenever possible. He was promised a position as soon as there was a vacancy, but that did little to alleviate his difficulties. He was ill, destitute, and homeless. Fortunately, he met a thirteen-year-old boy, George Duvall, while seeking accommodations. In his customary fashion, Van Buskirk befriended the lad, and shortly after they met, the Duvall family agreed to provide the bankrupt invalid with room and board, presumably at a price commensurate with his $3.25 monthly pension. By April he was a resident of their spacious Annapolis home, sharing a bed with young George. Mrs. Duvall objected at first to the sleeping arrangements, claiming the ex-drummer would be uncomfortable with her son in his bed, but for reasons never made clear she finally allowed them to bunk together. Van Buskirk was irritated by her initial wish to keep them separate. He believed her opposition was rooted not in a concern for his comfort, but because she did not trust him in bed with her child. How could she believe such a thing of him, he wondered.[39]

While it is unlikely Van Buskirk's relationship with George Duvall ever became overtly sexual, it had a physical component. The former Marine wrote of the ecstasy he felt when near the boy and of his rapture when he gave him warm kisses. He even celebrated their closeness by penning a doggerel anthem to their bond. As he had done with his shipboard loves, Van Buskirk appointed himself the moral tutor of his young friend. The task was eased because there were no pederastic crewmen to guard against, but there were serious dangers within the Duvall household. His boy "angel" was vulnerable to the depraved examples of his older brothers, and his classmates at St. Johns' College were ill-suited as models for him. More distressing for George's self-appointed spiritual advisor were the boy's habits of looking at pornography with his friends and fornicating with Jane, a Duvall family slave.[40]

In July he was notified of his appointment as a watchman at the academy, but that did not immediately mitigate his difficulties. He was not scheduled to begin work until September. It was only then that he would start drawing his $9.60-per-month wage. Meanwhile, he continued at the Duvalls throughout the summer without paying them for the food and shelter he received.[41]

Once it began, Van Buskirk was notably unenthusiastic about his job at the naval academy. The college-trained son of the late William Van Buskirk surely deserved better, he thought, than sweeping walkways and spending endless hours keeping track of who entered and exited a school gate. Neither did he care for his associates. They were a dull-witted, churlish lot in his estimation. Not surprisingly, he paid little attention to his tasks. He frequently left his post for meals or for other reasons, cattle wandered through the gate and into the academy's quadrangle, he forgot to ring bells on time, and when he remembered to ring them, he often did it incorrectly. The level of ineptitude he displayed earned the anger of both officers and faculty. In the hope of driving him to perform at a higher level, they prohibited his reading on duty. They also objected to the band of small children, mostly male, who collected around him when he was on guard. As was his practice, he fed them treats, worried about their levels of purity, and developed crushes on some of them. At one point, when the boredom of his job overwhelmed him as it often did, he compiled a list of boys "for whom I have entertained great fondness." The nineteen entries ranged back to his childhood and included Roderick Masson, the friend from his Georgetown days, a lad only dimly remembered as "Norman of Frostburg," and of course the Hibbs brothers, John and Emery.[42] His diary entry for March 6, 1860, is typical for the period:

> I was on watch this morning from 3 to 7, and was napping at my post being snugly ensconced in the arm-chair of the officer-in-charge when an alarm of fire was raised in the town, and carried swiftly to the gate of the academy, and reached me just in time and in the manner to admit of my saving myself by quickly calling up the officer-in-charge and reporting the alarm, before it had spread, thus making it appear that in going the rounds as my duty required I had myself made timely discovery of the fire.

As was usual for Van Buskirk, his young loves caused his life to oscillate between extremes of ecstasy and pain. The ones who hurt him most during his years guarding the naval academy were Essex, Charlie, and Theodoric Porter, the sons of David Dixon Porter, the future Civil War hero. The watchman was certain they needed the moral instruction he could provide. Each of them cursed unremittingly, masturbated regularly, and spent the small amounts of money Van Buskirk gave them with little thanks to the donor. When they moved from Annapolis in the autumn of 1860 they stole his best pair of boots, boots that had cost him seven dollars. At least some in Annapolis noticed the watchman's seemingly indecent interest in small children. A woman identified only as Mrs. Upshaw instructed her young son to never let Van Buskirk kiss him. Another woman gave two small daughters similar instructions. Later in the year, the captain of the watch issued an order requiring men on duty at the west gate to keep children out of the watch house. Van Buskirk understood the officer's intent. "I may almost take this as leveled at me, for I believe I am the only watchman that is known to be partial to children," he wrote.[43]

During his tenure at the naval academy, Van Buskirk regularly lamented being troubled by sexual notions, although he did not specify their exact nature. He claimed in his diary that the presence of small children helped rid himself of such thoughts, but whatever the role of juveniles in his imagined sexual cosmos, his concupiscent fantasies began to shift at Annapolis. While he maintained his interest in beautiful boys, he also began noticing pre-pubescent girls and commenting upon them in the diary. The relationships with the girls closely followed the familiar pattern of his relationship with young boys. The watchman, now in his late twenties, offered advice, treats, and love. The girls reacted to his advances more negatively than boys had done over the years. They categorically rebuffed him. The three who figured most prominently in his writings were his young cousins. Sally, a fifteen-year-old, was disgusted by his repeated attempts to kiss her. The thirteen-year-old Rebecca rejected all of his proffered advice, and the youngest sister, nine-year-old Rosa, penciled permanent marks across the back of his best coat.[44]

During his stint as a naval academy watchman, as he tried to cultivate the friendship of an assortment of small boys and girls, his sexually-specific fantasies involved young women. He thought regularly of patronizing local brothels, but always found excuses not to do so. There was no opportunity for such visits because of his work schedule, he explained to himself, or he was concerned that knowledge of such visits would tarnish his reputation. For a time, a slave girl belonging to an academy faculty member occupied his mind, but he was unable to realize his wishes with her. As he explained in the diary, there was no opportunity to speak to her let alone arrange a meeting.[45] Jane, the slave girl he met at the Duvalls, seemed more accessible. He knew her, and knew well that the three Duvall sons regularly had sexual relations with her. On November 7, 1860, Jane and a friend visited him, and he immediately decided he should take her to his room, but something akin to panic followed the thought, and his ardor died immediately. The watchman gave her and her friend fifty cents and sent them away. Jane returned the next week, and for reasons that he clearly could not understand he sent her away again. In his puzzlement, he considered taking an oath of chastity, presumably to give him sound reason to reject opportunities for sexual relations he was unable act upon.

Van Buskirk's self-esteem deteriorated substantially during his stint as a watchman. In the fall of 1860, he was disgusted with himself for smoking a pipe and cigars. It has become a "confirmed vice in me," he noted in a September diary entry, "to the great prejudice of all my interests, temporal and eternal: there can be no mistake in this ... it will make me an inferior man, and eventually ruin me." He drafted a pledge to abstain from tobacco entirely, but the pledge, or at least the copy of it in the diary, remained unsigned. At the same time that he was implicitly chastised for entertaining children while on duty, one of the academy faculty members, a Professor Hopkins, offered to help him with his mathematical studies. The watchman demurred, explaining the reason for declining the proffered assistance in his diary. "I am a watchman — no gentleman," he wrote. "[I] cannot go into Mr. Hopkins's house — into his parlor — may go into his kitchen — how can he instruct me."[46]

Almost his only rewarding moment in that difficult autumn came when he gained at least a small measure of righteous satisfaction from his actions after receiving a sexually explicit advertisement in the mail. The circular offered "White India Rubber Safe" condoms and a number of presumably salacious books, pictures and cards for sale. Inquiries were to be sent to C. F. Sherwood in Lowell, Massachusetts. "The precious circular," he wrote, "I have placed in an envelope, and mailed to the following address: "To His Honor the Mayor of Lowell Mass."[47] His mood was slightly improved in October when he heard a rumor that he might receive his sought-after commission as a lieutenant after all. The paymaster's clerk at the academy, a man he hardly knew, said to him, "I hear you are going to get a situation in the Marine Corps — let me see who told me about it.... O! It was Dr. van Bibber — there is little doubt about it.... That shows that you have friends notwithstanding that you happen to be in a low situation." The watchman's elation over the news was tempered by several factors. He had never heard of Dr. van Bibber, and so was unable to evaluate the reliability of what the man might have said. Neither did it seem to him that a paymaster's clerk was a solid source for such information. The concluding sentences of his diary entry on the matter exhibit his frustration: "That I expect to be a marine officer. I wish I had never said anything myself upon this subject to persons unconcerned. But foolish babbling was until very lately one of my constitutional sins."[48]

Near the end of the month, Van Buskirk learned of the impending resignation of Marine lieutenant Edward Jones.[49] On the October 24, he wrote to Secretary of the Navy Isaac Toucey, hoping to be considered for the post. He marked the envelope carrying the letter "Private" to insure it would not be opened and read by a clerk. Still, his optimism was dampened by the recollection of previous failures. "I alternately hope and despair in this question of my promotion," he sadly confided to his diary. His agony did not last long. In a short note, the secretary explained, "I beg respectfully to state in reply to your letter ... that the vacancy in the Marine Corps to which you refer, has already been filled."[50]

There remained only one other chance for advancement after the dashing of his dreams. He occasionally performed clerical chores for Captain George S. Blake, the academy's superintendent, and he hoped that his work for him might lead to a clerkship in the navy. The chances, he reasoned, were far better than being appointed to a lieutenancy, and the level of prestige the job carried was far higher than that of a watchman. His previous education made him well-qualified for the position, in his opinion, since one of his friends, former Marine sergeant Joseph Mundell, served as a clerk to the commandant of midshipmen, and his qualifications were far inferior to Van Buskirk's. Yet even the small chance of such an appointment was hardly sufficient to lift him out of the depression he endured after his failure to become an officer. When the clerkship did not materialize, his dark mood turned to despair.

Van Buskirk's state of mind naturally impinged on his work. His performance level as a watchman declined from its previous level of ineptitude to utter incompetence in the months that followed. Early in November he feared being called to account for allowing several sailors without passes to slip beyond the gates. He suspected that if the matter were pursued, he would be fired. He tried to justify his conduct in the diary, but finally admitted, "I somewhat betray my trust in permitting a sailor to pass the gate even for a moment unauthorized."[51] Within days after he escaped unscathed from the pass episode, he was in difficulties again. A bottle of whiskey was found in his watch house. He tried to explain that a sailor passing through the gate on his way back to a ship left it with him, the man knowing full well that he could not take the bottle on board. A panel of officers summoned Van Buskirk and the sailor to explain what had transpired, and after at least a perfunctory debate on whether or not he should be dismissed from the corps of watchmen, they let the entire matter drop.[52] He was also forced to fend off additional charges at the end of the month. He was accused of leaving his post on two occasions before he was relieved and of lounging in his room when he was scheduled to be manning guard posts. When called to the commandant's office to answer for his dismal performance, he explained that the first complaint was caused by scheduling confusion. He categorically denied the latter charge. The matter went no further.

Although Van Buskirk suffered no consequences from his incompetence, the failure to obtain either a lieutenancy or a clerkship continued to weigh heavily upon him, and his depression deepened even further as 1860 came to a close. He worried about his mother, he thought about migrating to the west, and he considered changing his name, presumably to avoid heaping further odium on a family that had once produced a Maryland secretary of state.[53] He summarized his feelings in the diary's concluding note for that year:

> This is a revolution of time that I have need to be ashamed of. I have by no means advanced myself in acquisition of knowledge, and have done little or nothing in the way of disciplining my mind, or of reducing my thoughts to the rule of virtue.... As regards "social status" I have remained throughout the same degraded "*pariah*" — rejected from all respectable society — simply because of my "low position." In all this year I have not presumed to look up from the ground. And my duties are of a nature, that combined with other causes of disquietude, tend to stultify the mind, and keep the man sunk or sink him deeper in moral degradation
>
> Mentally, I must blame myself that I am no better off than I was at the beginning of the year, a young man with a smattering of book learning, but no sound education, even the commonest.
>
> Morally, then, on the whole, I may claim for myself that if I have not improved perceptibly I have not retrograded at least perceptibly.
>
> The weights that hold me down are in the mind, and rest upon the mind like an incubus — these are faint-heartedness and mental indolence.
>
> So the year has gone.
>
> P. Clayton Van Buskirk
> Watchman at the Naval Academy

Van Buskirk had almost no interest in politics or political parties. On November 6, 1860, he cast his first ballot in a presidential election for John C. Breckenridge not on the basis of his feelings about slavery or any other issue, but because he learned that Senator James M. Mason was a Breckenridge supporter. He hoped as late as election day that this might in some unspecified way improve his chances for securing a lieutenancy in the Marine Corps.

The day following his trip to the polls, long before his vote could have been counted and added to the Breckenridge total, he wrote of the *Baltimore Sun*'s proclaiming Lincoln's victories in states that had voted earlier than Maryland. His record of the event indicates no strong emotional reaction to the final result. He wrote only that "Abraham Lincoln is President Elect of the United States."[54] In the weeks following his first ballot, Van Buskirk did not ponder the question of secession. It was not until late December that he set down his thoughts on the subject with an inchoate but melodramatic flourish:

> In this month men's minds have been much occupied with the question of union or disunion — war or peace. We fear the politicians are bringing us to the verge of ruin. I deprecate from the bottom of my soul a civil war. If however it is to be ... I will not refuse if called upon, to join the side espoused by Virginia. My hope and prayer is that the Union may be preserved! That Virginia may be on the side of union. Then God with us! I will join in the battle, and not seek to avoid a friendly bullet, for fall or survive, it will be all the same — victory will be ours![55]

January 4, 1861, was a day of fasting and prayer, and by mid–April the tension at the naval academy was palpable, according to Van Buskirk. Word of the battle at Fort Sumter created a national uproar.[56] On April 15, he wrote:

> Today came the president's proclamation, following the news of the capture of Fort Sumter. Intense excitement prevails. Alas! War is close upon us. I remain here for the present. If Virginia don't secede, I may escape military service. If she does I have no alternative than to go and take my chances with my people in that state. Gen. McKay of Allegany told me this evening I ought to join the Confederate States Army, where I might be a lieutenant.[57]

He was acutely conscious of being considered disloyal by his associates at the naval academy, but his natal ties to Virginia, despite the fact that he had been raised in Maryland, and the lure of a commission prevailed. By the 22nd of the month he had made his decision. On that day he recorded that "the captain of the watch enters at my dictation the following remark upon his watch report: 'Buskirk ... respectfully asks attention to his application for discharge, and declines all further service.'"[58]

After leaving the naval academy Van Buskirk had little time for his diary. He was in Washington, D.C., for a short period, visited with the Schultz brothers, and gave them a cased ambrotype of him dressed in his watchman's uniform. In due course he was wandering about Baltimore with his "boyfriend," little Henry Hale. The two attended the theater and then kissed goodbye.[59] On June 16, he enlisted in the 13th Virginia Infantry.[60]

It was not long after Philip Van Buskirk became a Confederate soldier in the summer of 1861 that he began his Civil War diary and went off to fight the Yankees. He was present at the First Battle of Bull Run, but it is unlikely he saw any combat. His regiment was on the right and not involved in the fighting.[61] By February of the next year he was at Camp Walker near Manassas, Virginia. The winter quarters of the regiment were relatively comfortable according to one southern officer who was stationed there in 1862. He wrote of tents and log huts, and provided a description of Confederate garrison duty:

> One who has never been in an army or seen camp life would be surprised at the pleasures and comforts the men were surrounded with as well as the many ways they found in which to pass away their idle time. Cards were the principal source of amusement. Chess was sometimes played. Papers and books were sought for men in camp will read anything.[62]

Despite the pleasant nature of army life at Camp Walker, Van Buskirk deserted.[63] The difficulty of army life, particularly in winter, was a reason many men abandoned their units. Other reasons spurring desertion from the Confederate ranks included homesickness, resentment, boredom, the knowledge that they would not be severely punished if apprehended, and a concern over the suffering of families. Southern soldiers frequently abandoned their units during that first winter of the war, driven by the government's decision to extend some enlistments for three years, secure in the knowledge that they would be welcomed home by their kinsmen, and motivated by the Union policy of encouraging desertion by offering a host of incentives to men who would cross the lines, especially with their accouterment. The decision to desert could not have been too difficult for Van Buskirk. He was, after all, no stranger to desertion. He walked away from his post in Pensacola years before and knew that the consequences of his act were hardly severe. Then, too, his friend and the former object of his devotion, George Schultz, also deserted the navy for a short time in 1858, and was punished only with a few days in the brig before being assigned to another ship. Still, these factors probably played little part in his decision to abscond.[64] Van Buskirk's flight was more likely the result of his disappointment at failing to gain a commission in the 13th Virginia. Elections for officers were held that month and he was not one of those chosen, but whatever the cause of his precipitate departure, he made no note of it. His only comments on abandoning the Confederate cause were made a quarter of a century later when he wrote in his diary that he had made an "escape" from the regiment.[65]

Introduction

Unlike most Confederate deserters who set out for home or for the safety of Union lines, the former warrior wandered for his first few weeks of freedom before being captured on May 26 at a place called New Creek in western Virginia. His captors, troops of the Potomac Home Brigade's Second Regiment, took him to nearby Camp Jesse for interrogation. Union army records describe him as 5' 9", having gray eyes, blond hair, and a dark complexion.[66] He was quickly transferred to military authorities at Wheeling. The reason for the haste in moving him from one post to another is apparent in the note written by Camp Jesse's commander, Captain George H. Bragonier, to Major R. M. Cotwine, the judge advocate of the Mountain Department in Wheeling:

> Sir:
> I have the honor to send you a prisoner arrested at this post, named P. C. Van Buskirk; the particulars of whose history, as connecting him with the rebel army the major will find contained in a private "pocket diary" found upon his person, which Capt. Petre will deliver, from which in addition to a personal examination, I hope the judge advocate will find justifiable grounds for the arrest. He refuses to take the oath of allegiance and I believe him to be a spy.[67]

In a postscript, Bragonier, again urged the judge advocate to "give the 'diary' a close examination."

The notebook that persuaded Bragonier his prisoner was a spy failed to convince the judge advocate. After examining its contents, he decided Van Buskirk was only an infantry deserter. He was then sent to Camp Chase military prison in Ohio. The pocket-sized diary volume was not returned.

Van Buskirk wrote nothing of conditions during the six months he spent at Camp Chase. It is likely he was well-fed and comfortably housed. Union commanders hoped in 1861 and 1862 that word of humane treatment and decent rations in northern prisons would spread throughout the southern ranks and encourage desertion. Even a fulminating southern partisan who spent time at Camp Chase later in the war admitted that blankets were available, although he raged against the poor diet that was by then being provided.[68]

Since living conditions at Camp Chase were tolerable, Van Buskirk's chief concern quickly became the loss of his diary. Regaining possession of the just-confiscated segment of the record he had been compiling obsessively since the late 1840s became a consuming task. On June 5, he sent

Introduction

an awkwardly-worded letter to the camp commander explaining his frustrations:

> Prison No. 2
> Mess No. 4
> 5 June 1862
> Colonel:
>
> When taken into custody on the 26 of last month at New Creek, I was deprived of a private and entirely personal diary kept during my year's service with the Virginia Volunteers. The commander of the post ... forwarded me next day to Wheeling, and directed the officer having me in custody to deliver the diary to the Judge Advocate of the Mountain Department, or to the Governor of Virginia.... I have no choice but to throw myself on the kindness of the commandant here. All that I have to ask is the restoration of my diary: if the colonel will kindly take the necessary steps to affect this, I will put myself under personal and deep obligation, and [3 words illeg.] in all future time to hold in grateful recollections the favor [illeg.] me.
>
> > Respectfully submitted,
> > P. C. Van Buskirk[69]

The letter produced no result, and by the end of the month, the prisoner was truly desperate. He penned another letter intended to persuade the authorities at Wheeling to assist him:

> Mess 14, Prison 2, C. Chase
> Columbus, O.
> 28 June 1862
> Capt. E. [W.] Over
> Deputy Provost Marshall
> Wheeling
> Sir:
>
> I beg respectfully to submit whether the purposes intended in restoring my diary will not be as well attained by taking a transcript of those positions (certainly few) which were deemed important enough to arrest the attention of the officers in command respectively at New Creek and Wheeling.
>
> If the labor of transcribing be the sole objection, I cheerfully offer to perform it myself under the eye of the secretary of the post here ... with every passage marked with a cross that it is intended shall be copied. Or if this favor cannot be accorded me, I will still be satisfied to receive such a fragment of my last year's diary as will remain after all the portions adverted to are removed. I presume I will then have all the strictly personal notes which I have entered during the past year. I know how

entirely I am in the hands of the provost-marshal-general. The disposition which is to be make of my diary rests with him. If therefore a favorable reception is given this communication, which I beg you will submit for his consideration, I will not fail to have and retain a proper sense of obligation.

> I am, Sir,
> Very respectfully, etc.,
> P. C. Van Buskirk[70]

The second missive, like the first, failed to gain the restoration of the diary, and by mid July he was frantic. He wrote again, this time offering a bargain to get it back:

Hospital in Prison 2
Camp Chase, O.
15 July, 1862
Capt. Ed. [W.] Over
Sir:

I would respectfully ask attention anew to my letters addressed last month to the Provost-Marshal's General's office, requesting restoration in whole or in part of my last year's personal diary, and in reference thereto beg to state that I have signified by letter to the War Department my willingness to take the oath of allegiance to The United States and the (New) State of Virginia.[71]

May I under these circumstances indulge the hope of the early restoration of my diary?

You will oblige me by submitting my communication to Major [Joseph] Darr.[72]

> I am very respectfully your obedt servt,
> P. C. Van Buskirk[73]

Beneath the signature, in a hand not Van Buskirk's, is the notation, "Answer, the diary is here & will *remain*."

In late summer, the United States Army included Van Buskirk in one of the prisoner exchanges effected early in the war.[74] He was a member of a consignment of 1,100 Confederates who left Camp Chase on August 26, 1862, for Cairo, Illinois. At Cairo, the prisoners were loaded onto eight or ten transports for the trip southward. They were heavily guarded during the journey, and many became ill or died due to cramped conditions, bad food, and contaminated drinking water. The flotilla reached Vicksburg in early September, and the men were released. Van Buskirk then wandered northward over the next several months, but recorded little of his peregri-

Introduction

nations.[75] By December the repatriated Confederate was settled in western Virginia, and in April of 1863, he resumed the journal keeping he had abandoned the year before when Union troops confiscated the diary volume he had kept since early 1861.

Van Buskirk's diary from early 1863 onward is far different from the vast number of chronicles kept by Union and Confederate soldiers, and it is these differences that make it a uniquely valuable record. Almost all military journals written during the war, particularly those that have been published, set down the careers of men who served with fortitude and honor, and often with distinction. This is not the case with Van Buskirk's small diary. His is a deserter's story. The chronology of this obscure Confederate is not the usual register of marches, rain, snow, bone-chilling cold, fatigue, poor rations, misery, battles, wounds, and death. Instead, it is a story of men and women caught between and behind the lines. Union policies of depriving Confederate forces and sympathizers of food, shelter, and supplies made life difficult during the years from late 1862 to 1865, and Philip Van Buskirk not only cataloged the deprivation and pain of the residents in the mountain valleys where he lived, but he recorded a singular collection of information on the lives of ordinary, mid–nineteenth-century Americans as they struggled to survive amid the warfare that engulfed them.[76] He wrote on subjects as diverse as child-rearing, sartorial standards, women using snuff, the definition of a gentleman held by the rustic aristocrats who employed him, and of holiday observances, those for religious celebrations as well as those proclaimed by the warring governments.

The diary entries deal with local matters for the most part. He gave short shrift to all that occurred beyond his immediate cognizance. Lee's surrender and Lincoln's assassination receive a word or two, but the substance of the diary concerns the military, economic and social settings where he found employment and support after deserting his regiment on April 18, 1862. During war years he tried his hand at a variety of occupations, several times establishing schools for rural children.[77] When not teaching youngsters to read or begging tuition from their fathers for lessons already taught, he took whatever jobs he could find: farmhand, railroad laborer, and the like. He often recorded intriguing snippets about his work. While employed as a log samsoner at Davis's sawmill, he wrote of the hard physical nature of the job. At other times, he described tapping trees for sap to make sugar, bartering his labor for goods, plowing, and

a successful lawyer, legislator, and high public official. After his father's suicide, his widowed mother acquired an aged slave named Isaac, who helped her with chores about her farm. Still, Philip was never a rabid partisan of slaveholders, although from time to time he expressed the view that "Negroes" were the mental and moral inferiors of whites. Toward the end of the war he had come to believe that slavery should be eliminated. Like so many abolitionists, he argued that forced bondage was essentially evil and that southerners were unfit to be masters, but he also had personal reasons for favoring emancipation. One of the most wicked features of the south's peculiar institution, he explained on several occasions, was that it almost guaranteed the debauching of the young sons of the masters.[84] White boys were regularly corrupted by slave girls, in his view, and he was appalled by it. Everywhere the young sons of slaveholders, from ten onward, were victims of the blighted practice. He wrote of one family, possibly the Duvalls, where the sexual contacts between one son and a slave girl became so frequent and flagrant that everyone knew of it, parents, brothers, and sisters. The awkwardness was ended by hiring the girl out. The son received a mild reprimand, but to Van Buskirk's horror, "he ceased not to be the pet of [the] family, and such he continues to be."[85] Although beautiful lads still exerted a profound attraction for Van Buskirk in the early 1860s, the one sexual encounter recorded in the diary during the Civil War was with an unwashed slattern he met at a sugar camp. His narrative of their awkward trysts provides a splendid example of nineteenth-century male-female byplay, from introduction to temptation, and on through reluctance, hesitation, seduction, and fumbled consummation.

At one point, Van Buskirk tired of farm labor, and sought less arduous work by signing on as a drumming instructor for the Confederate 22nd Virginia Infantry. In April 1863, he and the six or seven hundred men of the 22nd joined with several irregular units under the command of newly-promoted General John D. Imboden. The purpose of the combined force was to conduct a major raid into northwest Virginia. It is unlikely there was the slightest hesitation on the part of Imboden's command to accept the drummer into their ranks. The unit already contained a large number of deserters from Lee's Army of Northern Virginia, and additional men, no matter what their provenance, were more than welcome.

The orders for Imboden's expedition came directly from Robert E.

Lee. Part of the plan was to launch a lightening strike into the territory and catch the Federal armies completely by surprise. Accordingly, the mission and its objectives were to be kept secret from the men of the units involved. The plan called for two columns to march into the areas under Union control, one under Imboden, the other under Brigadier General W. E. "Grumble" Jones. The mission of the combined force of approximately 5,000 infantrymen and cavalry was to drive the Federal armies out of the Kanawaha Valley, secure supplies for the Army of Northern Virginia, gather cattle, horses, and recruits for the Confederate cause, and sabotage the Baltimore & Ohio and the Northwest Virginia Railroads.[86] Attacking the B. & O. Railroad was a particularly important part of the mission, since it was the shortest route from the Potomac to the Ohio River and was the primary artery for supplying Federal troops in the Shenandoah Valley and the Trans-Allegheny region.

There are no diary entries for the period Van Buskirk served under Imboden, although he did manage to dash off missives to a favorite boy while on the move. The failure to chronicle his service during these weeks was due, in all likelihood, to the difficulties encountered by the expedition.[87] The first week of the march along the route from Staunton westward was made through driving rain, across swollen and fast-coursing streams, and over deeply mired roads. At one stage during the expedition, the raiders managed to cover only fourteen miles in three days, even after abandoning spare wheels and some of their shot to lighten artillery caissons. Throughout the thirty-seven days of marching, countermarching, and raiding, the expedition traversed 400 miles despite two solid weeks of rain, inadequate rations, and a lack of forage.

Although the northern troops in the area invaded by Jones and Imboden far outnumbered the Confederates, they were widely disbursed and poorly led. Their commander, Brigadier General Benjamin S. Roberts, was conspicuously non-aggressive in the face of the invaders. Despite the ineptitude of the Union commander, the two-pronged offensive obtained only a portion of its objectives. The southern force was too small to eject their enemy from the Kanawaha Valley permanently, but they managed to disrupt railroad operations to some extent. The raiders also destroyed 150,000 barrels of oil, commandeered a large number of cattle and horses, and captured 700 prisoners. In addition, the Confederates managed to sign up several hundred volunteers, although their recruiting effort was not as successful as they had hoped.[88]

Introduction

After his return from the expedition with Imboden in mid–May, Van Buskirk went on only a few more military adventures. Most of the time he lived as a deserter, with ample time to record what he did and what he saw. It was not until over a year and a half after he last marched with Confederate forces that Union authorities arrested him on suspicion of spying and confiscated the volume he was then using as a diary. Along with two Irish prisoners he was placed on board a railroad car and sent off in custody to Cumberland, Maryland. The letter sent along with him was addressed to a Lieutenant C. A. Freeman, one of the officers at the Cumberland military prison. It contained information on the prisoner's background and state of mind:

> I this day send to Cumberland under guard *P. C. Van Buskirk* whose father was once secretary of state of Maryland.... On his person was found some letters, a "diary" and sundry papers all of which accompany this.... He professes to have been coming in to deliver himself up and take the amnesty oath. He, however, since being here suggested to a gentleman whether he could not be let loose or paroled awhile and be permitted [illeg.] afterwards take the oath or be treated as a prisoner of war as he might [illeg.] elect. He is an intelligent, educated man, as his diary shows, and may be here for the purpose of spying out our means of defense.... His diary is a curiosity and will pay for the trouble of reading it.[89]

Van Buskirk's captured diary quickly moved upward through the Union chain of command. It was on July 18 that he first met General Benjamin Franklin Kelley, who personally summoned him to his office. The general made it clear immediately that he did not intend to accuse the former Confederate of spying. He explained that the diary had the ring of truth about it. He then asked the prisoner several questions, and evidently satisfied with the answers, advised him to be loyal to the Union in the future. The diary was returned to its owner along with other personal items that had been taken from him. Kelley asked Van Buskirk to make a transcript of the diary for publication, then ordered him released. Before departing, the grateful Van Buskirk asked the Union commander to help retrieve the confiscated 1861-1862 volume of the diary, but it was never returned.[90]

When the Civil War ended in the spring of 1865, Van Buskirk's services as a farm hand and laborer were no longer required, and his status as a vagabond appeared to be permanent. He wandered despondent, hungry, homeless, rejected, and often unemployed through the area where the borders of Virginia, Pennsylvania, West Virginia, and Maryland are in close proximity. In desperation, he returned to Washington, D.C., in September, and on October 2, 1865, went to the headquarters barracks of the United States Marines and asked to rejoin the Corps. It was six years earlier in the same building that he had been denied reenlistment on account of his persistent dysentery. This time he easily passed the physical examination, and, as he explained, took "the oath which binds me to *penitentiary* service for four long years."[91] In November he was ordered on board the "little steamer" U.S.S. *Swatara* as a member of the ship's guard. He was desperately unhappy with the new post, and tried on several occasions to get permission to go ashore, but was rebuffed each time. The entry for December 31 summarized the year that concluded with the months on board the *Swatara*. He wrote, "1865 is gone. My God! What memories crowd it! It has passed over me like an ugly dream."

The Civil War
Diary of
Philip C. Van Buskirk

1861–1862

The entries for 1861 and 1862 that follow are Van Buskirk's ineffective attempt to reconstruct the diary volume confiscated when he was taken prisoner by troops of the Potomac Home Brigade's 2nd Regiment on May 26, 1862. Complete diary entries do not begin until April 1863.

1861 July

21. Battle of Bull Run.

1861 December.

Sunday. [Illeg.]—13th Va. Vols. At Centerville, anticipating a battle.[1]

1862 February

3d. 13th Va. Vols. Camp Walker, in winter quarters.

1862 March

18th. Deserted the 13th Va. Infantry.

1862 May

26. Arrested while returning from a visit to Elijah V. Buskirk. Had departed from the V. Buskirk home this morning. Taken as a prisoner to military camp at New Creek, where stay tonight.[2]

27. Taken from New Creek to military prison in Wheeling W. Va

28. Taken from Wheeling to Columbus O. and committed to Camp Chase military prison.

1862 August.

26th. Depart from Camp Chase in a draft of prisoners to be exchanged. (The imprisonment at Camp Chase began 28 May last.) Can't recall how or where headed this night.

27. Still a prisoner of war in transition. Can't tell how dormitoried.

28. Depart from Cairo on prison transport steamer

1862 September.

9. Steamer arrives at Vicksburg. Prisoners (including myself) put over the lines and turned loose.

1862 November.

13. Depart from Grayson County, Va., and arrive Marion, Smyth County, Va.

14. Depart from Marion, Smyth Co., Va. and arrive (via Dublin) at Giles C. H.

19. Arrive at Richlands, near Lewisburg [Virginia].[3]

1862 December.

17. Depart from Richlands. and arrive at the home of Col. Davis, where take up my abode for remainder of the year. Open school at Col. [James Lucius ?] Davis's with two pupils, to wit a son of the Col. and Lewis Jefferson (or Llewellin) son of Gen. A. W. G. Davis.[4]

What have I been in this year 1862? In turn soldier, vagabond, prisoner, and vagabond again.

1863

PRIVATE DIARY OF
Philip Clayton Van Buskirk
Begun this 1 day of April, 1863, in the 30th year,
1st month and 28th day of my age.

April 1863

Greenbrier County [Virginia].

1. I returned here yesterday from Mr. [Lieutenant Governor Samuel] Price's in town,[5] where I had been staying some nine or ten days. In this time I did something in the way of instructing the drummers of the 22nd Virginia Regiment, giving them an hour or two each day.[6]

And yesterday completed a period of 7 weeks and 5 days, throughout which it was my supreme happiness to have for almost constant companion, a noble boy [Lewis Price, son of Lieutenant Governor Price], [illeg.] whom none that I have ever known is more worthy of love and esteem.[7] In this boy my best affections centered. He became my idol. In me he found a playmate, a familiar friend, his teacher. I trust in god my teachings were faithful. I know they were earnest, unremitted, prompted by a powerful Love, and founded in my best wisdom. God be his guide — his teacher — this noblest of boys.

3. End of the sugar making season, which lasted 5 weeks. On Mr. [Charles L.] Peyton's place were three sugar camps, tended by a force made up as follows: 8 men, 1 woman, 9 children.[8] One thousand trees. The yellow maple were tapped, and the yield is found to be 1679 pounds of sugar and 121 gallons of molasses. The former is selling at the sugar camps at one dollar per pound, the latter at five dollars per gallon. Pork costs 50 cents a pound and corn meal 4\frac{50}{}$ a bushel.

13. The 22nd Virginia Regiment (Infantry) being ordered upon an expedition to the northwest, and departing today, I have arranged with the drum major and adjutant to join it in the capacity of volunteer drummer, to draw no pay, nor be enrolled, but retain the liberty of discontinuing my services when I please. This step is prompted by a curiosity to see the country and people north of here, and to see the end of the expedition. It may be, rather than patriotism, for I would not have joined the regiment had Mr. Price found employment for me on his farm at Richlands, where I desired above all things to stay and work, and have Lewis for the companion of my evenings and nights.

May 1863

17. The 22nd marched into Lewisburg today, and thus ends my participation in the expedition.

At Hightown [April] 15, the 22nd joined Imboden's Brigade,[9] consisting of the 62nd, 25th, 31st Va. Infantry; Jackson's and Dunn's Battalions, (on foot,) 19th Va. Cavalry; 6 pieces of artillery; which with the 22nd made up, it was estimated, 3700 men.[10] On one of the early marches I met unexpectedly my cousin John Chipley, captain of a company of the 62^{d}; and at Buckhannon, his brother Tom, captain of cavalry. Tip was a member of Tom's company, but I did not get to see him. In this expedition I did not forget to write frequently to my loved boy at Lewisburg, only to find on my return that he had not himself read three lines of all that I had written. It seems impudence to expect this boy's love. Yet his regard for me is very great. He "likes" me very much. He all but loves me. I have exercised almost unlimited control over him. For me he has strived manfully along in paths entirely new to him, and such as it required great self denial to pursue. I have engaged to teach the drummers of the 22nd how to beat. Twenty-six dollars per month is the compensation allowed me, with a ration. I live at Mr. Price's and spend two or three hours every forenoon in the regiment. Camping two miles out of town for the purpose of attending to the practice of the drums.

June 1863

MEADOW BLUFF.

6. Whew! I figured in a scene this night very disagreeable indeed to the parties principally concerned, and amusing no doubt to the spectators. A scene that will bear mentioning again, the story of which may travel to Lewisburg. I've been boarding and lodging at a Mr. Renick Kincaid's, whose fine brick house overlooks our camp, and this afternoon with the consent of the boy's mother, I took one of his little children on a visit to Mr. Dietz, about a mile distant.[11] Parson Fisher called to stay, and that put in course of preparation such a savory supper that I was tempted to remain till after nightfall, this delaying the return of the child in proper season. Of course the parents were anxious, and when I least expected it, the father made his appearance a picture and pantomime of rage.

I did not lose my own imperturbability, but having in mind through-out the sacred characters of Father with which Mr. K. was invested, and aching as he was in behalf of his child, untroubled with fears, I governed my deportment according to what I thought (and now think) was just and proper under the circumstances. Mr. K. bid me take my "traps" from his house. (They consist of only a book and a haversack.) I acted at once upon his suggestion, and though he relented so far as to tell me I needn't leave till morning, I preferred finding shelter elsewhere, and have had a pallet spread for me on the floor of an Irish cabin (Mrs. Hughs) within a short walk of camp, where I propose resting tonight.

18. Drew $21^{25} from the adjutant today, the amount of pay due me up to date, at the rate of 26 dollars per month. After leaving Mr. Kincaid's (6th) I found boarding and lodging at Mr. W. R. Sharp's near camp, and stayed there till yesterday, when I was notified to leave. The bill presented me is at the rate of $1^{50} a day, from which I am allowed to deduct 50 cents for my rations. Certainly twice the fair price. Avarice is the pervading trait in all this section.

July 1863

6. In my boots, socks, pants and shirt, I weigh 142 lbs. Out of them 134 lbs. Sick at heart these days.

12. Today we part, Lewis Price and I. I never met a boy who more needed a friend. I came by degrees to idolize him, and had he chosen to accept my offer, I would now go to the farm at Richlands to stay and work on the farm, and teach him English rudiments, and teach him virtue.

I could never gain his love. He grew tired of me, and though it is appointed that I depart forever tomorrow, he did not love me enough to stay in town with me today.

13. Though I stay often at Mr. Price's, the days of my sweet companionship with Lewis are past.

September 1863

21. Marches and battle. On Monday the 24ᵗʰ of August, the brigade (called the First of the Army of W. Va., Col. G. S. Patton in command) was put in motion, assembling at Frankfort to march, I had no clear idea whither. I chose to accompany the 26ᵗʰ (Edgar's Battalion), whose drummers I had been instructing.[12]

Two miles from Dry Creek Hotel, early in the forenoon of Wednesday the 26ᵗʰ we unexpectedly came upon the Yankees, and a battle ensued that lasted all day. I must say of myself that in the beginning I was full enough of courage, and in the discharge of duties assigned me I rode the adjutant's horse through fire without being troubled with fears, and recrossing, under the same fire, I choose, having regard for the life of a valuable animal, to come on foot, leaving the horse in a safe place. I had intended to serve only as an assistant to the surgeon — help to carry wounded off the field, a duty usually assigned to musicians in this army — but came afterwards to take a place in the ranks, and so remained with the battalion to the end of the battle, and through the subsequent pursuit of the enemy as far as Callahan's Station. When the battle waxed hottest I think I rather found the measure of my courage: but I did not show any trepidation: but thanked my stars we were so well sheltered [by a breastwork of rails] from the enemy's bullets.[13]

October 1863

8. James E. Arbuckle, little fellow of 10, became my companion for a day or two, and much of a friendship sprung up between us.[14]

10. Exodus of "undomiciled foreigners." Today a long train of wagons filled with families. I claimed to be of that class, and asked the brigade adjutant for a pass to the United States, but that dignitary of the army refuses to recognize Maryland as a foreign state, and says that I, as a Maryland refugee, am liable to conscription, unless a medical board exempts me.

13. Spy captured today. Evidence of his guilt found in his stockings. Sad fate awaits him. Sad disgusting exhibition will be his public execution.

Another embellishment for the annals of Lewisburg. Received 30\underline{^{00}}$ Confederate scrip from Adjutant Craig.

15. Good bye Lewis — a kiss and Good-bye! Good-bye the Prices and Peytons, and Lewisburg! Gen. [John] Echols begins an expedition to the west (Kanawha Valley) and I accompany Edgar's Battalion as a volunteer.[15] I bring my Burnside carbine, and exactly what duties will be assigned me I cannot say yet. I've said to Lewis, "Keep a faithful diary, and remember, it depends upon your conduct, whether you ever see me again."

16. Army camped at Meadow Bluff last night, and at daylight this morning, took up its march westward, but had not gone a mile when orders came for its steps to be retraced, so that each command is back where it camped before, and I am here.

19. Said Gen. A. W. G. Davis to me yesterday: "If you can get released from the army, and will teach this boy of mine (Lochlin) I'll give you more pay than you get in the army.

November 1863

6. Mr. Tiddler, a hatter, said to be the most skillful workman in the country, lives at Mr. Schisler's. I heard of him, and came here Monday night to offer to work for a hat — a fur hat of the first quality for a boy thirteen years old, (Lewis,) and agreed with Mr. S. to work at old time wages (50 cents a day) payable in the hat at the old time price, 5$\underline{^{00}}$. These hats are selling at 25\underline{^{00}}$ Confederate notes. Three days of my ten had been worked out, (shucking corn in the field,) when the enemy made their appearance in force, and advanced within miles of Mr. Schisler's. The brigade is expected today, so I lay down my husking pin, and take my old place among the music of the 23rd Battalion to see them through the engagement that is expected to come off today.[16] Saw Runnels Davis (Commanding company in the 19th Cavalry) and asked him to send me the first spare horse and accouterments that he may happen to have on his hands.[17] The 23rd Battalion held a road and did not go into action. The battle went against us, and I am at this house tonight, a straggler among a dozen "demoralized" soldiers, all astray from the battalion.[18]

9. Day of grief! Said Lewis to me yesterday: "I don't want you to stay with me this winter, but I'd like to hear from you once in a while." Gen. Davis wants me to stay at his house, and teach his children. Mrs. Arbuckle extends me a similar invitation, and so do others, and all seem to love me but Lewis.[19]

10. A heavy heart — grief! The world has lost its beauty.

11. Such traveling today. Carrying a heavy heart too, till having found Dixie restored at Schisler's. I turn my steps again in the direction of Lewisburg.

16. Benighted, I applied in vain for shelter in the Irish cabins ½ a mile from there, so I am glad to take shelter where I am.

27. Rode Lieut. Davis's horse and John Price's saddle, and go there in time today to put in half a days work (shucking corn) for the hat I am getting made for Lewis Price, if the services of my horse do not count me, I have 6½ days more to work.

28. Weather too bad for work in the field, so I chop wood to day, all for Lewis's hat.

30. Snow, and too cold to do anything. I however get to shell corn, and go to mill. So I can call it half a day. I have now five days to work for a hat.

December 1863

7. At Robert Renick's today, where I happened on my way to Falling Springs, an old fellow took it upon him to lecture me for being out of the army. He judged of me by my hat and boots, and talked such stuff as put me out of all humor. His name which I have taken pains to find out, is [no name follows].

10. At Hillsborough, at Col. Beard's house in the room where Lieut. Balderman and other wounded lay. Col. Beard sold me a fine pair of cavalry boots, for which I paid him $10 and am to pay $20 more. My coat, vest, pants, and boots are now unexceptionable. Had I another hat, no old fellow would mistake me for an ignorant lout of the country. The fine fur hat which I had making for Lewis is done, and I am taking it to him.

12. Excitement all last night. I went to bed as usual and tried to sleep. Today a battle was anticipated. I reported mounted to Col. Edgar, who employed me as courier. But the army falling back, I was excused from further service, and went to Gen. Davis's and joined Allen and Sam in running off the cattle. So that's what [sic] I am at now.

24. Mr. Price's Negroes ran away when the Federals were here last. As two of them were bright mulattos [*sic*] of the tender sex, and notorious for their prostitutions, I rejoiced at the event, as the great danger which threatened the morals of my loved boy was now removed. The Negroes all gone from Richlands. I am in demand to go there to live with the two old ladies (Mr. Price's sisters) and keep things in order on the place. At the same time I am invited to stay this winter at Gen. Davis's to teach two children, and have another invitation to live in Mr. Arbuckle's family, and there teach two children. At the latter place I would be most comfortably fixed. But I choose to stay at Richlands, and work hard this winter, if Lewis will be my companion and pupil. It is given him to choose. I am sorry he exhibits indecision. It is night. Boys are in crowds in the street firing off fire arms. I am just in from one of the crowds. Small boys ripping out big oaths were there, and drunken men too. Lewis is at the farm. I am alone.

27. "Today we part," so I wrote months ago, and I thought this unloving boy had indeed drove me from him.

I expected to leave the country, but remained and wrote of our sweet companionship as past. True in one sense only. Lewis does not, will not love me. Still, we have been often and for days together. Often slept together, and say our prayers kneeling together hand in hand, I repeating each portion of the "Lord's Prayer," which if Lewis understands, he repeats after me: then Lewis repeats the "Child's Prayer." "Now we lay us down to sleep," and kissing each other our devotions end. This looks like love, but I have Lewis's word for it that no such feeling exists in his breast, yet for his docility, for his truthfulness, for his childlike piety and innocence, though he will not call me brother and love me, I still love him, and today have accepted his promise to obey me all the coming winter as his instructor.

SECOND MEMORANDUM.[20]

1. Pigskin Box and clothes press entrusted to care of Smith Capron, Annapolis, Md. In May, 1861, was seized by the provost marshal and never restored. Col. J. P. Staunton, military commandant at Annapolis, during the period of my imprisonment was addressed in reference to the subject, but returned no reply. George Schultz requested to effect if possible their restoration.[21]

2. Diary. Seized by commanding officer at New Creek and transmitted to Major James [actually Joseph] Darr, Provost Marshall General at Wheeling, by whom retained.[22]

4. I am pledged to [unidentified Chinese character] and the L O of N and TC not to use tobacco nor drink ardent spirits during the years 1862 and 1863.[23]

5. Letters received at Camp Chase entrusted to Lieutenant Cutler, 85 Ohio, for transmission to George Schultz.

1864

PRIVATE DIARY
OF
PHILIP CLAYTON VAN BUSKIRK
"As we beat thro life to make a lee,
In poverty or riches,
Should Heaven send a head beat sea —
Damn it! Ease her when she pitches."

January 1864

<u>Remarks</u>. The house at Richlands is a comfortable brick containing four small rooms. Its inmates are two old maids (sisters of Mr. Price) with Lewis and myself. Sometimes a soldier on short leave is employed on the place, and sleeps in our room. As winter approached, Mrs. Arbuckle, a wealthy lady, living in good style, invited me to stay in her family, as instructor of her two little boys. Gen. Davis also offered to pay me well, if I would teach his children through the winter. But Mr. Price's slave family went off, leaving his farm without a man upon it and I chose rather to go there as a farmhand, to work and to tend the cattle through the winter upon the sole condition of having the lieutenant governor's little son Samuel Lewis placed with me during that time as a companion and pupil.

Samuel Lewis Price was born in Lewisburg on the 10th of July in the year 1850.

February 1864

<u>Remarks</u>. This month, as last, Lewis and I live happily together, fellow students and intimates. We pursue our studies like two boy philosophers, the one a boy of fourteen, the other a boy of thirty.

A Mr. Lawhorn, a soldier hired to make troughs, etc., during the latter half of the month was given a bed in our room, and trespassed upon our hours a little.

19. I am ill at ease. An irascible man addressed me in language the most insulting — called me a "d — ned Yankee son of a b — ch" — and yet I did not knock him down. He was an old man. I sidled up to him, and, I think, put him in some fear by my own words and demonstrations. But old as he was I ought perhaps to have given him a box on the ear, for to have not done so seems like having pocketed an insult, hence an uneasy feeling possesses me tonight. The man of whom I speak is a Mr. Alexander. He is preparing to work a sugar camp rented from Mr. Price, and had hauled a quantity of wood. On the late "cold day," our wood being exhausted, I and a Mr. Lawhorn, borrowed a sled load from Mr. Alexander's pile, intending to repay it, with some additional big sticks by way of interest.

Today while I was hitching up oxen to bring wood in return for what had been taken, Alexander appeared and asked "Whether I knew who had taken a load of his wood?" I replied that I had taken it myself. Then came the torrent of insult of which I have written.

26. Said Lewis last night: "Mr. Alexander says that he saw a man who knew you in Charlestown, Va. This man says that your mother lives in Charlestown. Mr. A. thinks it's all a story about your coming from Maryland."

The man adverted to by Mr. A. I have learned today is George Cordell, son, I believe of Dr. Cordell, of whom I heard so much in times long passed. Mr. A would, I have no doubt, be pleased to see the agents of conscription hunt me up, and place me in the army. As a Marylander I am exempt from conscription.

27. Cannon heard.

28. Smoky day. Sat up quite late last night to write out something for Lilburn [Peyton] to use in his debating club next Friday.[24] It is probably the first "speech" I ever wrote, and I doubt not, is a puerile performance, though Lilburn thinks it a masterly composition.

March 1864

THE RICHLANDS FARM.

7. I am guilty of a grievous sin this day. May God forgive me! I am humbled. Not before man, for my sin is my own secret. But before Heaven, and in my own eyes, I am indeed a pitiable wretch. I have been like a master to Lewis. Let me never again assume the bearing of a superior towards this noble boy, whose shoestrings I am not worthy to tie. Lewis is away. In his absence has this misfortune come upon me. May God forgive me![25]

9. Hair cut. Started early in the forenoon to visit Gen. Davis. Lewis accompanying, but I didn't get any further than town. A pleasure party was to meet at Gen. Davis's and more young ladies were anxious to go than had horses to ride. I gave up mine to one of them, and returned on foot to Richlands. Lewis proceeded with the party. On my way back I passed by a sugar camp tended by a squalid woman, and accepted her invitation to come again that way and spend the night.

10. Wild geese migrating. I passed last night in the sugar camp of the dirty, uncombed woman, and had for company besides, a girl of eleven, almost as dirty as the woman. Low propensities induced me to steal over to this woman's den, and though I pigged in with her and the girl through the night, and had come for lewdness only, yet nothing like fornication took place between us. We pigged in with our clothes on. There was no "stylem in pixide," but I am nevertheless guilty of sin — a sin approaching to that of Onan. I am now in our room washed and divested of last night's rags. Cleaned of everything but last night['s] sin.

I have a high character here for morals. Only a little perseverance in conduct like this, I am aware would speedily reduce me to infamy. I am resolved to take better care of my reputation. It may be I can not hope before marriage to become chaste in mind, but my heart is not entirely reprobate. I would that virtue sat enthroned in my heart.

Pleasure party at the General's were alarmed in the night by news of the approach of the "Yankees." They all took horse after midnight, and got back to town as best they could through the darkness and rain. So says Lewis.

12. Grieved today. My boy detests books. He hates learning, and is willing to resign himself to ignorance. I have failed to raise in him the ambition to be intelligent.

My dear child, Lewis, whom I love with more than a brother's love. I reasoned with him. I strove with him today, and tears coursed down my cheeks. But the boy sat immoveable.

25. Good Friday. Good Friday, but it is no part of the religion of the people of this section to observe it as a fast day. Indeed the people here never have [illeg.] fast days, and know of none, save such as the president may appoint by proclamation, and not then to observe it.

31. Sugar making ends. Mr. Prices Sugar Camp No. 1 was vacated today, after a season of 5 weeks. Three men and one horse were employed, and 250 trees were tapped — two spiles being inserted in each tree. Mr. Price gets as rent one third of the sugar made.

April 1864

8. Fast Day. Molasses making. Lewis and I hung onto two kettles, after the sugar makers had vacated Camp No. 1. We gathered in about 40 buckets of water, and with much trouble boiled it down, obtaining not more than 3 quarts of molasses. We probably boiled down more rain water than sugar water.

Congress of the C. S. before adjourning, appointed this day for "fasting, humiliation, and prayer." In this neighborhood it is kept as a sort of half-holiday only, and I suspect it is very little regarded in other parts of the county.

17. WHAT THEY SAY OF ME. It seems I am not too insignificant to be the subject of remark now and then. Thanks to Lewis I can make a note of some of the sayings which it may interest me hereafter to look over. (1.) He is a very childish man, and seems to have little judgment about things." This is the opinion of Mr. Price, concurred in by all the young ladies. (2.) "He is an educated fool." So a Mr. Lawhorne expressed himself in conversation with Mrs. Price one evening. My sin against Mr. L. consisted in my excluding him from our chamber during hours devoted to privacy and study. (3) "He is the finest scholar I ever seed." Mr. Knapp. (4) "He is a very childish man, but is willing to work if somebody will show him how; but hasn't himself the least judgement." This is from Mr. Price. He came out the other day, and undertook with my assistance, to put a wagon in order for carrying hay. To complete the job some small thing needed to be properly adjusted. Mr. Price didn't know how to do it. Neither did I. *His* judgement (ingenuity) did not avail him in this case; and as for mine — if it is allowed that I have any — I must confess its exercise was suspended.

My intercourse with Mr. P. has always been marked by a diffidence which few others inspire, and the manners resulting from this feeling doubtless deserves to be called "childish."

21. Yankees a coming!

23. Steal away after supper under pretense of going to visit the Peytons, and spend the night in the camp of the filthy woman mentioned 9th and 10th March. the woman's name is Julie. She is about 20 years old, rather large, red-haired, ugly, clumsy in her manners and exceedingly *filthy* in her person. A little child of her own (she has two) and a somewhat sprightly girl of eleven years, are in the sugar camp with her; also a boy who gets asleep, and stays in the camp all night, as does the girl of eleven. Her own child is after a while taken to the house in which the woman now lives, and left there. Julie begins with a song that for rank obscenity beats anything of the kind I had ever heard. Then follow jokes equally obscene, some leveled at the little boy, who takes it all in good part, and shows us that nothing in these doings is new to him. The girl of eleven at first exhibits some faint signs of offended modesty, which are evanescent, however, and then proves herself a worthy disciple of the abandoned woman. To remain and see how far it can go, I must perform a bad part myself. Accordingly I proceed with a smutty story quite to the taste of my auditors. The night wanes, and in the end we all pig in together to get a little sleep. and yet, but two of us ... [Van Buskirk's ellipses] the young 'uns really become wrapped in slumber. The woman only pretends sleep. She wants to be *forced* as it were. And I have resolved this time not to fail in effecting the gratification of— say impure desire. At least eight years have elapsed since I put myself to woman [*sic*].

Imagination, and all I have read, and all I have heard of it, bid me anticipate ecstasy inexpressible. But the sin the *adultery*. Are the religionists right in classing simple coition with no man's wife as adultery? And then, I am subject to nocturnal emissions, which occur as often as three or four times a month, a distressing complaint, for which I have read and believe, that coition is the only available remedy.

I have excellent general health. Then why did I fail to experience the transports ecstatic the bliss indescribable? I had disappointment instead — sensations unpleasant — and a feeling of disgust remaining. I'll not touch this woman again, unless I think it helps my case. Truly, if that were not the motive, there would be none other to tempt to a repetition of this act.

As to the scenes I have mentioned as preceding it, I think, I may safely say that nothing would induce me to take part in such again.

Before the morning uncovered these deeds of darkness and filth, I hie me back to my home, pretending to have come from the Peytons!

? Mr. Price says he will endeavor to obtain for me a pass through the lines. I am anxious to get into some district in which is a U.S. Post Office, so that I can hear from my mother.

May 1864

3. Lewisburg
   May, 3, 1864
   Gen. John Echols
   Dear General:
      This note will be handed to you by Mr. Van Buskirk, the gentleman of whom I spoke to you for a pass to go through our lines.
      He comes to take the *oath* of secrecy [*sic*], and to get the pass.
                                        Very truly yours, etc.
                                        Samuel Price

Presented the foregoing note at the brigade headquarters today, and after waiting about an hour, was called into the general's tent, only to be politely informed that it was not deemed expedient in the present juncture of affairs to grant the desired passport. The general had promised Mr. P. that "if I would present myself I should certainly get the pass." Well! I didn't think much of the disappointment. Maybe I can get along without the billet.[26]

4. The rumor of "Yankees a coming!" is spreading alarm among the people.[27] All work in the field is suspended, and everybody is thinking how he or she can best save the little stores of sugar and bread and meat-stuffs on hand. Horses are being gathered up to be run off. Lewis did some milling this morning for town [*sic*] and came out this evening in a fever of excitement to secure his colt. His father is refugeeing again.

6. I am just in from the field, where I've been all forenoon (nearly) helping an old black man to lay up fence. Miss Mary Ann says it has been reported that the Yankees are at Meadow Bluff, with one hundred wagons, from which it is argued that they are coming this time to stay. We are hurrying to get our grain in the ground.

P. S. All afternoon helping Mr. Knapp to furrow out for corn, my first ploughing of the kind that I can remember.

8. Eventful day. U.S. forces arrived in town about the middle of the forenoon. All the male inhabitants were gone save some fifty non-conscripts, about a dozen of whom, including myself, formed little parties of spectators in the streets, meeting for gossip here and there, sometimes altogether, like a town council. The advance squads of Yankees passed us by. A brigade came up in the course of the day, and halted a short distance out of town. Their behavior extorted the admiration of the inhabitants. No person in town that I have heard of has as much as been annoyed. The soldiers I am informed, are forbidden to enter enclosures without license, much less houses.

And so far as I know, there has not occurred a single instance of violation of this order. No person complains of the loss of as much as a fowl. I was directed to invite an officer to take up his quarters at Mrs. Prices, for the sake of protection, and I found opportunity to converse with several, each of whom impressed me with a high opinion of his character as a gentleman. Only one I did not admire. A surgeon, whose sayings and doings were otherwise unexceptionable, sat down near me, and in conversation let drop an intimation that he had that morning given two pounds of coffee to a "lady" in exchange for her <u>favor</u>. The Yankees had not been in town a quarter of a day before they had opened the way to a whorehouse, or had opened the whorehouse itself, for if such an establishment had a pre-existence in this town I did not know it, but then I am not posted as to what are the brothel facilities of Lewisburg.[28] (Thank goodness! my little friend is equally ignorant with myself of the existence of such haunts near his home.) One is accountable to his God alone for his secret deeds; but if they are of a licentious character, and he unblushingly avow them, he, in that, much poisons the moral atmosphere, and earns for himself the detestation of all men who think as I do.

In the evening came orders for every man in the streets to return to his company, and as the sun went down not a soldier was to be seen in the town. The officers invited to stop at houses did not come. So far as protection was concerned, they were not needed. The women however do not retire without misgivings.

9. Unless in his dreams no Yankee disturbed the sleep of a single inhabitant. I arose late and walked down street before breakfast. Not a Federal was to be seen. The "fight before Richmond" is now the absorbing theme. It is going on, and the daughters and wives of the "secesh" are already cheered with the news of victory, on the Confederate side. Hateful war! One man's glory is a thorn in another's bosom! Came out to Richlands. Having a letter from Lieut. Col. [A. R. ?] Barbee, C. S. A.,[29] to his wife living within Federal lines. I proceeded to the Camp at Bungers Mills[30] to find an officer who would take charge of, and mail it to its destination. Fell in with a drum-major (a fellow who swore me out of countenance) and asked him some questions, which put him into the notion that I was a spy, and caused him to run off with that information to Col. [Abia A.?] Tomlinson.[31] My arrest followed.

The colonel accepted the account which I gave of myself, and released me at once. He asked me questions about the stock of provisions in the country, which I could not answer otherwise than to say in all sincerity "I did not know." And right glad am I that I did not even have the curiosity to pry into the affairs of even the family in which I live, much less peep into the barns or meat houses of my neighbors to know anything about the character or quantity of their stores. In short I had nothing to divulge — knew nothing.

The colonel understood my motives, and respected them. I have returned to the Richlands farm. I devote a small portion of time to write this note, and then I will busy myself with corn planting. I will testify by that service my sense of gratitude to the Father of Lewis for his kindness and protection these past twelve months. And then — can I see my mother? Can I hear from her?

P. S. And yet there was no corn planting today. It seems that nothing can be done without a horse; and the horses have been sent beyond the reach of the enemy.[32]

11. Yankees gone! Returning from town this morning, I learned that the Yankees had visited the farmhouse and helped themselves to a considerable quantity of bacon, but had not disturbed anything else.[33] But one instance of rudeness has occurred at this farmstead so far. Mr. Peyton had flour, bacon, and some grain taken from him — suffered no other damage. I believe it is the design of the authorities impressing these things to leave a sufficient supply with the families to keep them till harvest and hog killing. In the afternoon comes the very glad tidings that our hostile visitors have departed westward. Horses can now be brought in from their hiding places and agricultural labors be resumed. Our late visitors were I believe regiments designated respectively the 36th and 5th Virginia. The latter, I learned from one of its members, was composed almost entirely of Ohioans. There were some intelligent looking men to be seen among them, but as a body of men they very unfavorably impressed me. Their behavior as soldiers on this expedition was on the whole very good, for which we feel indebted to the discipline enforced by their officers.[34]

15. WAR NEWS! Lee has gained a complete victory over Grant! [General Frederick] Steele has surrendered to [General Sterling] Price! [General John C.] Breckenridge has defeated [General George] Crook! Southerners are victorious at Plymouth! In every quarter are southern arms triumphant! All hold this to be the eventful week of the war, and all believe these victories will speedily bring it to a close. The reports which are given above were received today, and are not doubted.[35] The southern heart is elated.

16. Cry of "Wolf" again! Our quiet and farm labors are brought suddenly to an end by intelligence sent us that [General William W.] Averell is on retreat through Lewisburg this way!" Gather up the horses and put out to the mountains!

18. Worse and more of it — so the inhabitants of the loyal town of Lewisburg aver. Col. Tomlinson came up with his infantry from Meadow Bluff yesterday Monday evening, and camped very near the town. I walked from the Richlands yesterday evening. Found everything quiet — good order and discipline prevailing.

This morning I paid Col. Tomlinson a visit to beg the privilege of using on the farm one of our own horses. Was referred to Lieut Blaizer,[36] whom I never got to see. Meantime the inhabitants busied themselves in what I will call gossip for want of a better term. Rumors and conjectures employed the tongues and filled the minds of all. In the afternoon it became known that Averell's forces were coming from the river, and this occasioned much apprehension. Surely Averell's men will respect nothing! They came. Sentinels were posted at almost every crossing, and it was astonishing to see how quietly the whole command formed their encampment, and retired within its precincts without disturbing in the least any of the townspeople. An officer, Captain Farrand, stays with us tonight by invitation. We have besides a house guard assigned us, and so feel entirely protected.

19. Foraging parties of 4 and 8 men scoured the country adjacent to Lewis-burg today, and I judge, swept away the whole remaining stores of many families. I went up to Richlands in the morning. A party of four (includ-ing young Carter, late slave to the Prices) came up to the farmhouse, and insolently demanded to be shown where our provisions were stored. The man's intolerable manner led to an altercation between us, in the course of which he threatened me with his pistol. I did not yield to him, and I gave him to understand that if he took our seed corn (contrary to Averell's orders) I would certainly make out a charge against him before the gen-eral. The party searched the house, but departed without taking anything. Not so another party, which arrived during my absence about an hour — a party of eight or nine. They ransacked the house and carried off every-thing of the provision kind they could lay their hands upon, leaving the old ladies absolutely nothing besides half a loaf of bread and a small piece of bacon. A pair of shoes, a coat, and one other article. I missed immedi-ately, having arrived at the moment of the marauding party's departure. Another party soon after came up, but there was nothing for them to take. These acts were perpetrated at every house, I believe, in the Richlands neighborhood, so that the people there are almost at the verge of starva-tion. Or probably that is too strong a term. Roots and some livestock still remain in the country. Great distress however will certainly follow. Vis-ited camp to ask the favor of house guards for three families in town. Scraped acquaintance with Adjutant Clark of General [Alfred Napoleon Alexander] Duffié's staff.[37]

20. Courtesies are interchanged between the southern families and Duffié's officers. Adjutant Clark called with Captain Rucker last night, and passed, it may be an agreeable hour with the young ladies. With little to say myself I was an attentive observer of this interchange of civilities. A considerable army is now bivouacking around us. The telegraph is being put up, and everything looks like permanent occupation. This sorely annoys the citi-zens. They are persistent Southrons. I remain today at the house in town, and have been, I think, very serviceable to the families in this quarter as a medium of communication between them and the military authorities.

Loyal slaves. Loo, slave of Major Bowen, 8 Va. Cavalry, and Peter, slave of ____ now acting as cooks to Federal officers, and retained in their present places by compulsion (say they), claim to be still loyal to their old masters. They were captured by their present employers. Loo is cook to

General Averell. One is a full blooded African. Loo, I think, has some Caucasian blood in him. The ladies here sympathize greatly with the two servants, especially Peter, who appears to be in great distress.

Col. [John H.] Oley, 7 Va. Cavalry, U.S.A. At the request of some ladies I repaired to Col. Oley's headquarters to ask for officers to stay overnight at their houses. A surgeon, a quartermaster, and a captain accepted the invitations tendered them, and obtaining leave from Col. Oley, returned with me to town. The deportment of all these officers was without exception gentlemanly. Dr. [L. L.] Comstock[38] came to Mrs. Price's, and I think has favorably impressed the family.

Devastation. A Federal officer rode up, and reported to Col. Oley that "every house between here and Frankfort had been turned upside down and pillaged." Children are now crying for bread and receive it not. Averell's men had been some days without rations, and dispersed when they arrived here, in little parties all over the country for foraging, and very many of those parties entered into the indiscriminate plunder of houses. Wretched — wretched beyond description are the hapless inhabitants whose abodes were adjacent to, and not within the precincts of Lewisburg. No houses in town, that I have heard of, have been openly pillaged. Some attempts at house breaking in the night have been frustrated by the house guards who were fortunately present. It is due to Col. Oley and his officers to say that the report of the officer abovementioned was received by them with marks of disapprobation. Col. Oley exclaimed "It is a shame. I wish some of these rascals could be detected and brought to punishment. They ought to be shot."

21. Repaired in the forenoon to General Averell's headquarters with an invitation for the general to call at the house of Mrs. Price. The chief of his staff said the general was absent but he had no doubt the general would take pleasure in according the interview desired, and promised for himself, that he would come anyhow.

Returning by way of Richlands, I met parties bearing turkeys and chickens. On one man's bayonet was carried a very handsome coffee pot of Britannia ware. Another carried a little brass kettle. This party was not afraid to expose these articles of plunder to the view of their officers. Some officer at headquarters told Mr. Peyton that two soldiers were being tried for their lives for pillaging houses. I saw a man at Gen. Duffié's headquarters undergoing examination for the same offense, and believe that it is the general's desire to repress gross outrages, but it is the opinion of the people here that Gen. A. has deliberately given up the country to pillage.

Certainly the devastation could not be more complete had he done so. I have met some hardened rascals, and then again I have spoken with men of conscience — all engaged in this foraging. The latter restricting themselves to legitimate plunder, the former devastating ruthlessly and indiscriminately. The camps, where I have been, are so abundantly supplied that flour, meal, and bacon, milk, beef, and fresh pork are found wasted, and thrown about in great quantities, to be picked up by the boys and women that always appear like turkey buzzards in quest of what soldiers leave behind when vacating a camping place.

Found that C. H. Willis, 2nd Va. Cavalry, had undertaken to guard Mr. Price's house at Richlands from further outrage. We are indebted to him for what little that may remain of provisions or portable property. Speaking of cupidity, Mr. Kenny says that those people who before these terrible times, hoarded their stores and would hardly as much as bestow a crust of bread to appease a soldier's hunger — the grasping and extortionate are the very ones who now suffer the most, while some generous people have almost entirely escaped injury.

A poor crippled Negro woman came in this evening from Mrs. McClintock's to inform us that starvation had arrived, and was peeping through the doors of her mistress's house. They were four mouths, and not a morsel to eat. The soldiers came yesterday, she said, and took away our last bushel of potatoes. "I asked one of them," continued the Black, "if you please, Sir, will you leave us only enough to make our breakfast to-morrow, but he damned me, and said he would not." The Negress applied to the doctor who stays with us, first, and learning from him that nothing could be done for her until the trains came up, next applied to some of the town ladies, one of whom (Mrs. Mathews) offered to divide her little remaining portion of flour with the distressed family.

I conducted the woman to Col. Oley, and that officer promptly filled her basket with crackers, coffee, and sugar. Mrs. Mathews did not have to divide her scanty store of flour.

23. On the farm again. This morning invited an honest intelligent looking orderly sergeant of the 2nd Va. Cavalry to bring his rations to be cooked in our kitchen in town, and if he desired, take up his board at the home and charge of himself with its protection. Then came out to the farm, bringing a quantity of shelled corn on my shoulders. The soldier (C. H. Willis) who had guarded the Richlands place was still on duty, and Mr. Knapp was allowed to use his horse to open furrows for planting corn. And besides this soldier was another, Woodrum by name, whom Mr. Willis had associated with him in the homestead defense. Planted corn in the evening, Woodrum helping. Two soldiers came to buy milk this evening.

Devastation and pillage, it would seem is at last at an end. But who can say?

26. Early in the forenoon, took a ham of mutton to town. Lewis went to mill on Mr. Willis's horse, Woodrum riding by his side as guard. In town I found old John ploughing with the two horses Dr. C. was kind enough to furnish us.

Town well guarded. Learned that orders had been given to withdraw all the guards stationed at houses in the country, and this because of the capture by a Confederate scouting party of a soldier stationed as guard at Mr. Arbuckle's. He was deprived of his horse and arms and released. The ladies at Mrs. Price's requested me to ask Gen. Averell whether a flag could be sent with one of them to the Confederate headquarters, in which case, one of the ladies would cheerfully go and demand the restoration of the horse and arms. Returning to Richlands I found our guards preparing to leave, so I repaired at once to General Averell's headquarters. and preferred the request of the ladies.

The General had reasons for not granting it. I next called at Gen. Duffié's headquarters to ask the continuance at their posts of our guards, as we thought our house, being only two miles from division headquarters, was within the line of pickets, and Gen. Averell said his order was for the withdrawal of the guards from houses outside of that line, but Duffié's adjutant general decided that our house was not [illeg.] the prescribed line. So it is likely that we will part with our guards, which we regret, as they are good men, did their duty faithfully, and we came to like them very much. Their names are C. H. Willis, of Jackson C. H., Ohio and J. J. Woodrum, of Marion, Lawrence Co., Ohio, both of Company H, 2nd West Virginia Cavalry, and both orderlies to Brig. General Duffié. We have plowed with the horse of one, while the other has helped us to plant corn. Adj. Gen. Clark gave me leave to retain our guards one night longer.

27. Adj. Gen. E. W. Clark visited the farmstead today.

29. Cattle taken.

30. Our guards were withdrawn as intimated two notes back. The farmstead is about two miles through the fields from Bungers Mills, where are the headquarters of both Averell and Duffié. We are regarded as <u>without</u> the lines, and subject to certain orders recently issued concerning the citizens whose houses are so situated. Today I walked over to camp with Mr. Knapp. Before getting back we were overhauled by an officer who required us report to Adj. Gen. Clark. That officer did not retain us, nor treat us at all as suspicious persons. And here let me observe that I have not upon any occasion since the departure of the C. S. forces been examined, paroled, or treated in any way by U.S. officers as a man under suspicion. I have been permitted free access to town or to the camp from the farmstead, and both Mr. Knapp and I are sensible of the implied obligation "not to abuse a privilege to the injury of the party by whom the privilege is granted." We therefore are bound by the laws of honor to refrain from what Mr. Knapp terms the "packing of news." Marauding parties do not threaten us almost every hour of the day, as was the case during the first three days after Averell's arrival. Those were the terrible days long to be remembered. I speak of the country. The town has been from the very beginning wonderfully protected. But those days are passed. Trains came up for the army.

Guards were placed at houses. We have had no trouble since our guard left us greater than what are occasioned by strolling parties in search of provisions and of what can be picked up. In some parts of the day the neighborhood is overrun with these stragglers from camp, and they exhibit every disposition from that of the honest man who courteously offers to pay for what can be spared him to that of the ruffian who avows his determination to take by force <u>what he</u> wants. And for begging and stealing, it doesn't seem to me that these stragglers are anywise behind the "<u>Rebs</u>." They have the same stories to tell, and the same tricks to perform that I long ago observed of our own men when placed in like circumstances. The poor people on the lines have really an anxious time of it.

<u>P. S.</u> After dark a party visited one of our hen houses. Mr. Knapp and I reached the spot in time to save a few fowls.

31. The cavalry are scattered over the country all round us grazing their horses. With grazing and reaping our meadows are destroyed. Our wheat is, however, protected. A party of seven or eight came <u>to the house</u> today, and gave us considerable trouble. They were for breaking into the cellar and helping themselves to whatever would answer their purposes, and threaten us with violence if we dare to follow them to camp to report them, but Mr. Knapp and I set out for camp, accompanied by a friendly cavalryman, whereupon these men, who were infantry, beat a retreat.

Our old black man set out from town, in company with Lewis today, and had nearly reached here when he was overtaken by a little party, who robbed him of about 75 cents in silver. I judge a great deal of this kind of waylaying is going on.

June 1864

1. Great day in town. Gen. Crook's Division —10 infantry regiments, 10 pieces of artillery, 103 wagons, 6 pontoon wagons, and 33 ambulances passed through.

Had a tooth extracted today. I had taken the greatest pains to get Lewis to adopt the rule "to return from the company of such persons as would use filthy language, or descant obscenely in his presence," and for three months he had faithfully observed the rule. The other day he was working the garden with two Negroes. They began some filthy discourse. Lewis left them, and asked his mother what he should do under the circumstances. "Go back to your work," said this mother, "and don't mind what they say — let it go in one ear and out at the other." The indifference which this woman exhibits as to her sons morals is perfectly astonishing to me. While I have labored to teach this boy of 14 that it is of the first importance that he should avoid the company of the obscene, his own mother, upon every occasion of his consulting her, seeks to inculcate an entirely different principle. The woman's counsel to her son may be summed up in these words: "It is well to avoid the company of the obscene when you can do so conveniently; but whether you do so or not is a matter of very little moment." In all my trouble and care with Lewis, I never had his mother's or his father's cooperation. They permitted me to stay in the family in consideration of my services as a field hand, and I believe it would not have made the least difference to them had my moral character been bad. They would have been equally satisfied that Lewis should be my intimate associate. The boy's mother has the reputation throughout the community of being a perfect lady. Rich and poor join in her praise. Neither do I discern anything unladylike in her manners. The boy's father is a self-made man; a successful lawyer, an elder in the church, and highly esteemed. They are devout Presbyterians, and yet shamefully recreant to the duty of instructing their children. This boy of 14 cannot read and understand the story of Robinson Crusoe. Today I made Lewis promise to keep from listening to obscenity, as the sole condition of my staying in the family. I love the boy. I must say I despise his parents.

2. MARAUDING continues almost as bad as ever. A party came to the farmstead today, pretending to be a provost guard, and filled the kitchen for a while, acting with great rudeness to the Knapp family. I read the "safeguards" to them. Shortly afterwards they betook themselves to the woods, and we soon heard them shooting our sheep. Mr. Knapp and I first repaired to the spot whence the firing was heard. A wounded sheep was there. The marauders seeing us coming, had taken to the bush. We then repaired to camp. One fellow whom we met on the way, said "It is dangerous to go to camp." Why? "Because there's a row about some boys that have been reported for being out, and doing something, and if you go, they'd just as leave shoot you as not." We went. The man was lying. I had scraped a sort of acquaintance with the adjutant of the 34ᵗʰ Ohio Cavalry. This man I next met, and talking over the matter with him, became convinced that this officer at least was very far disapproving of the outrages complained of. Next talked over the matter with our friend Woodrum. Informed that it was confidently expected that Averell would leave tomorrow with his command, we let the matter drop. Got permission for Woodrum to come over and stay all night with us. Hear that during our absence in camp, some soldiers came, and drove off a portion of our sheep with one of the cows, and addressed abusive and filthy language to Mrs. Knapp.[39] When I applied to the party grazing their horses near the house to turn out a little guard to prevent depredation, they alleged inability to act without orders. I suggested to the adjutant 34ᵗʰ that the people of the country could be easily protected from outrage if he would give the non-commissioned officers sent with those grazing parties instructions to act with their men as provost guard in the immediate neighborhood of their grazing grounds.

3. The FIFTEEN DAYS WITH AVERELL are past! Days of Terror were these! Generals Averell and Duffié took their departure eastward this morning.

5. First swim.

21. Yankees coming! David Creigh, a citizen of this place, was arrested when Gen. Crook was here last, upon the charge of having last fall murdered a Federal soldier who came to his house and set to plundering. Creigh was taken east, and today comes intelligence deemed reliable, that he has been hanged!

The Prices call him cousin. Creigh was a man very much esteemed by his neighbors. I will say nothing of how such news affected the people. The distressing intelligence has gone to his wife and family. I have taken some little note of how our "cousins" can bear up under such afflicting intelligence.[40]

Pshaw! It gives birth to <u>momentary</u> grief, succeeded by feelings of indignation, after which cheerfulness returns, and our cousin and his fate is consigned to oblivion. In the case of the young ladies, it didn't seem their feelings were moved enough to suspend their usual good appetite for dinner, which came on an hour or two after receipt of the sad news.

<u>Afternoon</u>. The startling report has reached town that a train of 270 wagons guarded by 500 cavalry are advancing this way via White Sulphur. The prominent men are preparing for flight again. Horses are being gathered up and galloped off. Terror is depicted upon the countenances of the females. Later we hear that Therman [Capt. William Dabney Thurmond] is advantageously placed to intercept their march.[41] Lieut. Liggit has gone to the river to bring us certain intelligence. Towards sundown the impression obtains that our troublesome visitors are taking another direction, and <u>will</u> not pass this way. This is a comfortable conjecture. We retire to our beds in hopes that it is well founded.

22. <u>Forenoon</u>. Liggit not returned. Painful suspense pervades the community. Between times I employ myself learning something about the counties lately traversed by Crook and Averell. I have a map suspended against the wall of my room. At ½ past ten a small party of Federals, numbering fifteen or more, arrived, and took the Frankfort road. A gang of our own men came flying through the town before them, and took the direction of Bungers Mills. All now anxiously await <u>the arrival</u> of the main body.

Afternoon. No main body arrives. Still no satisfactory <u>news</u> from the river. Liggit has not returned. The party of Federals which had taken the <u>Frankfort</u> road return this way, and continue on towards the White Sulphur.

Near sundown we are surprised by the arrival of <u>Therman</u> and his men, who bring the astounding news "That the whole army commanded by [General David] Hunter, Averell, Crook, and Duffié are in full retreat this way, closely pursued by [General Robert] Ransom, [General George E.] Pickett, and Breckenridge, and that the discomfited army may be expected to arrive at White Sulphur tomorrow at ten o'clock." It is added that this retreating horde is completely "demoralized," a word of terrible <u>import</u>. Therman and his men are in town getting something to eat.[42]

23. Nothing startling. The impression is that our threatened visitors have gone up Anthony's Creek, and so will not come this way. And as to the "demoralized" army, it takes a direction away south of us.

25. Until about nine in the forenoon many indulged the hope — faintly — that after all no <u>army</u> was coming. Then a foraging party came into town, and we learned our fate. I was glad from what I heard from the man in charge to be enabled to give Mrs. <u>Price</u> some assurance that it was not intended to burn the town. Her anxiety was still distressing. Governor Letcher's house had been burned in this raid by order of Gen. Hunter.[43] Before any parties reached Mr. Price's house, I was fortunate enough to find an officer (Capt. Hume, 15th W. Va. Infantry) who was willing to accept such provision as could be made for him and his men and to place guards at Mrs. P.'s and neighboring houses. This was opportune. Several parties who exhibited a disposition to ransack were prevented from entering. The house in town protected. I found a soldier willing to go to the farmstead and act as house guard. Him I conducted to the country, being obliged to use much persuasion, as there was a general <u>dread</u> of bushwhackers.[44] Returning in the afternoon, I learned that a great part of the forces had gone through town. Captain Hume had remained with his guards till his brigade came up, and then (most opportunely) Dr. Webb and subsequently Dr. Comstock dropped in, the latter to stay all night.

Captain Rucker (of Duffié's staff) was kind enough to send an orderly at my request. So that with guards and officers the house in town escaped being ransacked. At dusk a man was shot just around a corner from where I was standing. I heard his groans. Probably he is dead. And this was <u>not</u> a man engaged in forcing an entrance anywhere, or plundering, but came riding along in the middle of the street. At least it doesn't appear that he was. The incident seems forgotten in the next half hour after its occurrence. This is bushwhacking. A representative young lady says of the act "It was not wrong but I think it was imprudent."

At Price's the demand for provisions was complied with to an extent not ruinous. Other houses unprotected, suffered terribly. The town has suffered this time. Last time it was protected. The passing army doesn't appear to be "demoralized" in the military sense of that term, but the men are suffering from hunger. I met party after party as I was coming in from Richlands. In several instances they seemed to take me for a bushwhacker, but after a little questioning, allowed me (upon the strength of my good countenance it may be) to pass on. I have just picked up three men, who have undertaken for a little to eat, to guard this house tonight. I have come myself to stay, as they think my staying may lend to the protection of its inmates. It is midnight. The rumbling of wagon wheels indicate that trains are still passing through the town. I have been active today for the protection of property.

P. S. All night long trains lumbered through the street, and regiments of cavalry poured through the town.

26. It turns out this morning that no one was hurt round the corner where I heard the report of firearms, followed by groans and shrieks. It is thought some soldier was shooting at a hog, and that his ball barely grazed the head of a man who cried out "bushwhacker! I am killed," and groaned terribly. there was much of a scene in the neighborhood of the firing, when the guard sent by Averell arrived, they did their duty, and saved the property, and protected the persons of those upon whom the straggling rabble soldiery seemed bent upon fastening the guilt of bushwhacking. Today no efficient patrol was out to repress irregularities, nor has anything like a provost or town guard been established. But we have done very well. At those times when Dr. Comstock was absent, I kept watch on the house guard (one Pastorius, 14 Penn. Cav.) sent to Mr. Spoots's that he would reenforce me if I found it difficult to expel any threatening intruders. Three o'clock was fixed for the departure of the army (Maj. Gen. Hunter commanding) now resting between here and Bungers Mills.

A little after that time we had a scene at the house. A quartermaster (Lieut. McCollum, 14 Penn. Cav.) appeared, and stated that he had been informed that a considerable quantity of provisions was concealed in Mr. Price's house. He was accompanied by Lieut. Wakefield, in charge of a small party of soldiers. The lieutenant conducted the search. This officer was by no means a Chesterfieldian, but I don't think he intended to be particularly offensive. The females however made a scene of it. One of the daughters accompanied the officer never ceased chattering. Another took a crying spell. Dr. Comstock engaged to see that the officer didn't exceed his instructions. Two pieces of bacon were found. And here let me note that the lady who had anticipated quite resignedly only yesterday the misfortune of having her house burned down, today displays a most undignified tenacity when a foraging officer seeks to wrest a piece of bacon from her hands. O Education! Children forty years ago escaped thy wholesome discipline! Two pieces of bacon and a half bushel of corn were taken.

The quartermaster left a certificate. Personal feelings are so blinding that this search came to be seen in any other light than as an outrage, as witness the following terms meant to be descriptive of the officer: "O Mr. Barr we have just had here the most horrid and most impudent of officers."

Dr. Comstock departed soon after the quartermaster had gone, and not two hours afterwards the rear guard of the army passed. I met a little bugler (Leonard Seis, 15th N. Y. Cavalry) last evening and brought him to the house. To my surprise the young ladies brought me privately enough evidence to convict him of having been party to a plundering match where he for his part had laughed in the face of a crying woman. This boy was alarmed about the shots fired in our neighborhood, and sought safety with me. I thought if he had committed a wrong — made a false step — it was an additional motive to keep him, and give him ~~the~~ kindly warning and counsel, for he was a boy. I did so, and the boy denied the charge made against him, and sifting the evidence today, he was proved entirely innocent.[45]

I also performed an act of charity. A sick and famished soldier — a native of Prussia — a man who did not beg, and assured me he would not steal — who straggled now only because he was too sick to keep up with his command — this man I brought to Mrs. Bell's and asked the lady to give him the breakfast she had invited me to eat. And I was happy to see her place nice biscuits, with preserves to spread on them, and good milk before him. I got them to bring ice too, that he could have the "cup of cold water" which it is a merit to give in the name of our Great Teacher of Israel. Near sundown I started out to Richlands, and stay at Mr. Peyton's tonight. The guard I brought to Richlands proved to be of no account. He gave way, and the houses were plundered over and over again.

(27. New rumors today upsetting all our hopes of yesterday. It seems the Yankees are to pass this way after all. Reported to be at Sweet Spring this morning, they are expected here to-morrow morning. The Prices feel sure that their house will be burned.)

28. Things are settling into <u>status quo</u>. Concerning Davy Creigh, if accounts are true, he was a noble man, one of nature's noblemen. He was charged with murdering a soldier who came to plunder his house. He was tried and hung. The man was shot by his own pistol being inverted in a scuffle, but not killed instantly, and Creigh expressed his desire to remove him to the kitchen and there resuscitate him. To which a Mrs. Jim Arbuckle (who had helped Creigh in the scuffle) replied that she would not quit him till she heard his last groan, whereupon an axe was brought and this woman gave him the <u>coup de grace</u>. It is thought that Creigh could have saved himself by turning state's evidence, but he chose rather to die himself.

29. Lewisburg,
> June the 29ᵗʰ 1864
> Mr. P. C. V. Buskirk, a citizen of Maryland, son of Wᵐ V. Buskirk, Esquire, late secretary of state of Maryland, is the bearer of this certificate. He has been residing with me for some time, and is now about to start to Maryland by way of Clarksburg. He is nearsighted and exempt from military service, and I write this certificate to prevent, so far as my acquaintance extends, any annoyance for military purposes.
>
> Samuel Price

Just received the foregoing from the lieutenant governor, together with two dollars in Confederate money and ten in Virginia treasury notes.

July 1864

2. Good-bye Lewisburg! The family of the lieutenant governor are not wanting in professions of regret at my departure. Mrs. Price repeatedly urged me to stay. "We will never get tired of you." And she tells me further on! "Come back to see us when "you can." They seem grateful for the protection which I obtained for their property and household in the terrible days during which the northern army passed.

Mr. Barr too, who is the Presbyterian minister, and Mrs. Bell — many indeed whom I cannot well name — all seem to regret my departure. Dr.

Caldwell urged me to stay a month or so longer and reside with him. The townspeople have from the beginning certainly shown me great favor.

(I bring away with me the ambrotype likeness of Lewis Price, taken some year and a half or two years ago, when he was ten years of age. Also a little "housewife," or needle holder, which one of the sisters of Lewis made for me, and embroidered on it, in blue silk, the initials PCVB.)

4. Early in the forenoon I took my departure from Mr. Peyton's at Richlands, bidding my two boy friends Lewis and Charley [Peyton] a long and affectionate adieu.[46] My haversack was weighty with provisions. A shirt, and a change of socks, a duodecimo volume within which were one or two letters, my Testament, diary, a keepsake needle-case, an ambrotype, and a snake-cane, (this last a memento of Camp Chase) made up my burden.

My money amounted to some eleven dollars in Virginia treasury notes, with two dollars in Confederate scrip. The latter I bought to preserve as a curiosity. It is currency so depreciated that I never like to offer it in payment for anything. I came whistling and rejoicing on my way. I promised myself to be in a few days in Clarksburg, in the family of my father's friend, W. W. Harrison, a good old Union man, I thought, surrounded by a Union family. He shall know my whole history. I will keep nothing from him. He will befriend me. I will enjoy the advantage of his councils. I will review my past conduct, and if I have indeed (as I begin to suspect), deviated stupidly and inexcusably from the path of duty, Mr. H. will nevertheless assist me to make my peace with the government. I will make directly for Clarksburg if I can, without going too much out of my way, avoid guards, I will do so, and knock quietly at the judge's door: unescorted by sentinels. I will surrender myself to him, and if he chooses, he may surrender me to the government. Then — my mother — thoughts of her — of the return of her rebel son, at once to his allegiance to the "Old Flag" (my mother's term) and to his duty as a child. Anticipations the pleasantest filled my heart to the exclusion of the regret which I know I could have keenly felt at parting from the little people I loved so well. As to their seniors, the Peytons, the Prices, the Davises — their kindness protracted through two long years, certainly exceeded my deserts, and won my grateful appreciation, and yet I care to remember only two names in all Greenbrier, as entitled according to my way of thinking, to a high place in my esteem: these are Lewis and Charley.

The only incident today consisted in my being accosted by an old man in language like the following:

[OLD MAN]: "Stranger, what is the news?"

[VAN BUSKIRK]: I repeated the latest that had been noised in the Streets of Lewisburg.

[O. M.]: Where is Echols Brigade?

[V. B.]: I told him where I supposed it to be.

[O. M.]: I have a son who was conscripted, and forced into that company, and I can never get to hear what's become of him.

[V. B.] It is a sad thing that men are forced to serve against their convictions.

[O. M.]: Stranger, I've heard it said that New Jersey is somehow in this war. Now I don't think that is right.

[V. B.]: Why not New Jersey take part in it?

[O. M.]: Why for this reason: New Jersey, d'ye see, wasn't one of the Old Continentals. Now this war is just like two men planting a field together, and then having a quarrel about the crop: I think they ought to be allowed to fight it out themselves, without any outsiders interfering.

Passed through the little assemblage of cabins called Williamsburgh. The boys recognized me, though I had only been there an hour or two, over a year ago. I expect I am taken to be a deserter from the army by some, and by others a Yankee soldier making his way home. I find a house at the foot of Cold Knob Mountain, on the very outskirts of Sinking Creek settlement — what I take to be the border settlement of Dixie in this direction. The people are kind.

5. Bright and early ascended the Cold Knob and pursued my course seventeen miles through a dreary wilderness — thinking sometimes of bears, wild animals, and footpads, but I saw nothing but a fox (I believe) and a few pheasants. At last signs of a settlement began to present themselves. I knocked at the door of the first house. "If you are white, come in: of you are a nigger stay out!" answered a voice — a child's voice — from within. I answered, "I believe I am still white," and walked in. A little girl of some twelve years, I found mistress of the premises. She exhibited some confusion at seeing me. Her joke was intended for her mother, whom she supposed did the knocking. This was a girl of some beauty too. I rested here, and eat of my own little store, the family supplying milk. Grain is packed thirty miles, and then obtained with difficulty. The road I traveled today leads from Cold Knob to Summersville. After crossing Cherry Tree River, and ascending a mountain some three miles, I abandoned the road for a path that took off to the right, and this brought me late in the evening to the cabin of a jolly woodsman, with whom I put up for the night. I suppose I had traveled twenty-five miles. I had now arrived in a district said to be infested by a kind of armed bandits made up principally of deserters from the southern army; as witness the following colloquy that passed this evening between me and a man that I met in the woods:

> Did you come through such a lane? Yes. Well a fight took place there last night between a party of horse thieves, and a party of home-guards.[47] They come unexpectedly into collision last night, and nine or ten shots were fired. The people of the house knew nothing of the presence of either party until they heard the guns going off, and the words. <u>Charge 'em boys, charge 'em</u>! I've walked out this evening to see what has happened, but I know I am liable to be shot down any moment.

This man's name was Clemons. John Hinkle was proprietor of the cabin in which I took shelter for the night. Though he lived in the midst of dangers and alarms, it didn't disturb (it seemed to me) in the least the jolly tenor of his way. He seemed to laugh the oftenest and heartiest, and enjoy it more than any man I ever met before.

6. Continued on through the wilderness. Crossed the Gauley River at Proctor's Ferry (or ford rather), and stopped to take dinner at a Mr. Robin somebody's, where a stable was being raised by a party of thirteen or fourteen very good looking fellows. The rulers of this little party were secesh. Here I was joined by a youngster named Overton, who had heard of my going on ahead, and had striven very hard to overtake me. Overton informed me that he was a noncombatant that had been four years sojourning in Albermarle County, and was now making his way to his home in Missouri. A companion had started with him, but turned back upon hearing of the dangers which beset the path of any one traveling across the belt which separates Dixie from Yankeeland. My new acquaintance came dressed in a military shirt and cap, and carried an oil-cloth blanket. He informed me his age was under 18. I liked his appearance. We agreed to travel on together, and to that end he thought proper to change his course, and go with me to Clarksburg, where he could take the cars for the west. Towards evening we arrived in a beautiful valley through which flows a stream called (I think) the Big Birch. On its banks resides a very intelligent Italian. I stopped to talk with him. If I am a judge he was true Union.

A mile or so below him stood the cabin of a Mr. Dodrill. I applied for a night's lodging. "We are neither Yankees nor rebels," said I, "and I shouldn't think you ought justly to incur the displeasure of either Confederate or Government by giving us shelter." The family kindly bade us welcome. Here I met with a little miss that decidedly pleased me. Before leaving this house I wrote a letter for the family, to be mailed in Clarksburg.

7. Four miles from Dodrill's (or it may have been only two) we reached the turnpike, which runs northwardly from Summersville to Clarksburg. Where the roads meet, we first met with what we took to be home-guards. They turned out to be <u>sang</u> (ginseng) diggers. Our route was now along the turnpike, and we made good speed. As we traveled, we learned enough of the home-guards (State Scouts) who do duty in these parts to not wish to fall into their hands. We heard too that a company which bears the sobriquet of "Bug-hunters" was ordered to occupy Bulltown that day, and believing them behind us, we resolved to keep them in our rear.

8. At Bulltown we learned that a wagon train, with a guard, had come out from Weston, and was halted from Jacksonville.[48] It became now a question whether or not to pass around this guard. We could not do so by taking a by-road near Bulltown, which comes again into the turnpike just six miles south from Weston. We decided to take the open road, and trust that the "Swamp Angels" (for so we learned the Lewis County state troops were designated) if they arrested us at all, would at least forward us on in the direction we wished to go. Sure enough we met the guards at Jacksonville, who conducted us before an orderly sergeant, their noncommissioned officer in charge. I informed the orderly sergeant of our character and destination, taking out the certificate I had received from Governor Price and presenting it to him for inspection. I carried this paper neatly folded in my Testament which contains also my diary. This latter did not attract the sergeant's attention, but I afterwards most imprudently volunteered a certain note for his inspection, which led him to turn over and cast his eye uninvited upon another page, where these words met his gaze: Battles, 1. Near Shanghai, China., etc., etc., etc., when a new idea seemed to strike the sergeant, who explained: "Sure he has run the blockade and been to hell and back."[49] It was as much as I could do to keep the sergeant from going on with his investigation. He at last consented to roll the diary and papers up securely for transmission to the provost marshal at Weston. And feeling that he had an important prisoner, he prepared to

conduct us at once to his superior at Weston. This exceedingly foolish act of volunteering a note of my diary for the sergeant's inspection has cost me a deal of trouble. The letter which I brought was to be handed so as to attract the attention of a man likely to seize it, and pass it along, to go from hand to hand. But to my story: The sergeant, taking a musket himself, called an additional guard, and set out for Weston. On the way, we met a Major Rollison, commanding state troops. He stopped, gave our papers a sort of hurried examination, and directed the sergeant to retain us and our papers, until he got back to Weston, which would be Monday. Late in the evening we arrived in Weston, and were put under guard in an upper room of the barracks occupied by the "Swamp Angels."

9. Become acquainted with Captain Wilkinson, who commands the "Lewis County Company, state troops," a squad of about eighteen undisciplined fellows, mostly boys, glorying in their fine hats, and uniforms of blue, and luxuriating in exhaustless stores of coffee, sugar, and crackers, with pork and beans. I liked Captain Wilkinson. In this eighteen men are included four sergeants — no lieutenant. The men and boys were noisy, rude, profane, and obscene; but of the eighteen there were but two that appeared to me to have bad hearts. They look upon us as suspicious characters, guard us closely during part of the day, while at the other times they don't seem to have any guard over us at all. The "orderly sergeant" is a young Irishman, whose father is cook to the gang — for gang it is. We have liberty to visit any part of the town when it suits the convenience of a guard to accompany us. Having enquired for Matthew Harrison, he came to see me today. I was pleased with my new cousin.

10. Sunday. took a swim in the river; attended church; and took dinner with a German family, where I had dropped in during Imboden's raid. I made acquaintance during Imboden's raid, [with those] who remember me, and welcome me now.

11. I had hopes that Major Rollison would restore may diary after examining it, but he didn't. Today he rolls all up, and forwards the package, and myself, under guard, to the provost marshal at Clarksburg. My poor diary is doomed to go the rounds of the circumlocution office.

Delivered to the brigade provost marshal whose name is [probably C. F. A.] Yahrling, I solicit the favor of a parole to the house of Judge Harrison, but am denied firmly, but courteously withal, and now find myself an inmate of the military prison.[50]

12. Addressed a note to Judge Harrison "respectfully and earnestly entreating him to accord me the favor of an interview." Paid a boy ten cents to deliver it. Lieut. Yahrling came in. His language and manner created the impression that I need look for no favor in his sight. He informed me that my papers were placed before the brigade commander — a Col. Wilkinson. I begin to realize that I am a suspected person. The guards, I learn, have orders to keep an eye especial on me. I cannot say, though, that any of my fellow prisoners — 17 or 18 soldiers, and 7 or 8 "rebs," so classified — evince unfriendliness. But the day wears away, and I hear nothing of Judge Harrison. The boy assures me that he gave my note into the judge's hands. It is plain that I am deemed unworthy of notice by the old gentleman. He has heard evil reports of me. I am in his eyes a traitor. The family discard me. I am not to be named among them again. That terrible feeling came over me — the sense of being utterly friendless — scorned where I looked for sympathy. Terrible indeed is this feeling. Yet it is an affectation that works to our souls' advantage. I never felt more like drawing nearer to my God, than when I began to realize that my earthly friends were drawing away from me. This is a prison day long to be remembered.

13. A day spent in suspense. A merry, jovial crew are my fellow prisoners. Their room is kept clean. The soldiers are cleanly and tidy, I believe without an exception. They are an entirely different class of beings from the "Swamp Angels." There is no end to the amusements with which they indulge themselves. I am sorry to see that mock religious services and obscenity enter largely into their schemes of fun. The "Rebs," who occupy the same room, are seven or eight in number, half of whom are ragged and lousy.

14. Lieut. Yahrling came up today with notice that two ladies wished to see me. They proved to be Mrs. Harrison and my cousin Sude, accompanied by my cousin Tom Harrison, also a judge. I asked them to see Col. Wilkinson, and get him to grant me an interview. I told cousin Tom that I desired to take the <u>benefit</u> of the president's amnesty proclamation. It seems my note did not reach its destination till today. Judge Harrison, Sʳ, is away from home. The boy to whom I entrusted the note to deliver told me a lie. Later came a basket of cakes for me. I eat some, and shared my good things with the most wretched of the prisoners.

I learn now that my diary, etc. is to go to the judge advocate at Cumberland. Three others with myself are to be sent there tomorrow under guard.

15. Intransitu. Overton, with two Irishmen and myself, were placed under guard this morning, to be sent in the cars to Cumberland. A sergeant and the prison orderly are our guards, who keep a vigilant eye upon us, and do not even allow the little window slides in the cars to be raised lest we should attempt to escape. We have arrived at Grafton, and are confined in a little unventilated shanty, yclept the "Guard House," where we are to stay till the Cumberland train passes, which will be at 4 o'clock this afternoon. It is in this pen that I have perched myself in a corner bunk to write the present note. The evening train brought us to Cumberland, where being lodged in a small room of the guardhouse, I spread a newspaper upon the dirty floor, and laying myself down, slept soundly.

17. Sunday. We are confined in an elongated shanty divided into four apartments, three of which are small rooms, and one long, well ventilated room. To one of these smaller apartments, called the "Dungeon," our little party was committed, to be kept under strict guard. By oversight of the <u>sentinel</u>, however, I got to enjoy the liberty of the long room all day. Its windows afford me a good view of the town. This has been a day of good resolves. I am amid scenes of my childhood again. This is the place to sit down in, and reflect, and begin anew. Allegany County is sacred ground to me. Prison scenes are varied by the performance of a drunken sot, who, among other things, persists in chewing a roll of greenback money in the place of tobacco. An Indian is among our number, who either can't or won't indulge in any talk with us. Two prisoners of war were brought in who prove to have been comrades of mine in the 13th Va. Infantry. A native of Saxe Meiningen, now a soldier, confined for having turned his little finger over his thumb too often (as he pantomimed it to me,) walked and talked with me part of the day.

18. No day so important to me as this. Very much to my surprise, I was called for early in the afternoon, and conducted to Brig. Gen. B. F. Kelly; who received me in his little private office, and, adverting to my diary, which he had perused, said it contained internal evidence of truthfulness throughout; asked me a few questions about Mr. Price's family, and that of Judge Fry; about Davy Creigh's case; then about my own views concerning the right and wrong of this war; and finally, bidding me to be loyal and true to the government in future, against which I had erred, and which now reextended to me its favor and protection, he said I should be released, and directed the provost marshal (Capt. L. Pierpoint, 6th W. Va. Inf.) to release me, and furnish me with "transportation to wherever I desired to go."

As to where I wished to go, I named Clarksburg, to the general, as Charlestown where my mother resides, is just now, I believe, beyond Federal lines. After taking dinner with Capt. Pierpoint, I was released from custody, but directed to call sometime in the evening at the provost marshal's office to take the oath of allegiance. In due time I called at the provost's office, where the oath prescribed in the president's amnesty proclamation was administered to me by a sergeant, clerk to the provost marshal; by subscribing to which oath, I formally ceased to be numbered among the adherents of Jeff Davis and the Confederacy. I have ceased to be a "confederate," and have become a "Yankee," after being three years ostensibly, though never heartily, and enemy to the "Yankees."

If I understand myself these are my sentiments:

1. I wish the Union arms to prevail. I can now honestly be glad when I hear of Federal successes. It was like a traitor to indulge that feeling when I was in Dixie, and yet I could not entirely repress it.

2. The Confederacy was the work of conspirators. The secession of Virginia was a fraud, and the result of intimidation. Thousands, really Union-loving were misled, I in the number.

3. I will be glad to see an end to slavery. The Negro would make a good servant, but the white man of the south is not fit to be his master. His slaves grow up around him untutored to common decency: he debauches their females, and they in turn debauch his children until the moral atmosphere of a slave holding community is fetid with importunity. Even the slave holder who is correct in his own conduct, will submit to see the morals of his children corrupted under his very nose, rather than lose a few dollars by ridding his family of a servant of bad character. For this, and other reasons, I will be glad to see an end to slavery.

Gen. Kelly returned my diary, ambrotype, etc., and kindly promised to use his influence to get that one back which Joseph Darr seized two years ago, and retained — my diary of 1861. Once more at liberty, I indulged myself in a stroll through some of the streets. Six o'clock tomorrow is the hour fixed for my departure. Cumberland is not the Cumberland of my boyhood. Twenty years have passed since I a boy of ten years, ranged the streets, swam in the Potomac, roved along its banks, and played with my fellows over and under the Wills Creek Bridge. But Cumberland has grown from a town to a city. The bridge familiar to my boyhood is supplanted by another unlike it. Wills Creek is a canal. The Potomac does not seem to be the same Potomac. I cannot find the houses in which my father successively resided. They were diminutive dwellings, and have long since given way to elegant private residences. I must except one. It is a little house, now occupied by Mrs. Mary Coffee, cheerful, active, healthful and ever so glad to see me. This lady, who in the days of my childhood was a poor Irishwoman living in a little shanty near the courthouse. Her son Matt was my playfellow, and if I had other playfellows, I do not remember them. I don't know why it was, but the tears gushed unbidden from my eyes today when Mrs. Coffee, speaking of Matt, said that he was devoted to me, loved none so well as Clayton, and then added that Matt died two years ago.

Mrs. Coffee insisted that I should stay all night, and left nothing undone that would make my stay pleasant. She lives with another son who has some employment connected with the railroad. I accepted her kind invitation to come back to supper, and to stay all night, then walked out to pay two visits which I thought I was in duty bound to pay. The only Cumberland names which remained unerased from my memory, were the following:

Samuel M. Semmes
Thomas Perry
Daniel Blocker
Mr. Black
Mr. Wade — the jailor

All I had long reverenced as old friends of my father. I learned upon enquiry that Blocker was away in a rebel Maryland regiment; Mr. Black was dead; Mr. Wade gone no one knows where; but that Mr. Semmes still lived a mile or so from town; and Mr. Perry occupied a fine house in close proximity to the courthouse. I proceeded accordingly to pay my respects to first one and then the other of the last named gentlemen. Little did I think what a mortifying reception I was destined to receive at their hands. Their manner, more emphatically that their words, bid me "begone as one we do not wish to have anything to do with."

An incident occurred today which is worthy of being noted. As the provost marshal and I were walking up Courthouse Hill, we were overtaken by a lawyer — Parrée — so the name is pronounced, who recognized me, had a word or so with the p.m. in which he mentioned my father as having been a prominent lawyer and politician of this county, and then, reminding me of an interview we had in the Maryland State Library some four years ago, he continued: "You had a place then in the naval academy, if you remember and I advised you to keep it — not to secede, but to stay where you were and stand by the old flag." I said nothing to all this, but the fact is that Mr. Parrée's advice, given about the time he mentions (I remember perfectly) was exactly the reverse of what he now states.[51]

19. Bid my good friends, Mrs. Coffee, Patrick (her son), and a young woman living in the house, good bye, and took the 6 o'clock morning train. They had almost filled my haversack with sweet cakes. At about two in the afternoon, arrived at Pour [West Virginia], and found my way to the dwelling of W. A. Harrison. Here were cousins

> Anna (the judges wife)
> Susan
> Rebecca

They welcomed me affectionately. Rebecca I had not seen before. The judge was absent. So were:

> Sallie.
> Sibbie.

The latter I had not seen. Sallie was my favorite cousin five years ago at John Boyd's.[52] We afterwards corresponded. Changing into a clean shirt, and greetings over, I employed the evening hours in transcribing such notes of my diary of this year as I have no objection to see in print, Gen. Kelly having requested me to do so, and to mail to him the transcript.

23. Cousins Sallie and Sibbie came home this forenoon. And a little later in the day arrived Mr. Harrison. He gave me a kind reception.

25. After sending off the transcript required by Gen. K., I employed myself between times writing cards to the following purport:

> A Refugee desires to spend the Fall and Winter in the mountains of Allegany County. He thinks he has learning enough to enable him to be very useful as a TEACHER OF SCHOOL. Or he is willing to live in any family, where there are good and intelligent boys, and divide his time between helping the boys along with their studies, and helping the farm work along. Has no objection to living in a poor family — is poor himself — always was. Only moderate compensation will be asked. Address: P. C. Van Buskirk, care Hon. W. A. Harrison, Pour, W. Va.

And letters to the following tenor:

Mr. Postmaster:
I will take it as a great favor if you will give all the enclosed cards but one, to persons going into the country. The reserved card I would be glad to have tacked up somewhere in your office.
Respectfully,
P. C. Van Buskirk

30. Therm 96° in shade. Saturday, last day but one of my stay at Judge Harrison's. I have had no responses to my advertisements mentioned 25th. My welcome here is about eaten out, my two shirts are getting into rags, my credit is worth nothing, and if I protract my stay beyond tomorrow, I will feel exceedingly uncomfortable. I asked cousin Susan to provide for my present necessities out of her own pocket money, of which I would keep an account and reimburse her sometime. She did so to the following extent:

    July 20. Straw hat 40
    " " Postage and stationery ... 1.00
    " " Repairing boots 1.20

When her means run out. My next demand (which if I except a small sum, say three dollars, to put into my pocket upon setting out for Allegany County, would have been the last) was for $2^{25} to pay for half a dozen photographs. Sue applied to her father, who declared he would advance no such sum; and has intimated to me that when my visit is out, he will pay my way to Cumberland, "where I have friends," and "where with a little exertion I can get into business." The photographs which I sat for five days ago, remain uncalled for. Yesterday I walked a circuit of eight miles in quest of employment as a field hand. I propose making similar exertions today, for I would be glad to pay for the photographs which I have engaged, nor am I willing that Mr. Harrison should "pay my way to Cumberland" or any where else. Mr. Harrison is not wanting in kindness. He has a large family, with increasing expenses, and his means, I would judge, are limited: no wonder then if he takes alarm at my threatening inroads upon his money drawer. I did, but he could not, see where my demands would end. To be sure, when I had money, I acted towards persons situated like I am now, in a different spirit; but I was then, as I am now, a man without family. I once met a son of this Harrison without money at a railroad station, and though I had but little, I didn't hesitate to supply his need, and that without knowing who the stranger was.

The absent members of the Harrison family are:

(1) Mabe (2) William — somewhere in the C. S. army; (3) Charles — a prisoner on Johnson's Island; (4) Matthew — lives with his father at Weston; and (5) Thomas Willoughby Harrison — judge of circuit court under the State of West Virginia. He lives with his family only a few yards from here. I call them cousins, though the relationship must be very distant.

Cousin Tom's children are: (1) Willoughby. (2) Matthew. (3) Sammy, and (4) a little girl. Willoughby is a manly boy. A cousin of his, George Safford, is here, on leave of absence from the naval academy, and has put it into Willoughby's head to try the naval profession. A vacancy exists, and Judge Harrison thinks he can get his son appointed to it. He leaves it to Willoughby's choice. Willoughby is undecided. Has been consulting me. Matt is a fine little fellow, and so is Sammy.

<u>Afternoon</u>. Walked out on the railroad towards Parkersburg 6 miles, and find that I can get work by joining a railroad gang, all along the road. All I have to do, say the "Bosses" to whom I have spoken, is pitch in, and go to work, and I will be paid for what I do. I was fully in the notion of joining a railroad gang, and going to work right here without thinking myself degraded, or caring who might see me at work, but upon second thought I cannot but feel that this imaginary degradation would affect my cousins unpleasantly when they came to know of it. And I have concluded to accept Mr. Harrison's offer to "pay my way" in the cars to Allegany County, where, somewhere along the railroad, unknown to the people here I can earn by hard labor money enough to repay Mr. H., and those who have been at expense on my <u>account</u>. Pride forbids me accepting the "aid" tendered by Mr. H., and if I governed myself by its dictates, I would go to work on the railroad near here, or on Monday morning. Without scrip, set out on my journey to Allegany County.

31. *Lorenzo, or the Empire of Religion. A Catholic Story.* Baltimore: John Murphy, Publisher, 178 Market Street. 1853. I have read nine chapters, and cried over the scenes it depicts, something uncommon for me since attaining to man's estate. What wouldn't I give to be able to place this little volume in the hands of my dear Lewis?[53]

1864

August 1864

1. Have a good coat, pants and boots, but no money. Mr. Harrison being informed that 4^55^ was the fare to Cumberland on the cars, put 5^00^ into my hands early in the forenoon. I lost no time in paying for the photographs I had engaged. 2^25^ remained. This had to be transacted privately. My cousin put up a snack of biscuits, sweet cakes, and bacon for me. Cousin Anna also put a good shirt up for me. At 10 o'clock I kissed them all, and took my departure. At the depot I bought a ticket to Cranberry Summit for 2^20^ leaving 5 cents, which at Grafton enabled me to add a quart of buttermilk to my snack. At Grafton I had to wait for the train coming east. While sitting outside the hotel door, a soldier came up, whom I remembered to have met soon after the Droop Mountain battle, in which I was among the defeated, he among the victors. Escaping from that battle, or rather while making my way the next day to a given point, I was obliged to hide my jacket and haversack, and take my stand near a log as if engaged chopping it, when the soldier I speak of rode up, and entered into conversation with me and with the old woman of the house, little suspecting that he was talking to a "reb." He behaved so well that I was glad to see him again. I reminded him of where and under what circumstances I had seen him, and asked him to write his name on one of my cards, which he did as follows: Richard Shahan, Fellowsville, Preston Co., W. Va.

At Cranberry Summit I got out of the cars and took the road eastward. As night approached, I asked for lodging at a house on the railroad, and was denied. Further along I saw a light in the distance, and as it began to rain, I hastened to reach it. It proved to be an Irishman's house, who with his wife, received me most kindly. They astonished me a little when I came to learn of their politics. They were all good "secesh." In due time I was put to bed, and then began my torments. The bed seemed alive with fleas and bed bugs. A bedfellow I had, and he didn't mind them in the least, but slept soundly. I had to get up, and sit by the window, looking out, and getting a little sleep by spells.

2. Tuesday. Kept along the railroad eastward. Passed the Maryland line. Enquired for "Bosses of the railroad hands." Heard of one whose name was Stanton, and that he would not be at home till night. Resolved to "knock about" the country till evening. Then go and see Stanton, whose wife had assured me of a welcome for one night under his roof. The family in a shanty near by Stanton's gave me my dinner. At night saw Stanton. He could not, he at first said, take me into his gang without authority from the supervisor at Oakland [Maryland], but observing how kindly the children took to me, and taking notice of my "discourse" to them, he changed his mind somewhat, and at one time proposed taking me into his gang without more ado. Stanton was "secesh" too, and so, Mr. Holland tells me, are all the Irish along the R. R. They remember "Knownothingism" and that it came from the north. Democracy and the south were the Irishman's friends in the days of the Knownothing excitement. All the Irishmen here seem to know this, and the south has now their gratitude and sympathy.

Tonight, as last night, bed bugs were my torment. The people who live in these cabins are utterly regardless of cleanliness in their bedding and cooking. Mrs. Fox, who gave me dinner I think was an exception.

3. Wednesday. Breakfast at Stanton's and take the road to Oakland. Avoid the railroad guards by making a detour. Halt no time at Oakland, but push on to the country, and by sundown, arrive at a little village called Johnstown. Asked for a night's lodging at the best cooking house. The lady replied that her husband was not at home, she therefore could not keep me all night, but could give me a supper, which she set about preparing. Meanwhile an old gentleman residing at the house accosted me, and quite a conversation sprung up between us, in the course of which I asked, "Did you ever know a William Van Buskirk?" The old gentleman replied that he was just about to ask me if I was any relation to William Van Buskirk: he had seen so strong a resemblance in me. "He was my father," said I. Then answered the old gentleman, "I will make it my business to try to get you a school. I knew your father well." And he went on to say a great deal about my father, after which he informed the lady that I was a son of William Van Buskirk, a piece of intelligence that caused her to change altogether in her demeanor towards me. Very soon afterwards when I said something about going out to find a lodging place, she rejoined: "Oh we can keep you. We consider you an acquaintance since we've learned who you are."

Accordingly I prepared to stay all night. The lady's father came in during the evening, as did also one of the village gossips, and I gave them some account of my travels. Thomas L. Drane is the name of the old gentleman who knew my father, and who seemed so disposed to befriend me.

I have advertised in my own way for a school and enquiring for some employment in the intervening time. I learned at this house that a sawmill some four miles distant, owned by H. G. Davis and Co. of Piedmont, needed hands.

4. Thursday. Leaving my haversack and cane at Mrs. DeWitt's (the house where I had stayed overnight) I set out this morning in quest of the sawmill. Lost my way, but succeeded in reaching the place about dinner time, and finding the overseer (a Mr. James Anderson), informed him that I wanted employment. "Do you know anything about working for a sawmill?" he asked. "No, Sir, but I've been told that it is work that can be done by anybody who had strength and activity." There is not much slight of hand about it, but the work is heavy, and we are in want of hands that can do it, you can go to work, and if you can stand it, we can give you permanent employment." I went to work. The labor of this afternoon was new to me and hard. This mill employs something over a dozen hands, two or three of whom are deserters from the rebel army. The steam sawmill (which runs a circular saw) is situated about nine miles NE^dly from Oakland. Two frame tenements lately constructed are close to the mill. One is the dwelling of the engine man and his family, the other is the boarding house (very neatly kept I think) for the work hands.

5. Friday. At hard labor. When night came on my bones ached. The dormitory of my boarding house (one room) contains six beds. Two men occupy one bed. I as yet have no bedfellow. But I notice a boy here who is about fourteen years old, and if I can, I will get him for bedfellow, lest some one may get in with me whom I would not choose.

6. Saturday. "Rebels coming!" More hard work, but not so steadily at it as yesterday. It is a custom here to quit labor at half past four on Saturday afternoons. We quit a little earlier today, on account of the rain.

7. Sunday. Glad to enjoy a day of rest. Have availed myself of the opportunity to bring my diary up to date.

12. Friday. Astonishing things this afternoon brings forth! I came in at dinner time with the other work hands from a forenoon of hard labor at "samsoning up logs," and was astonished to meet with a sergeant, who with a companion in arms had come out from Oakland with orders to bring me a prisoner to that place. Me — Van Buskirk — that was the name. Not understanding how I had become obnoxious to the government, I nevertheless thought it was a matter of great uncertainty whether I would be released or not, and so packed up my whole wardrobe, (sufficient to swell out a haversack,) and accompanied my captors to Oakland. They arrested another young man at the same time because his brother had deserted from the army.

To testify in favor of my fellow prisoner Mr. Anderson came with us, so we made a cheerful party. At Oakland we were delivered to a captain in command who committed us to custody, but soon released my fellow prisoner. It then turned out that my conduct when passing lately through Oakland had attracted observation, which led to enquiry as to my whereabouts, and finally caused my arrest. I had come into Oakland — nobody knew me — went to the hotel — looked attentively at the map — and then disappeared without saying anything to anybody — very suspicious behavior!

I gave the captain who now held me under arrest an account of myself, but he didn't seem to credit it, and observed to me that I differed essentially in point of education and intelligence from all refugees whom he had ever seen before, which he deemed an additionally suspicious circumstance.

Luckily Gen. Kelly was at his farm near Oakland, and soon afterwards walked into the Depot Hotel. My case was referred to him, and I was released.

Blackening up my boots and donning a clean shirt, I waited upon the general at the hotel to thank him for this second deliverance from the hands of the officials. The general had a kind word for me. I then learned that my diary as transcribed for Gen. K. was being published in "The Cumberland Union."

Mr. Anderson had paid me off as soon as arrested. My board bill (45 cents per diem) deducted, the pleasant looking little sum of 7\frac{10}{}$ remained for me. This enabled me to make the following purchases:

Pair of common shoes 2.50
Stationery .... .40
Postage stamps .... .50

Quite late in the afternoon I set out from town, and arrived to put up for the night at a Mr. Brant's who knew my father, and was prepared with his wife and children to give me a kind reception. Here I find a copy of the "Union," and for the first time in my life see myself in print. (If I except a scribbling of a few lines of mine that went into the *Baltimore Sun* some years ago.) What a treat! This afternoon then has been a holiday from labor. Money has found its way into my pocket. I have had the great pleasure of seeing Gen. Kelly. And to-night I will enjoy the satisfaction of reading a published copy of my own diary! What an afternoon.[54]

24. During the first half-week of my service here as a work-hand, the labor went very hard indeed with me. I was very glad when Sunday came. Gradually I became more and more reconciled to it. But it is "hard labor" yet. I come in this evening very tired and with something of a headache. By this time I am more used to my fellow workmen and their ways, and I like some of them very well. The mill has its complement of hands when sixteen are employed. This laboring force is usually distributed as follows: 2 sawyers; 2 off bearers; 1 fireman; 1 lathe sawyer; 2 wood choppers; 2 hands with cross-cut saw; 2 samsoners; 2 teamsters; and 2 carpenters. The mill, owing to scarcity of men in the country seldom has its full complement employed. The hands are illiterate, so far as I can see, and most of them are habitual and hard swearers. I get along very well among them. I think they pay me a marked respect. They have an idea that I am an educated man. My manners I hope recommend me, but probably above all my father's name in this county is the cause of my being held in respect. Some of my fellow laborers are like myself, refugees from Dixie. Some are married, some single. The woman who keeps our boarding house is a sour and disagreeable creature. Old man Henry Hammil is a carpenter working here. He went to school to my father once [*sic*], and ever after was an attached friend.

25. The other day some of our hands went over to a neighboring steam sawmill, owned and managed by a Mr. Richard Fairall, and returning, surprised me very much by saying to me: "Mr. Fairall wants to see you. He says he knew your father, and knows you; that a man of your education and talents oughtn't to be working out in the woods; and that he has a situation for you — something higher than samsoning up logs. He wants you to measure lumber for him down at Swanton."

27. Saturday. I told Mr. Anderson that if he had no objections I would take today for myself. Putting myself in my best attire, I walked over to Fairall's Mill, and thence to Swanton, where I met the proprietor. He recognized me by my resemblance to my father, and gave me a most kindly

reception. Mr. Fairall was at work with a few hands, so to not interrupt his labor any further, I arranged to call at his mill next Saturday evening and ride out with him to his house in Accident [Maryland]. Then walked on down the railroad five miles to Frankville, and across a ravine, and up the sides of a steep mountain to the residence of Ex-Gov. Francis Thomas. This was a home in the wilderness which the ex-governor had chosen, and beginning years ago with a little clearing around the log cabin he then inhabited, had by this time made a very pretty seat of it. A handsome barn, two neat outhouses, and a commodious cottage, all newly constructed, adorn the place. Its designation is "Mont Alto." An old lady and her daughter keep house for the governor: he is rearing a boy besides: and two or three refugees from Virginia do the labor upon his farm.

The governor was not at the house when I got there, but came riding up soon afterwards. As soon as I named myself he said: "I loved your father. He was a man of noble qualities. He was one of nature's noblemen." He then bade me welcome, expressed his gratification at seeing me, and added that I must make my home with him as long as I pleased. I was a little boy of ten in Annapolis when I last saw the governor. It is a real and great pleasure to see him again after the lapse of twenty years. He is hale and hearty. Father of Mercies! What have I not passed through since I last reposed under the roof of Francis Thomas! And what have those years made me? I am now beginning my fourth decade. Let me see to it that I render a good account of these years, and by the use I make of them atone for the crime of wasting the seed time of my life. The governor's conversation is in the highest degree edifying. I expected to find in him a great man in retirement, and I am not disappointed.

28. Col. Stephen W. Downey, a young man and protégée [*sic*] of the governor came to Mont Alto today, and I was introduced to him. I was very much pleased with him. These two, the governor and his protégée are emancipationists, and if I am to take them at their word, are in favor of giving the Negro political equality with the white man in this country. Indeed the colonel and the governor astonished me not a little with their radical views. Took leave of Mont Alto in the evening and returned to Swanton. There I called at the house of Patrick Hammill Esq., who was a co-laborer with my father years ago in the legislature. Meet Mr. White. He was teacher of the academy in Cumberland when I was a child and pupil there in the primary department. Mr. H. was not at home, but I staid all night, and became acquainted with some of the inmates and visitors at the house.

September 1864

2. Friday. Having a sprained wrist, I didn't work this day, but requested Mr. Anderson to pay the wages due me, which, after deducting board bill, amounted to about $17.$\underline{^{00}}$ With a great deal of satisfaction, I enclosed 10\underline{^{50}}$ to my cousin Sude Harrison at Clarksburg, for payment of what I owe them there, and also what I owe my cousin Matt Harrison at Weston. Then walked to Oakland, and took the cars to Rawlings Station [Maryland], near which, and close to the railroad lines lives Mrs. Wilson. To Mrs. Wilson's I went. The old lady was away from home. So were all who knew me in my childhood. But such as were about the house had heard of me. A son of Mrs. W. was there, an intelligent, educated young man. He gave me a kind reception, and walked out (about a mile) to the old log cabin where my father once kept school. The old barn is standing. I remember it well. But a brick house occupies the site of the old-time domicile. I believe the young ladies at Judge Hammill's were pleased with me, as I was with them. I felt conscious of such being the case when we parted. But it is not so here, albeit the young ladies are not wanting in measured courtesy.

3. Saturday. Mrs. Wilson not having returned, and I being under an obligation to see Mr. Richard Fairall on Sunday at Accident, I took leave in the morning, and set out on my way to Accident, by way of the old National Turnpike — getting upon the turnpike some 9 miles West of Cumberland. Come at night to Mr. William Frost's, where I am received at first reluctantly, and then treated with respect, which I know is owing to my manners and conversation, but later when I let it be known that I am a son of W$^{\underline{m}}$ V. Buskirk, the kindness of my hosts becomes marked.

4. Sunday. Continued my travel along the National Turnpike. Westward. It was a very disagreeable day. Took shelter for a little while in the "Stone House" (Little Meadows) [Maryland], not thinking then that my grandfather John Van Buskirk once kept this inn for something like two years, and my father, a little child, played there. At Kaiser's Ridge I turned off, and late in the afternoon, reached Mr. Fairall's.

6. Tuesday. Squire Fairall and his family were not wanting in courtesy. The squire said nothing about engaging me to act as his clerk in the lumber business. He said much about my father. He has papers which were on my father's person at the time of his death. I was not prepared to see them. Bad weather kept me longer at Mr. Fairall's than I intended. A young man, son of John Slicer, of the Selbysport neighborhood, being at Mr. Fairall's, I accompanied him to his home.

8. The family at Slicer's treated me with middling cordiality. Some young ladies were visiting from Cumberland. I soon used up my welcome at Slicer's, and after looking about a little for a school, with no idea of filling such a situation here, I set out on my return to Brownings.[55]

9. Arrived at Browning's, seemed like getting home again. It is only to stay overnight, however.

10. Went on to Swanton and thence to the governor's. The governor hears of my project to open a school, and offers to do much for the encouragement of such an undertaking right here. The people are intensely selfish, especially the native population, which latter are lying, thievish, destitute of all principle (so says the governor), but he is willing to do what he can to educate their children. The governor has accordingly given the basement room of his storehouse at Frankville (just a mile and a half from Mont Alto) for a schoolroom.

11. Domesticated in the household of the Hon. Francis Thomas on Mont Alto, which household consists of the governor, his brother, myself, the housekeeper and her daughter, a boy, and 4 or 5 hired men.

? It's fortunate about these times that I have a good jeans suit (the same which Mrs. Price had made up for me) so that my poverty is not patent to all eyes. I have a pair of boots (by this time unfit for wear) and a pair of shoes. My shirts are two, viz., a cotton one, given me by Mrs. Harrison, and a lindsey, recently bought. These, with two pairs of socks, and a handkerchief, make up my whole stock of clothing. I owe $3^{80} in the neighborhood, and have in my pocket $3.^{00}

19. Monday. Having previously talked with the heads of families, I open my school this morning. Only nine scholars make their appearance. I enroll them, and proceed to form classes as follows: 2 to learn their A B C; 4 to spell words of two syllables; and 3 to begin with their a-b-abs. The governor has given me a fine arm chair to sit in, and has caused a good table, with lock and key to its drawer, to be put in order for my use.

20. Begin our school labors with a short prayer, which I purpose always doing.

23. It is now the end of the school week. My school has increased to eleven.

26. I have met with only one discomforting accident. My very nice coat is damaged from being scorched last night. It is very unsightly.

27. A deserter from the C. S. A. — Brown by name — and a very good and intelligent man — is here working for the governor. He was in Lewisburg, in his time, and has seen Lewis. God bless Lewis! I don't think I have failed to include him in my prayers any one night since I parted from him in the road before Mr. Peytons.

28. General Kelly, it seems, "doesn't want to have anything to do with me." I wrote to him longer than a month ago, asking the privilege of enclosing a letter to him for transmission by some one of his scouts to Dixie. Though I sent also an envelope stamped and directed back to myself, the General did not favor me with any reply.

30. I sat on the throne of my little school with no very pleasant feelings. As yet my boys are partial to their master. They have yielded all the obedience that I could reasonably expect, but they are the children of sordid parents, whose selfishness is by no means of the "enlightened" kind, and from whom I cannot hope to extort the means necessary to procure school facilities. My bill, sent home to each patron today (the last of the month) I have no doubt will excite grumbling in half the households. A mail that had been accumulating for many days at Swanton, was brought to the schoolroom today. It contained several letters for me. One from cousin Sue. She thinks I am a man of unblemished morals. One from the provost marshal of Cumberland, who compliments me upon the "highly educated mind which I possess." Several from the governor upon subjects connected with the school and his farm. In one of them I am informed of a law requiring teachers to present themselves for "examination." My examiners, the governor says, will be three gentlemen residing in Westernport. I really know so little practically or theoretically about grammar, geography, or arithmetic, that it is dreadfully disagreeable anticipation — that of having to go before a board of examiners. But I will read and study all I can in the intervening time, and then if the examiners are themselves "rusty," I may have some hopes of getting through.

1864

October 1864

[Van Buskirk made no entries for October.]

November 1864

<u>Remarks</u>. Mother lives in Charlestown destitute of comforts. I hear from her at long intervals, and have been able to remit as yet only two dollars out of my scanty means. The ex-governor's household consists of himself, myself, 2 women, 5 men, and 2 boys. I never fail to offer up a prayer before going to bed every night. I repeat the child's prayer, and then another, in which I think of Lewis, and in which I use words that I caught from his lips, "Save us in Heaven."

11. The governor weighed a bundle of straw today, and came to the conclusion that his bundles averaged 25 pounds, and were worth 15 cents a bundle. He wanted to know how much that was a pound, and worked it out himself. The result, he said, was six tenths of a cent per pound, and asked me if his answer was correct. My attainments in arithmetic are very slender but I thought it entirely within their scope to undertake so small an operation in proportion, and yet I got confused, and amazed the governor and his visitors (two young relatives, Richard and Joe West) by failing to even state the question properly. After floundering about, the governor and visitors eyeing me the while, and I mumbling over incoherent snatches of the "Rule for Simple Proportion," learned from Ray only this year, finally got up, and went off to my school, without having obtained an answer. My Goodness! What a mortification this was! At the school house, out from under the governor's eye, I in five minutes relieved my mind of all murkiness and obtained an answer by two processes, as follows:[56]

$$25 : 1 :: 15 : .6 \qquad 1/25 \text{ of } 15/1 = 15/25 = 3/5$$
$$\underline{ 1}$$
$$25)15.0(.6$$

28. Monday. In the evening a dense smoke filled the valleys, and soon after came the report of "Rebels in Piedmont." Piedmont is about six miles down the railroad from the Frankville house. Mont Alto is about a mile and a half from the Frankville house, and on the side of a mountain opposite to that around which the railroad winds. Getting home from school I found much excitement among the governor's hired men — some six in number — all deserters and refugees from Dixie. After a hasty supper, this party "took to the brush" for the night, taking with them the horses.

Disclaiming, myself, the status of a "deserter," I chose to remain at the house and take chances with the governor. The refugees gone, our little remaining force at the house consisted of the governor, myself, two women, and a boy. As the governor has personal enemies from this county in the rebel ranks, he had reason to apprehend a night expedition to destroy his property or effect his capture, and determined therefore to keep on the alert. As the early part of the night wore on, our women reported lights on the railroad, and alarmed their imaginations with "the sounds of horses feet crossing the bridge, etc. etc," all which received due attention. Later in the night, the governor and I being out looking about, I called Tom, and both of us went to a field overlooking a switch to see what we could see, and from there we started through thickets for the railroad. The night was dark. We soon reached the house of a Mr. Templeton, foreman on the road, and learned that "all was right" in that direction; the moving about of lights was explained; and we were altogether assured that there was not the least cause for apprehension during the night. No danger can reach Mont Alto except by the railroad. So with alarming signs explained away, and with a very satisfactory report to make, I returned to the mountain. The governor had laid down with his clothes on, but could now undress, and go to bed.

Our refugees, very much frightened, I believe, camp out in the woods. And so end the alarms of today.

29. Tuesday. I walked over and opened my little infant school today as usual, feeling no apprehension at all of a hostile visit, though so far as my pet scrap book and papers were concerned, I took precautions against a surprise. Near 11^{00} a.m., one of the children coming from without, brought word that "more men than she ever saw in all her life before" were descending a steep mountain road to the railroad. I look out and saw that a large force of cavalry had reached the railroad at a point only a hundred yards or so from the school room. Feeling sure they were rebels I at once walked off in the direction of the Crabtree Bridge, accompanied by the boys, one of whom carried my haversack containing my papers and scrap book, the whole rolled up in a newspaper, which I put into a hole, and concealed with leaves immediately upon getting out of sight of the cavalry.

This was hardly done, though, before a cavalry man came into view, at which my three little companions broke away down the mountain side to a lower road running parallel, and I was obliged to follow. Reaching this road I hoped to get off safely, but in a moment cavalry came riding up to us. One little boy broke away again, but I called him back. Still impressed with the idea of these being rebels, I asked the advanced man what they meant to do; whether they intended to burn and destroy any private property. "Who do you takes us to be?" asked the man. "Confederates, of course," I rejoined. Some conversation then ensued in which I became convinced they were not rebels. I then walked down as far as the bridge, where meeting the officer in command, I answered his questions respecting the roads to Piedmont, etc., telling him, though, that the governor (if he could see him) could give him the most accurate information respecting the face of the country, the best routes, etc. The command took the road leading to Mont Alto, and I, supposing that the governor and his party would recognize them as Union soldiers by their uniform, and come in from their concealment, walked back to the schoolhouse.

Very soon my attention was called by the schoolchildren to a cornfield on the mountain side into which a party of soldiers had gotten. In great haste I clambered up the hill to the field in question, and thence repaired to the house. The governor had not returned, neither had any of our farmhands. The women were busy engaged cooking for the soldiers, whom by this time had learned were "Unions." I found the commanding officer in the barnyard, invited him to the house, and obtained his promise to prevent unnecessary destruction of property and waste of grain. He agreed to take no more provender that was absolutely necessary, for which he said he would give a receipt covering double the quantity taken. The party proved to be a detachment (150 strong) of the 6th West Virginia Cavalry, and was commanded by a major. The major being very anxious to see the governor, I took a ramrod with white handkerchief fastened to it, and set out in quest of the skedadlers. After going along the mountain ridge two miles or more, I gave up search, and returned.[57]

Near half-past two, the detachment remounted, and took the railroad towards Bloomington [Maryland]. When they were well gone a little assembly of loquacious old women convened in the kitchen, and after deliberations, very like a caterwauling, voted unanimously that our late visitors, notwithstanding all they had said to the contrary, were "rebels." My opinion was worth nothing.

Near four p.m., our hands came stealthily down with the horses, gave them a feed, got a hasty supper themselves, and put out again, for there was no persuading them that these cavalry were anything else than rebels, who meant to send a party back in the night to capture the governor. I told them to leave a horse for me, which they did. Mounting the animal I set out in quest of the governor. None of the men knew where he was concealed, and I supposed he had gone to a certain house six miles off, but in giving my horse a drink in Crabtree, my saddle and myself slid over his head into the stream, which wetting put me out of the notion of a long night ride. I then rode over to the railroad (the great place of danger in the imagination of the refugees and old women), and learning from Mr. Templeton that all was right in that quarter, returned to the governor's and put my horse up for the night. One of the refugees had come down stealthily to a position near the house, and ventured in when I arrived. I assured him and the women of the house (the caterwauling congress had dispersed to their several homes) that there was no danger, and they seemed to believe. A little later I heard the governor's voice outside, and he came in. To my surprise he too had taken up the idea of these being rebels in disguise, and it was some time before he could be brought to believe that the party were really Union soldiers.

Nothing would convince the refugees. Timid as sheep, and ludicrously suspecting they adhered to their determination to keep a great distance from the house. The governor took tea, and went to bed at his usual hour, and so ended so far as the governor and I are concerned, a protracted scene of skedadling from friends.

30. The neighborhood is still convinced of the rebel character of their late visitors, and our refugees hold the same opinion and it may be a week before they get over their fright.

December 1864

2. My school ends.

3. I had the pleasure today of setting before me, and opening my faithful old "Pig Skin box," the repository of my diaries and papers of old time. It came by Adams Express from Annapolis. For three years and a half it has been out of my reach, and in the hands of irresponsible persons. The books and papers, I observe, have been defaced a little, and carelessly, but not destructively handled. "Kate Leslie" is the only rummager who has left a scribbling autograph. The following are missing:

> All the naval books given me at the Academy.
> 2 fine blank books (accounts.)
> "Easy Lessons in Chinese"[58]

4. Sunday. Gen. W. C. Brown, of Baltimore, Md., called yesterday, and stayed till this evening, which necessitated my sleeping with the governor last night. Today I walked out with the general. In the evening the governor departs for Washington, to take his seat in Congress, leaving me in charge of Mont Alto.

25. The governor (who is returned to Mont Alto) discharged all his employees today. excepting Weeks, who was lately married to the cook.

31. My thirty-first year will in a very few hours more be at an end. I am seated in the "governor's room" in the house of Francis Thomas. It is night. I am alone. I have fasted since breakfast. I have this to deposit in an envelope, seal, and mark, and the hours between now and my sleeping will be for reflection. I am sensible of my <u>terrible</u> short-comings. Alas! 1864, you bear sad witness against me.

P. Clayton V Buskirk

1865

January 1865

14. The directors of School District No. 95, (in the Glades) having requested me to "take up their School" I quit the governor's [Francis Thomas] and come to live in the family of Mr. Browning.

February 1865

1. Am beginning to like my scholars.

4. Bad faith.[59]

9. Find employment in the engine house and shops of the B. & O. R. R. Co., at Piedmont, W. Va. Cost of boarding $20^{00} per month, lodging included.

25. The last seventeen days very wretchedly spent in a dirty crowded den among low characters. Change to-day for the better.

March 1865

23–31. These nights shiver with cold.

April 1865

10. Lee's Surrender!

15. Assassination!

24. The Misses Brown of Charlestown, Va., are old maiden ladies. They are sisters. Their names are Anne, Fanny, and Betsy. Visiting my native town I stay overnight in their dwelling. Mother has no place to keep me. The Misses Brown were of old friends of my mother's family. They were befriended by old John Dixon when he lived; and since he passed away, these ladies, growing old, have never ceased kind thoughts and kind offices for the unfortunate daughter of John Dixon. One of these old ladies nursed the baby Clayton. They bid me make their house my home when I visit Charlestown.

May 1865

2. Make a hurried journey from Piedmont, by the Georgia Creek Railroad, to Mount Savage, and thence to Wellersburg, Pa. on foot, in search of employment as a laborer. At Mount Savage I walked out to the house, where twenty-five years ago I lived with my father, during a term in which he taught school, and I found a family in this house, who had a child of just my age, when I played about the stream which runs close by. With this little boy whose name was Bertie Scott, I made friends at once, and getting his mother's permission took him with me down the stream, and on to Wellersburg. And a happy, pleasant ramble did I and Bertie have together. My means were scanty, but I had the pleasure nevertheless, of treating my little companion to cakes, and lemonade, and raisins, and candy for his sister, even beyond his desires, for Bertie was not selfish, and objected to having too much spent on him.

I found him a most intelligent child, and our little talks were agreeable indeed to me beyond expression. Bertie in a few minutes after we began our walk came to act toward me in the affectionate confiding manner of a little brother.

In our absence the child's mother became alarmed, and induced men and women to scour the neighborhood in quest of her son as a lost child. She worried herself a great deal, and without reason. Bertie and I heard of these things as we were nearing his mother's dwelling on our return.

June 1865

1. When I saw George Schultze in Winchester, he told me about Bill McFarland[60] getting a land warrant for service in China in 1854: so when I got back to Frankville, I wrote to a law firm in Washington about the matter, and learning that I too was entitled to a land warrant, notwithstanding my late defection to the general government (that being pardoned). I went down to Piedmont yesterday to make before a magistrate an affidavit, and also to execute a power of attorney. These were done

before a justice of the peace over in Westernport, two old gentlemen who knew me when I was a child kindly consenting to subscribe as witnesses, and this morning the papers were mailed for authentication to Horace Presley, Clerk of Court, Cumberland. I took supper, and passed the night with Frank Book. He is a painter in the employment of the railroad company at Piedmont, and he is indeed one of nature's gentlemen.

Today is by presidential and gubernatorial proclamation a day of mourning. I wear today a fine shirt, neat little cravat, nice hat, (borrowed,) white jacket, white pants, and heavy, clumsy shoes. I am not badly off for clothing. A trunkful that had belonged to me before the war, was kept in safety by Mrs. Streit of Winchester, and brought from there only a short while ago. But for this, I would be badly off indeed. Some of my clothing is tight fitting and entirely too small for my comfort. A silk flowered vest of this description, which the Bloomington storekeeper said was worth $4.$\underline{^{00}}$ I traded off to Mr. Baily for $3.$\underline{^{00}}$ and was thus enabled to pay the expenses of "executing" the papers for my land warrant.

Today is appointed for mourning. I procured a piece of black ribbon to be neatly tacked to my jacket sleeve. No similar symbol met my eye in Piedmont. Piedmont was as quiet as on the memorable nineteenth of April, and yet this was not (like that) a solemn day. The day is simply a holiday. Piedmont is quiet because it is depopulated. All Piedmont is gone a fishing.

? The deep cut is two miles up the railroad. They are prolonging an arch tunnel there, and laboring hands are in demand. This forenoon I walked up and asked for employment. It was readily given. The wages are 1\underline{^{75}}$ per diem, and I am to go to work next Monday. It is certainly my ambition to labor enough to pay for my board: so when the governor is absent, and he has been away some days lately, I have kept faithfully at work by the side of his hired man.[61] And yet the governor on getting home seems fearful that I have been idle and lounging, and have not so much as earned my board, and intimates as much, not taking note that his hired girls (who detest me) come frequently into the room while he is speaking.

? This hour is one of wretchedness. I am again homeless. The governor means me only kindness.

9. The governor means me only kindness — and I was going on to say — but he has given me a lecture this morning that makes me wretched indeed. I was getting ready to labor on the repairs of the railroad, and had asked him for a room in his vacant house at the switch (Frankville). I may say indeed that Francis Thomas has finally and pointedly turned me away from Mont Alto. Such was I going on to say. That was Tuesday morning three days ago. I sat under a tree on the roadside, waiting for the burden trains west to come along, on one of which I hoped to beg a passage to Rowelsburg. Templeton is a railroad officer at Rowelsburg. I had taught Templeton to write his name, and this man always professing to be friendly, might do something for me now. Exactly what he could do I had no distinct idea. The day before (Monday) I had worked at mixing mortar at a deep cut two miles off, where an arch is being built, and when night came on I dared not return to Mont Alto, but taking a small boy for company, went to sleep on the floor of one of the vacant rooms of the house at the switch. On that Monday morning the governor had "in all candor and kindness" said the words which amounted to my dismissal from his home, and more: it was formally reading me out of all caste. The governor has indeed all along treated me as a gentleman and as one of his own caste: he has given me a bed in his own room: and now he says to me:

> "A man to come here and be treated as a gentleman, must have associates when away from here such as fit him to be my associate."

(or words to that effect). I cannot labor on the road and be welcome at Mont Alto. The labor is hard and the associations are degrading: that is incontestible. But I am really a laborer. I have no money, no trade, and no profession. I am slowly and furtively, day by day, as I can find the time, making myself acquainted with English branches of learning, in order to become a schoolmaster or clerk. Of this the governor knows nothing.

On this Tuesday morning I had begged my breakfast, and sat under the tree waiting for the trains west.

Before they came, a little boy brought me word that the governor was at the switch, and wished to see me.

I went up, and had repeated to me pretty much the lecture of Monday morning, with counsel added, such as he would not have given had he known better my moral and intellectual condition, my plans, and my aspirations. Then he tendered me <u>ten dollars</u> "for my services on the farm." This was indeed a godsend, and I accepted it, muttering something, saying nothing. (It becomes a debt and must be repaid.)

So I got upon a burden train, and went up to Rowelsburg. Templeton was glad to see me. He thinks I can be useful to him. He will help me to set up a school. So I came down again on a burden train and am here at Mont Alto. This morning carried my trunk over to the switch (leaving only my box of manuscripts in the governor's custody), and took out a bundle of clothes for use at Rowelsburg. But I miss getting on the trains with my bundle and so have to stop here another night. The governor is not at home.

I need only a hat and shoes to be enabled to equip myself like a gentleman. I can buy these with a part of the governor's ten dollars.

10. Undetermined this morning what to do with a full belly to day, and ten dollars in my pocket. I waited at the switch for trains to pass (yet without any fixed intention to jump on any one), and brooked over my desperate predicament, filled with gloomy anticipations of the future. What will become of me?

If it were not for my mother and her wants through the approaching winter, anxiety would not so oppress me for I could creep into a place of obscurity and find work whereby to feed and clothe myself, and have time besides to continue with my plan of self-instruction.

But I want wages — winter is approaching — mother is to succor — and taxes are to be paid on her little property.

The portion of Scripture which (in pursuance of my plan) comes up today to be committed to memory, contains the words from the lips of our Lord:

> "Take ye Therefore no thought for the morrow; for the morrow shall take thought for the things of itself. Sufficient for the day is the evil thereof."[62]

In the face of this lesson I had no right to longer brood over evils that belong not to today, but are promised in the early future: so I aroused myself into good spirits, continued my lessons, played with a little Irish boy, and when the passenger train west came by, I got on board of her. At Rowelsburg I got off, and as luck happened, the conductor neglected to take my fare. Nine dollars have purchased me a hat, shoes, and light pantaloons, which with clothing that I brought up, will enable me tomorrow to appear like a gentleman: After taking dinner at Templeton's I walked three miles into the country, coming to the "North Western Turnpike" where the distance to Romney is 64 miles, to Clarksburg 44. Here preparations are being made for oil boring. On my way back I stopped to have a chat in the family of an old returned soldier whose daughter, a sprightly, and not bad looking girl of eighteen, who had never seen me before, made free to hide my hat behind her dress when I was about to leave, and had to be <u>wrestled with</u> (hugged and as good as kissed) before I could recover possession of it. This young lady is really prepossessing, and has but one fault (that I cared to notice), and that is the habit of rubbing snuff on her teeth. They tell me the custom is prevalent in this region for young girls to smoke tobacco, chew tobacco, and use snuff. Getting back to Rowelsburg, I attended church after night, and heard a sermon in which the preacher exhibited a woeful ignorance of grammar and sacred history.

18. <u>Robbed</u>. I had brought my trunk from the governor's and placed it in his storehouse at the switch some days before going to visit Eliza Van Buskirk.

This trunk containing valuable clothing, and souvenirs of my voyages to China and Japan, together with very highly prized letters and papers, constituted my <u>little all</u> of property in this world. It was broken open <u>and</u> robbed on the last day of my stay at Van Buskirk's. Soldiers of Sherman's army did it on their passage up the road.

22. Enjoying a little sleep in a fence corner in the early afternoon today. I dreamed of Lewis Price. Heaven protect Lewis! My love for this boy is unabated.

July 1865

<u>Remarks</u>. Change. This month, from the mountains of Maryland to the region wherein my family had its origin — from strangers to the midst of relatives. Luckily found early employment whereby a few shillings were earned.

4. P. C. V. B., and penniless, his lesson the 4th of July 1865, well learned. God bless the boy whom he kissed and parted from this day one year ago! O Lewis! O guileless boy! How solemnly I resolved a year ago to be like you, and how shamefully failed! Be my solemn vows this day renewed, and God help me!

5. Harriet Molila Welsh was born 31 July 1860. She is the daughter of T. S. Welsh and, I think, grandchild of Eliza Van Buskirk. We make a fire out of doors this hot July evening to smoke the mosquitoes away, and Molila and I pile up together on the ground near by, and we are a naughty two, for she likes to have her belly down to the little down-less mons veneris scratched, which I am wicked enough to do.

6. Eat nothing but buttermilk these two days.

? Old black man tells me about Grandfather Van Buskirk, and about William his son. These accounts and all else I can learn respecting my ancestors, will be noted in some appropriate little book.

23. John A. Thomson's wife died this evening. I sat up watching the corpse greater part of the night. Much lamented lady!

24. Today the funeral.

26. Over in the neighborhood where I've been working, they think I'll make a good primary teacher, and have invited me to take up school. I've looked about to try such an experiment nearer Charlestown, but meeting no encouragement, have agreed to open school in Mr. Messner's neighborhood, to commence the first Monday in August next.

Remarks. Mr. Messner, to whom I had last month hired myself to work by the day, being an entire stranger, judged by any language that I had education, and do suggest that I should take up a school in his neighborhood. A school I accordingly opened in the Old Jourdan Seminary, just 11½ miles from Charlestown: and by the end of the month find myself the Teacher of 8 children, for each of whom I hope to receive 1\underline{^{00}}$ per month.

September 1865

20. Have the satisfaction of knowing that I am "generally respected," but I [am] a "man without money" and without ability to make it.

22. Today, dismissed my little school, having kept it together one month; and so ends the Old Jourdan Seminary.

23. Entertaining no further hope of augmenting the number of my scholars I had given notice that on Friday 22nd I would bring my school to a close, and accordingly when that day arrived I instituted a "final examination" of my pupils, and at noon, announced the result, granted tickets to the deserving, and formally dismissed my school. Then calling upon my patrons I received half of what was owing me, and being promised that the balance would be mailed to my address, I took leave of my friends, and on Saturday morning, with four dollars in my pocket, bade a final adieu to the little settlement of "Arabia." The three patrons of my school behave with great friendliness towards me, and seem to regret very much the necessity which impels me to break up the school.

With my two shirts under my arm, my cotton pants beginning to look the worse for wear, and my shoes sadly in want of repair, I walk over to Summit Point, spend an hour with Warner Thomson, and then go across the fields to spend the night at his brother's.

24. The members of the household of John A. Thomson [Van Buskrik's cousins] constitute a happy circle, into which I have always been cordially received, and much kindness has at all times been extended to me. It is nevertheless and aristocratic home circle, and my poverty stands in the way of my feeling "entirely at home." All these cousins of mine sang for one last night just before going to bed. That which I called my favorite song, was one in which these words occur:

> "Then up stepped the Captain of this jolly crew,
> And a well spoken man was he."

This singing and music was all at my request. It in fact celebrates my last visit to "Hawthorne."[63] My cousins do not suspect it, but I have made up my mind to go immediately to Washington, and join the marines if I cannot do any better. John Throckmorton Thomson, aged about 12, has become my favorite. We sleep together and are as intimate as intimate can be. This attachment attracting attention, poor Jacky, in my absence, is by his aunts, and by Mrs. Steptoe, made the butt of ridicule. But he bears up against it, and much as they tease him, persists in his regard for me.

He shall not long be a little sufferer. Probably to-night we see each other for the last time for years. My cousins speak of me disparagingly. "Aunt Mary and Aunt Lucy say that you are a fool, and that your are crazy." I doubt not Jacky hears much else calculated to lessen me in a boy's esteem.

28. About noon, I am sitting on the river bank, close to the place where twenty years ago I and my college fellows came to swim. I am just after bathing again in the old stream. Behind one is the high canal bank, and only a little distance beyond that, is the college.

Leaving this spot my way leads through a passage under the canal, and my memory tells me that in the winter time twenty years ago, rowdy boys waylaid me in this passage, and robbed me of a pair of skates. What memories do these rocks call up! My heart aches at the retrospect I take from this point. I mourn the loss of twenty years.

October 1865

<u>Remarks</u>. I consider that I enjoy the favor of the commandant of the corps, of the sergeant major, and of the officers (Lieut. Kokes especially); for which I feel grateful; and by which, by fidelity to duty, I hope to render myself worthy. Inside the barracks Kearney the baker relieves me of a hundred daily vexations, by having given me from the first, a corner in his family quarters.

Outside, I find in "No. 150" now (what it hath' ever been), a home.[64]

2. The surgeon in attendance at the marine barracks subjected me to a rigid examination this morning, and pronounced me fit for military service. Not, however, before asking me questions enough to illicit an acknowledgment of my rebel antecedents, whereupon he heaped reproach upon me, and indeed made me feel bad enough. But I am told that when I left he spoke very favorably of me. The surgeon's certificate being obtained, my enlistment paper was filled out, and I appeared before the officer of the day, who called in Captain Houston, and the last named officer proceeded to administer the oath which binds me to <u>penitentiary</u> service for four long years. The sergeant major, and others of the old time corps who are here are not wanting in kindness.

13. From the day of my enlistment to this day, I have been a close prisoner in the barracks, excepting two occasions of liberty granted for a few hours according to custom to soldiers coming off guard. But his morning I handed the following paper to Major Graham:

Marine Barracks
Oct. 12. 1865.
To the Commanding Officer:

Private P. C. Van Buskirk respectfully states that his home is immediately in rear of the barracks, and asks that he may be granted such a standing pass as will enable him to spend the hours between <u>retreat</u> and <u>tattoo</u> (or between <u>tattoo</u> and <u>reveille</u>) each day among his people.[65] He will go no where else unless on regular liberty.

And if at any time he miss a roll call, or otherwise be remiss in his duties in consequence of this indulgence, he will immediately surrender his pass to the orderly sergeant.

Before reading it, the major ordered me to tell the orderly sergeant to put me on duty as acting corporal, and shortly afterwards, the officer of the day called me into his office, and causing me to read out my own paper, informed me that my request was granted upon the conditions I myself named.

The officer and the sergeant have (very favorably for me) attached a different signification to the parenthetical clause in my application from which I had intended, and so accord me the privilege of "spending the hours between retreat and tattoo, and between tattoo and reveille away from the barracks, more than I had dared to ask.

I am sure I am grateful for this kindness from Major Graham.

Day before yesterday I patiently bore with violent abuse from a sentinel who was himself intoxicated. I had violated no order of his post, but some days before, I recollected to have said something to him that did not please him at the time. The behavior of this man I reported to the officer of the day (Lieut. Williams), and the sergeant of the guard and others were called up, persons who saw all that transpired, but not a soul of them would corroborate my statement. I think they all very coolly lied, considering it a merit to screen the sentinel, and the officer dismissed the case.

November 1865

1. Yesterday I was promoted to the rank of corporal, and ordered to join a detachment consisting of a sergeant, two corporals, and twelve privates, detailed as a guard for a little steamer called the "*Swatara*," now lying at the navy yard. I handed in to the officer of the day, for transmission to Major Graham, the following paper:

Marine Barracks. Nov. 1, 1865.
To the commanding officer:

I beg to thank the commandant and the commanding officer for my promotion.

I enlisted with the determination to honorably perform all the duties of a soldier, whether in or out of the ranks, during this term of service, as the only amends I can make for an egregious mistake of four years.

The favor shown me by my promotion is an additional incentive, if any were needed. Considering myself the joint selection of the commandant and the commanding officer, I trust by faithfully discharging the duties of my new capacity to do honor to their judgment. And my mother (a loyal woman) is immediately benefitted by my advancement, I beg to present her thanks also.

By permission of the commanding officer.

Respectfully submitted
P. C. Van Buskirk

Of course I have a right to nothing, and should be, and am, grateful for any favor shown me, leaving the measure ~~thereof~~ to my superiors, yet I must confess myself greatly disappointed at being ordered to sea as a junior corporal of a little guard, over which a mere boy is placed as orderly sergeant. At 2$\underline{^{00}}$ p.m., the *Swatara*'s guard was marched to the navy yard, and quartered in one of the lofts. Evening came on, and there was a grand procession of working men through the city, which I would have been glad to see, but it was impossible to get out the gate. I find Sergeant McDonnough in charge at the navy yard, the same who was there as orderly sergeant with me near or quite six years ago. He seems disposed to treat me kindly — and that may be a little strange, as his habits and mine, now as well as then, are as opposite as can be.

Today, Major Thomas G. Field, commanding marines at the navy yard, kindly granted me the privilege of being absent each day, when not on duty, till "tattoo," in order that I may have the opportunity of spending as much time as possible among my people. He could not, consistent with the requirements of the service, continue the indulgence which had been granted me at the barracks, of sleeping at home.

13. Monday. Probably the hardest part of my hard lot, is the being compelled to borrow money, every week two dollars, to send to my mother; for I am anticipating my pay, and striving all I can to send to her regularly small sums proportioned to my wages. Mrs. Hilbran has up to the present time been kind enough to advance these little sums as I required them. But today I find that either her money drawer, or my credit, is at last exhausted. "Begging credit — my mother says — is the meanest of all begging." She is an authority on this subject, and my own feelings at this moment do more than verify her proposition.

Mrs. Schultze, or Mrs. Wunderlich would, no doubt enable me to continue the weekly remittance; but my goodness! my feelings rebel as much against begging loans from my best friends as they would rebel against unqualified mendicancy. I take comfort in the prospect of being in the early part of this week paid off, preliminarily to going on board the

"*Swatara*," for it is now a fixed thing that I am to go as junior corporal in that steamer.

15. The "*Swatara*'s Guard," consisting of one sergeant, two corporals, and twelve privates, was marched today at or near one o'clock, on board the vessel, where a small knot of young officers were assembled on the poop, and a motley crowd of blue-jackets amidships, when the ceremony of "going into commission" was enacted. Upon the arrival of Comdr. Balch, Capt. Jeffers read to his auditors an order addressed to him by the Navy Department, and added: (as near as I can remember:) "In accordance with the orders of the Secretary of the Navy, I assume command of this ship." Nothing more. A pennant was then run up the main, and the ship had gone duly "into commission." The *Swatara*'s guard, leaving a sentinel in the gangway, then marched to the barracks, and was merged as before into the body of marines doing duty in the navy yard. Since Major Fields departure, the navy yard marines have been subjected every day to unnecessary and harassing inspections and drills, far exceeding what they had heretofore been accustomed to.

Lieut. McCullom succeeded to the command pro-tem, and began at once introducing all these changes; and now that Capt. Haywood, the permanent commanding officer, has arrived, it seems they are approved and are likely to continue in force a long while. Major Field left on the 7th. I am envied on all sides my chance of getting away from the yard.

Coming off guard today, I have a permit to be absent till 6 o'clock tomorrow morning, and as it was late before I could avail myself of my liberty to go out, I begged the lieutenant to extend my permit two hours, but I begged in vain.

The manner which officers affect toward their men, has already made me feel some of the horrors which sprang from the consciousness of <u>caste lost</u>. And yet I cannot see why degradation should attach to the position of common soldier. He has a heavy burden to bear. He should be respected for his burden. True, the men who compose the garrisons at headquarters and here, are seventy-five per cent very low characters — thieves, liars, habitual swearers, and obscenists of the filthiest order, illiterate and puerile in intellect, and I suspect the same may be said of the whole corps. The non-commissioned officers are, as far as I can see, very little better than the rank and file: they certainly receive very little respect from the private soldiers, and are treated with very little superior consideration by their officers. Granting all this, I cannot see why a man who has enlisted with the honest purpose of doing right under all circumstances, should be considered as having by the act of enlisting forfeited all title to respect. I mean to serve out my time honestly. I will stoop to no mean thing. I will render to my officers an honest obedience, treating their commands and their persons with sincere respect. But I have no idea of exhibiting the cringing servility which they, I am afraid, are long accustomed to receive from "enlisted men."

17. Not much time to spare (these last sixteen days) from drills, inspections, and guards.

18. Saturday. Passed a pleasant hour this evening in the family of Thomas Johnson, who was drummer-boy with me in the *Portsmouth*; a good boy whom I loved and now a happy father of a fine baby.

20. Monday. At one in the afternoon, the "*Swatara's*" Guard was formed in uniform (watch-coats over), with knapsacks on back, and marched, preceded by music, to the vessel. Sergeant Cathcart is at last placed in command of his little guard, Corporal Hines ranks next, and I am second corporal of the *Swatara's* guard from today. We are only too glad to be away from the navy yard.

25. Restriction. This is my first note in any diary aboard the *Swatara*. I am sitting on a ditty box under one of the berth deck lamps, and the guitar, with singing, is going on around me. It is sweet music — how I love it! It takes me in spirit to the parlor of my cousins in the valley.

But I must by an effort bend my thoughts to the matter which it is the object of this writing to record. And I will hurry, for I long to enjoy the music. First to be mentioned is a little event of last night. One of our guard, sitting at the orderly table with me, opened and began reading aloud from an obscene book, soon attracting a crowd of eager listeners. Failing to convince the reader of the impropriety of his proceeding, or to induce him to desist, I had recourse to the officer of the deck. An end was put to the reading and my fellow <u>soldier</u> received some good advice from the young officer in charge of the deck. No sooner was word taken below <u>of my</u> having "reported" this offense than nearly the whole guard <u>were</u> up in indignation, and a delegation came up, headed by the orderly sergeant, to express the general displeasure. It was a queer scene. After a few demonstrations denunciatory of my conduct, the little party adjourned below.

One incident I thought particularly amusing. Looking down the hatchway when all had gotten below, I observed one fellow obstreperously repeat the exclamation, "<u>I am a Union man</u>!" until a big fellow (our cook) who was among the others in their hostility towards me, but who coming to conceive some how or other that these words were meant as a spiteful reflection on <u>his</u> loyalty, took them up, and retorted with — "I am a Union man too, and if you want anything I can [*sic*]," and this closed up our would-be patriot.

To turn to something else. Today I tried all I know how to get the poor privilege of going out to my home, only two or three squares from the navy yard gates. But it was of no use. The young sergeant interposed his authority to prevent my making application directly to the executive officer (Lieut. Comdr. Lull) that, he said, he would do himself, and he did it in such a manner as to bring back a refusal. I then entreated to be allowed to speak to the officer myself, but the sergeant persisted in refusing his "permission," and I had no alternative than to do so without his leave.

The lieutenant commander in a rough way replied that I had already received an answer, and declined hearing anything more in the subject. So I retired, restricted to the yard, and denied the poor privilege of going only two or three squares from the navy yard gate to my home were but for one hour. I believe there is not a Negro cook on board the ship whose privileges in this respect are not greater than it is intended to accord the "non commissioned officer" of the guard.

26. Sunday. About a week ago, a batch of twenty-one or twenty-two privates were taken with but little discrimination from the ranks, and promoted to be sergeants and corporals. The sergeant major could have had me retransferred to headquarters and promoted on this occasion. I judge that it was within his power, but he gave one no such evidence of his friendships. Some of the new sergeants are raw recruits, and I judge from what I hear said, that more than one of the promoted men are unable to read and write.

Sunday night. I open today a new column in my diary. A star in it will indicate that I am a prisoner — with a prisoner's feelings — for the day. When our ship lies in port, and I feel a strong desire to visit the town, I can not conceive — <u>all things duly considered</u> — any reason why my wish should not be gratified. Restriction to the vessel per force, and by the mere ill-considered arbitrary order of some persons who hardly know my name, is in effect <u>imprisonment</u>. A prisoner's feelings must be mine. I do not say that I am <u>undeserving</u> of all the incarcerations, and humiliations, and degradations that (I should have known beforehand) he must accept as a portion who voluntarily enlists as a common soldier in the navy.

This enlistment, dating from 2nd Oct., I must accept as just punishment for the shortcomings of <u>four</u> similar periods of time, either one of which properly improved would have involved me with intellect and attainments such as would at this juncture of my life have raised me far above the reach of the peculiar order of misfortunes which now environ me.

P. S. Upon second thought I believe I'll not continue the column for "Prisoner marks." I can in some other way indicate that kind of treatment.

December 1865

2. Liberty-requested. Today handed to the executive officer with request that it be handed to the captain the following letter:

Swatara 2nd Dec. 1865
Commander W. N. Jeffers
Sir:

I respectfully ask to be allowed a day and night in the city, in order to dispose of business connected with my family, which cannot be neglected without great detriment to myself, and to others. My home is hardly three squares from the navy yard gate, and not anticipating rigid restriction to the ship, I had hoped to find time and opportunities before the *Swatara*'s day of sailing for adjusting my little affairs and transferring to other hands the duties which now demand my personal attention. Five or six days ago, being unable to get into the city (where I suppose I could have borrowed money), and receiving intelligence of my mother being in <u>extreme want</u>, I put in a requisition for money from the paymaster, and, at some sacrifice of pride accompanied therewith a letter detailing my mother's difficulties. My effort was without success and my mother's wants remain unsupplied. I beg to mention one more particular. Today I expect will arrive in town to take his seat in the next congress, a gentleman who brings me a number of articles that I am anxious shall be received and lodged at my home, and whom I am besides anxious to see. To neglect submitting this statement would be to do injustice to myself and to others.

The commander's favorable consideration is asked, and if my request can be granted, I will be duly thankful.

> P. C. Van Buskirk
> Corporal, Marines

3. Sunday. Joe, in company with a little boy friend, came on board at noon.[66] Our interview gave me the pleasure which only a poor prisoner can feel who is visited by his intimate friend and brother. Joe must be principal manager of my home affairs while I am in this prison ship, and away on the cruise for which she is fitting out.

5. Today the captain's servant brought my letter of 2nd to the orderly sergeant, who in turn sent it to me. On its back is the following "endorsement:"

> After a crew is transferred, no leave can be given, except with the assent of the commandant, which I do not at all feel disposed to ask. Before sailing, such persons as have money due will be allowed to draw.
>   You have had plenty of time to prepare.
>   (Initials: cannot make them out)

Transferred today to what is called "petty officers port watch mess." This is a new thing. Marine corporals aforetime belonged to the "orderly mess," which was quite a privilege on account of conveniences and decencies appertaining to that mess. But in arranging messes here, the executive officer (Lt. Cmdr. Lull) left out the corporals, who continued to mess with the privates until today.

I'm sorry to see that my strict adherence to orders while doing duty as a corporal of the guard is creating trouble for me ahead. Many of the marines dislike me for that, and some of them (I have reason to believe) heartily hate me. I notice that cock-and-bull stories are afloat respecting my past life, all hatched in malice. Added to this, the orderly sergeant though he keeps up "appearances of cordiality," I am satisfied, is very unfavorably disposed towards me. It is certain that whenever I find any difficulty in carrying out orders on account of sentinel's neglect, he never gives me any "support," but always excuses the sentinel. One consequence of which is that the latter is becoming indifferent to my instructions, and I have already intimated to the young sergeant that it would suit me better to serve in the ranks.

6. Wednesday. Mr Crawford, who is a blacksmith in the yard and an old acquaintance came on board near sundown. I had sent him word that I wished to speak to him. Through him, and by the agency of his little boy, I hope to communicate with my home in town. We are not allowed the liberty of even the yard. I am anxious to earn the credit of having done my duty throughout the cruise of this ship, and I have no other intentions (whether I receive the credit of it or not) to keep faithfully the promise made to the country in my enlistment. On this head I hold myself responsible to God, and I certainly do not know myself if petty tyranny doing its worst can drive me to such a thing as desertion. The treatment which I am now receiving at the hands of Captain Jeffers and his lieutenant is bad, and regard for my oath of enlistment alone constrains me to endure it. I am sensible of the insult which is put upon me.

7. Thanksgiving Day.[67] Joe came on board today. I importuned the executive officer again for money. It is due him to say that he did not receive my application with a scowl. He promised to "see the captain about it." And this is probably the last I will hear of it. I joined a party of marines who were enjoying themselves under the hammocks spinning yarns (and such yarns! The most puerile of ghost stories), singing, etc., and this because it was "Thanksgiving Day." Of course it was impossible to be an hour in such a crowd without hearing filthiness.

31. I see how little I have done for myself in the past year, and with alarm at the flight of time, I earnestly resolve to labor on steadily through my book, page by page, till arithmetic is learned and let nothing put me back.

1865 is gone. My God! What memories crowd it! It has passed over me like an ugly dream.

P. Clayton Van Buskirk

Afterword

After Van Buskirk had been on the *Swatara* for a time, his frustrations became almost unbearable. Although he had earlier complained to his diary on a regular basis of poor conditions on board the *Cumberland* and the *Plymouth*, his life on the steamer exceeded in misery anything he had previously experienced in the United States Navy. He described her as a place where he was "penned up like a brute." A portion of his discontent was due to the design of the vessel. She was one of the newest of the *Resaca*-class, screw-driven gunboats, and he described the wooden-hulled iron clad as small, cold, uncomfortable in the extreme, foul smelling, and dark. A primary reason her men suffered discomfort in excess of that usually experienced on board sailing ships was due to the steam-powered engine. Although the gunboat was longer than many of the navy's larger fighting ships, her narrow beam and shallow, twelve-foot draft meant space below decks was at a premium for the men. Not only did the engine and coal storage occupy considerable cubic footage, but the exceedingly heavy structural members necessary to support the engine additionally reduced living space. Then, too, when the *Swatara* reached her maximum speed under power of approximately ten knots, the noise and vibration of the four screws amplified the level of misery. Not only was the ship a wretched piece of work in Van Buskirk's estimation, he firmly believed the officers did their best to make life even more miserable for the sailors and Marines under their command than would have been normal due to the *Swatara's* design. In early 1866, he referred to William N. Jeffers, the captain, as Henry Wirtz, the notorious commander of the Confederacy's Andersonville Prison. Lieutenant Edward P. Lull was at least as bad an officer as the captain, and the noncommissioned officers harassed him at every turn when he tried to carry out his assigned duties. The ordinary members of the crew were also a disreputable lot, in his estimation. Van Buskirk contributed in no small measure to his own torments. He adopted the same negligent attitude toward his work that he demonstrated as a monumentally inept watchman at the naval academy. In less than a year as a *Swatara* Marine, he was made to stand extra duty, officially reprimanded at least once, arrested twice, and demoted from corporal to private.[1]

What antagonized Van Buskirk even more than the incommodious ship, the hateful officers and crewmen, and the navy's niggling bureaucratic regulations was the fact that he was unable to leave the *Swatara* at any of the foreign ports she visited during 1866. As a drummer on the *Plymouth* he had been able to come and go as he pleased without much interference, but as a regular member of the steamer's Marine detachment he could go ashore only with permission, and it was rarely granted. Black stewards and cooks, boat crews, and musicians lived under no such restrictions, and the knowledge of their relative freedom and his confinement galled him. Despite knowing his requests would be routinely turned down, he badgered his officers for permission to go ashore and grumbled incessantly when it was denied.[2]

The captain eventually wearied of the complaints and constant requests. In October of 1866, he was reassigned to the naval academy. For a time things seemed to improve. He was promoted to the post of drum major, and when his mother died, the commander of the Marine detachment, Captain McLane Tilton, loaned him money to attend the funeral. Unfortunately, there were as many difficulties ashore for Van Buskirk as there were on the *Swatara*. He regularly quarreled with Tilton, who in January of 1867 sacked him as drum major. In retaliation, Van Buskirk tendered his resignation the next day. As a mere music boy, the job he descended to upon being demoted from drum major, he found himself in the same lowly post he occupied two decades earlier as a teenager on board the *Cumberland*. The loss of status increased his hostility, and he continued to antagonize his superiors. They responded as might be expected. He was denied liberty, arrested for no apparent reason, once placed in double irons, and subjected to constant rounds of humiliations. The continued ill-treatment not only stoked his bitterness but made him even more recalcitrant. He missed roll calls, took unauthorized absences from guard duty, and forgot to beat drum calls. In due course Captain Tilton was driven to extremes by his wayward drummer, and ordered him confined to a dark, unventilated, filthy 4' × 9' cell below deck on the U.S.S. *Wyandank*, a side-wheel steamer permanently anchored at the academy to serve as a water-borne barracks. The prescribed diet for the drummer and the other prisoner with whom he shared the tiny space was bread and water. His incarceration only provided fodder for more complaints. "I have a companion," he wrote, "dirtier still than the floor — a strange character, who has shuffled through the War, playing all sorts of roles in and out of the Army perpetrating villainies which finally consigned him to the Penitentiary of New York, from which an easy transition to the Marine Corps."[3] Van Buskirk eventually gained his freedom, but leaving the cramped and fetid cell did not improve his disposition. Continued dereliction of duty earned him another stint in the *Wyandank* brig, but his companion during his second confinement was more to his liking, a young fifer named Clinton Davis. Their plight was made less arduous by an opening from their cell into the adjoining cell where a Black mess hall attendant was locked away for unspecified offenses. He regularly shared his servings of meat and potatoes with the two musicians. When not engaged in a war of attrition against the authorities, Van Buskirk feuded with fellow Marines, whom he characterized as liars, thieves, habitual swearers, and illiterates.[4]

Service in the post-war Marine Corps was a dismal experience for Van Buskirk, but he had to admit that it had its compensations. After years of receiving depreciated southern currencies or trading his labor for food and shelter, he was once again being paid in specie. Another advantage of being a Marine was that there was little work to do. Although there were as many as seven drum calls to be beaten each day at the academy, there were enough drummers available so he need not be present every day or beat every call when on duty. Most of his time was spent reading, eating, and chatting. Indeed, so little of note occurred during these years that he gradually inflated the most ordinary events into epochs on his diary pages. He once expended considerable ink recording the saga of a pocket watch that disappeared during a visit to the privy. Then, too, there were boys to occupy his idle hours. At one point he worked at teaching a youthful fifer the rudiments of chess with a borrowed board and set of pieces. On another occasion he befriended a little boy named Johnny Jefferson. He often took music boys John McLane and Clinton Davis on visits and excursions. Although the former drum major once listed Davis as a "decent lad," it became clear in short order that he was a "blackguard" in need of reformation. At some point the three — Van Buskirk, Davis, and McLane — moved into a tiny 6' × 10' room together. Their cubicle had once been the province of the post tailor, but after some scrubbing with soap, water and sand they transformed it into a suitable bunkhouse. Acting fatherly, Van Buskirk set out to build little shelves for each occupant, but their private nest was far from secure. When the hated Captain Tilton happened by and observed what was afoot, he forbade the installation of the shelves.[5] After tutelage from the drummer over a period of time Davis was much improved. According to the proud mentor, he "now sides altogether with the orderly, the obedient, the decent — and perseveres in his efforts to gain knowledge, for all which I greatly respect him." Still, as was almost always the case with Van Buskirk's charges, his pupil retained many faults — his manners were deficient and he was so selfish that the diarist found it impossible to love him.[6] At about the same time he improved Davis, he actively pursued another friendship with a boy identified only as Tracy. The drummer described fifer Tracy in much the same fashion as he described most of the other lads with whom he was enamored over the years. He was "well favored," intelligent," and "of a higher order or morals." As was usually the case with his infatuations, the relationship with Tracy provided Van Buskirk with more anguish than joy. The connection between the adult and his young friend is impossible to follow closely since the diary entries recording it during the winter of 1867 are faded and largely illegible. The few readable snippets suggest that Tracy "was tracked from the cradle by misfortune," at least in Van Buskirk's estimate.[7] Characteristically, this gave the older man license to save the boy from what ever menaced him. In some way, now indiscernible from the pale script on the pages that recount the relationship between the two, Tracy was offended by his self-appointed mentor's actions. Van Buskirk was crushed when the boy rejected him, and attempted to regain his friendship with fawning obsequiousness. He summoned him to his room and later wrote of what transpired. "I am sorry I spoke so harshly to you this morning," he wrote, "and I ask your pardon. If you think that I have wronged you in any way, tell me what I must do to make it right and I will do it." Words only conveyed a part of his message, the diarist noted, explaining that "I am sure that my tone of voice and countenance bore witness to the sincerity of my apology, which even Tracy could understand." Unfortunately, neither soft words nor a sad face were sufficient. Tracy "turned away without a word," but Van Buskirk was unfazed by the rejection. "I am glad to believe," he confided to the diary, "that a wound is not left open to fester in my brother's heart."[8]

Afterword

Although Van Buskirk was cheered over his partial success with Clinton Davis and not entirely disappointed in Tracy, his assessment of the general run of music boys remained much as it had been when he was first inducted into the Marine Corps as thirteen-year-old in the early summer of 1846. Most were beyond redemption by his or any other hand. They were a collection of disgusting, debilitated, debased, and perverted reprobates. In one instance he recorded how this degraded gaggle whiled away a day gawking at obscene engravings and reading passages from a pornographic book. Suffused with righteous indignation, he reported the spectacle to the "Sergeant-in Charge," but had little expectation that his diligence would aid in reducing barracks depravity. "I doubt if ... there is a sergeant at the post who has courage enough to undertake a seizure of anything of the kind in the music den," he wrote. In a final blast, he added that Captain Tilton would not support noncommissioned officers who tried to deprive their charges of literature that contained material of dubious moral quality.[9] Van Buskirk undoubtedly forgot or chose not to remember that a dozen or so years before — when he, himself, was a newly-recruited Marine drummer — he had read the same book the boys found so enthralling. Its title was *Silas Shovewell*.

During the years after the war, Van Buskirk seized many opportunities to renew old acquaintanceships. He frequently visited the home of his former heartthrob, George Schultz, and virtually roomed there on visits to Washington, D.C. In Annapolis, he sought out George Duvall, the boy whose friendship had secured him meals and lodging with his parents six years earlier while he was waiting to take up his job as a watchman at the academy. Duvall by this time had attended St. John's College and was teaching a troupe of boys at a school he superintended. Despite Duvall's attendance at St. John's, Van Buskirk observed that his friend had not become his "intellectual superior."[10] Van Buskirk also corresponded with two of his former favorites, Lewis Price and Charlie Peyton. Their letters warmed his heart, and he rejoiced in the knowledge that after the passage of years neither of the pair excoriated "the vagabond soldier ... almost pederast ... I am not scorned for having been (as their memories must now testify) puerile in the days of our intimacy ... they heap no reproach on me." The fascination for the two Georges, Lewis, and Charlie was gone by the time he began exchanging notes with them, but his attraction to beautiful boys had not diminished. Between 1867 and 1873, the drummer kept a sharp eye out for handsome youngsters, took several under his wing, plying them with treats and endeavoring to encourage their moral progress and intellectual development. In January of 1869, he had a boy identified only as Parker coming to his room for instruction. Later in the month he opened a school in Annapolis to teach English to Portuguese men and boys. Throughout the few weeks' duration of the language academy, Van Buskirk regularly treated the two or three boy pupils to cakes, taffy, and candy at the local Y.M.C.A. The men were not included on these excursions. He occasionally planted kisses on the cheeks of his youthful favorites, sometimes paying them in dimes for the privilege. In addition, he cultivated another cohort of likely lads, a son of the naval academy's chaplain numbered among them. Typically, he took the boys on excursions, attempted to teach them one subject or another — English, Chinese, or how to read — and fed them lemonade, cakes, and other assorted treats. He managed to find young companions everywhere he went, whether in the Boston Public Library, in Malaga, Canton, or in "Pulo Penang." He met the "pleasant, intelligent" nine-year-old Theodore van Doren in Washington, D.C., and talked with him on a curbstone. In China he found a regular "Sancho Panza" of a boy whom he hired to help him carry his things. When he strolled through Wu-chang he had little George Purcell to accompany him. Spencer Liasun, the son of the vice-superintendent of Shanghai's Imperial Government School, became a "great" friend of the American in 1872, as did a Chinese boy he met on a steamer that same year journeying to the United States for an education. Liasun was sixteen. The unidentified Chinese boy only twelve. Another Chinese boy, a blacksmith's son with beautiful skin, caught his attention and received a dollar for being so attractive. Two boy prostitutes collected "cumshaw" from Van Buskirk during one of his on shore excursions, but there is no indication he purchased their services.[11] When a Spanish gentlemen boarded the same steamer that carried Van Buskirk at Montevideo in 1874, he immediately became infatuated with the man's ten-year-old son. The lad was "not less quick and intelligent than beautiful. To me he was like a ray of sunshine, and active, observant, enquiring, he penetrated like sunshine almost at the same moment every part of the ship."[12] At a mosque in Suez, a lad caught his eye who wore a "red fez, white gown and red sash. Try to get his name.... I liked his ways. He seemed [a] ... worthy follower of the Prophet."[13] Despite the easy availability of some of the lads that attracted him, none of the relationships apparently went beyond bussing. He left no record of any overt, explicitly sexual dimension in his encounters with any them.[14]

Afterword

Throughout the last two years of his enlistment in the Marines, from 1867 to 1869, Van Buskirk tried on a number of occasions to be released from the corps and obtain a clerkship or a police appointment. He approached his former employer Governor Francis Thomas at least twice, trying to secure his political leverage to assist him. He also solicited the aid of Reverdy Johnson, a powerful senator from Maryland who had attended St. John's College and may have been acquainted with his father. Neither man chose to help Van Buskirk, and in desperation he turned to Rufus E. Jordan, the Maryland state librarian. It is unlikely Jordan could have obtained a discharge for the hapless supplicant or gained him any manner of appointment even if he desired to do so, but Van Buskirk's misery was so intense, he was willing to explore any possibility to get free of the Marine Corps.

In addition to soliciting support from those in positions of power, Van Buskirk worked hard on his on his own to obtain a position in the military as a clerk, but his applications were rejected time after time. As his enlistment drew to a close, he suffered spates of severe depression. He was faced with two equally dismal alternatives, reenlistment or a return to vagabondage. The only ray of hope for him was an application he filed to be a mate in the navy. When he went to Washington, D.C., to be discharged in October of 1869, he was interviewed for the job. The examiners were evidently impressed with his experience, and by the end of the month he received the appointment.

Van Buskirk was overjoyed by the knowledge he was to become a mate. After years of humiliation in the lower ranks, he would now be by law an officer, with commensurate pay and privileges. In order of precedence, mates were beneath the lowest commissioned ranks, but were above the navy's warrant officers and petty officers. Mates messed together, occupied quarters far more spacious than those allotted enlisted men, and dressed in the same uniform as commissioned officers — frock coats, blue trousers, and billed hats. The only visible distinction was in the amount of ornament. Mates wore fewer brass buttons and less gold braid on their sleeves. Their hat insignia was also much less elaborate than that of the officers with commissions.

Though Van Buskirk had been appointed a mate, he was not immediately able to don the new uniform and proceed to his first assignment. Ratification of the Fourteenth Amendment the previous year prevented anyone who had fought in the rebellion against the United States from holding civil or military office.[15] His only hope was a provision in an 1870 bill before Congress which specified that such legal disabilities could be removed by a two-thirds vote of Congress. He again contacted Francis Thomas, who responded more positively on this occasion. He explained that the best tactic for the would-be mate was to go to Washington and personally present his case. When he arrived in the capital, his former employer introduced him to Senator Thomas Robertson of South Carolina, who was then maneuvering a bill through Congress to relieve some two thousand former Confederates of legal disabilities. This was a distressing time for Van Buskirk. The fate of Robertson's legislation was uncertain, and he knew without doubt that if it failed he had nothing to look forward to but a life of hopelessness and privation. On March 7, 1870, the bill passed. The southerners whose names it contained, including "P. C. Van Buskirk of Loudoun County" in Virginia, were restored to full citizenship.

During the difficult months after Van Buskirk was appointed a mate but was forced to wait in agony hoping the legislation that would allow him to assume the post would become law, he visited Francis Thomas at Mont Alto.[16] While there, he was initially attracted to fourteen-year-old Israel Spiker, but he developed a much closer relationship with his bedfellow at the Thomas home, the governor's eight-year-old adopted son, Frank.[17] "To my shame," he wrote, "I have the last two nights opposed no check to his taking just what liberties he pleased with me."[18] Van Buskirk was somewhat embarrassed by his and the boy's antics, but the former Marine could not resist the opportunity to mentor his little sleeping companion on sexual matters. He made a crude drawing for the boy, a sagittal section of a human being. It showed the mouth connected to the stomach via an esophagus, and the stomach connected by tubes to two unidentifiable organs. A small array of tubes connected the region near the genitals to a spinal column that extended upward to the brain. The purpose of the diagram was to demonstrate how certain foods upset the digestive tract and thereby stimulated the penis and testicles. The resultant expulsion of fluid caused debility, which was then transferred to the brain. The pedagogical point, he explained, was to let the boy know that immodest play in bed was not a healthy activity. Whether or not the eight-year-old was impressed with the instruction, the lesson indicated that Van Buskirk clearly remembered what he had read years earlier in a host of tracts and medical books when he was tormented by masturbation and nocturnal emission and seeking cures to his dual afflictions.[19]

Afterword

As was the case with others of Van Buskirk's boys, separation did not mean he had forgotten them. Over the next few years he corresponded occasionally with Frank Williams. The first note was posted a month after Van Buskirk left the Thomas household. Writing from the Ninth Street home of George and Jonathan Schultz in Washington, D.C., on February 28, he sought to curry favor with the boy. He told of seeing a congressional page, a "young gentleman [with] a good face, as only a boy who has no bad habits can have." When he inquired as to who the boy was, he discovered that the boy was Frank's older brother.[20] The next month, after the happy news that the legislation removing his legal disabilities has passed and he had become a mate in the United States Navy, he wrote to Frank's brother from on board his ship, the U.S.S. *Palos*, asking him to deliver a small gift to the boy. Van Buskirk sent another letter from Yokohama, Japan, on July 7, 1873, in response to a letter and a photograph he received from Frank. The youngster had written from Lima, where he had gone with Governor Thomas, when the latter was appointed United States Minister to Peru in March 1872. True to form, Van Buskirk's letter was filled with flattery and the promise of gifts. He also gave Frank information and instructions for the care of an exotic bird he was sending to the minister. In a final letter, he informed Frank that the gifts and the bird had been dispatched as promised.[21]

A new man had been created in 1870 when Philip C. Van Buskirk became a naval officer. On June 11, as the *Palos* was preparing for a voyage to the Pacific, he recorded his feelings on the occasion: "I mounted the official cap with gold cord for the first time today. Thus the long-cherished hope to wear the gold cord of an officer of the navy is realized. Proud day, proud hour."[22] In his capacity as a mate, he was paid a salary far in excess of any compensation he had ever received, and the petty restrictions that bedeviled his life both as a Marine and as a watchman no longer applied to him. He had been transformed into a gentleman, and could live comfortably ashore or on board ship, come and go as he pleased in foreign or domestic ports, explore the pleasures of any city he chose without galling restrictions on his movements, and finance his new life with a generous wage.

The elevation in his professional status that came with being a naval officer also benefited Van Buskirk in his liaisons with civilian society. In the years that he wrote to Frank, he also carried on a detailed correspondence with the boy's adoptive father. The day half a decade earlier in June of 1865 when Thomas evicted the Confederate deserter from his farm because his job as a railroad worker rendered him unfit company for gentlemen was forgotten. As a naval officer he now had sufficient prestige to engage in a cordial correspondence with his former employer. Thomas's letters to Van Buskirk cannot be located, but two lengthy, detailed, and descriptive letters to him from the mate survive. One of them, a travelogue of sorts, provided a comprehensive description of Hankow, in which Van Buskirk not only described the city, the people, and their customs, but mentioned the fine expatriate club where, as a United States naval officer, he was welcomed. It had billiards, bowling, a bar, and everything else that would be expected in a fine hotel. While on shore his associates included the United States counsel and his wife and several customs officers. It was a wondrous change from his earlier incarnation as an enlisted man who usually wandered alone in Pacific ports or on occasion cavorted with crude, inebriated sailors and Marines.[23]

In another letter to Thomas, headed "Boisée Bay (Lat. 37° 30') West Coast of Korea[24] June 3rd 1871," he described a preliminary skirmish that led to a largely unknown but shameful episode in United States naval history, the massacre of hundreds of defenseless Korean soldiers by a force of American sailors and Marines.[25] Although the United States and Korea had several minor diplomatic disagreements over seafarers and their activities during the preceding decade, the military operations in which Van Buskirk served were only peripherally related to these earlier disputes. In the spring and early summer of 1871 the presence of the United States Navy in Boisée Bay was part of a concerted drive to establish an American imperial presence in the Pacific and to intimidate the Koreans into signing a trade treaty. When it became apparent in late May that the talks between the two countries would not be productive, the navy made preparations to force their way up the Han River to Seoul. The Americans reasoned that warships positioned to shell the country's capital might persuade the Koreans to be more forthcoming in negotiations. On June 1, a small flotilla — including the *Palos*— began moving up the river. In due course a shower of cannon balls rained down on the tiny fleet from forts, hilltops and breastworks along the shore. The Americans returned fire for a time, then reversed their course and sailed back down the river to the shelter of their large fleet.[26]

The acting assistant secretary of the American legation in China, John P. Cowles, Jr., who was on board the expedition's flagship, the U.S.S. *Col-*

orado, described the engagement the next day in a note to Frederick F. Low, the United States minister to China, who also sailed on the *Colorado*.[27] "The pluck of all engaged, but especially of the launches, words can do no justice to," he said. "There is no lack of pluck in the American people."[28] The record of the incident that Van Buskirk wrote into in his diary had a very different tone. "Our gunnery was not very good.... We did not fight like a well-trained ship of war — not a bit.... The squadron hailed us — what we proclaimed ourselves — victors! Victors!.... Returning we blazed into empty breastworks, and our men were extremely anxious to fire at junks — stray parties, without troubling themselves as to whether they were combatants or not — into anything Korean."[29] Despite the proclamations of victory, the Americans decided the enemy needed more punishment. "The situation must be viewed from an oriental stand-point," wrote Frederick Low, "rather than the more advanced one of Christian civilization." If the outcome of the skirmish could be interpreted favorably by the enemy, since the American flotilla did not reach Seoul, the word would spread and all Asian nations would become more truculent in their diplomacy, he added. Rear Admiral John Rogers, the commander-in-chief of the Asiatic Fleet and one of the most distinguished officers in the Unites States Navy, agreed. A punitive expedition set out on June 10 to help the Koreans understand precisely who had emerged victorious from the skirmish.[30]

The ships and steam launches of the flotilla, again including the *Palos*, moved up the Han carrying an amphibious force of some six hundred and fifty men. All went according to plan. Marines and sailors streamed ashore at the designated location, and quickly moved to secure several forts and redoubts that had earlier fired on American vessels. Two days later, on June 12, the entire force was back with the main fleet at Boisée Bay.[31] Quite naturally, Admiral Rogers exalted over the affair, proclaiming it a success for punishing the barbarians. He heaped praise on his men, commending their "gallantry" three times, describing them as "gallant" twice, and mentioning a lieutenant who led him men "gallantly," all within the compass of a proclamation containing less than five hundred words.[32] The diplomatic dispatches sent to Washington echoed the admiral's assessment of the attackers' heroism and the salvaging of national honor. As had been the case when United States forces stormed Chinese forts along the Pearl River in 1856, the defenders of the riverside forts were routed after taking substantial casualties while the attackers suffered only small numbers of wounded and dead. What sets this action apart in terms of unequal confrontations between technologically sophisticated imperial armies and the indigenous forces they often encountered was not that the Westerners achieved an easy tactical victory. The official proclamations of triumph in this insistence were neither believed nor repeated by all of the media. Both the *Shanghai News* and the *North China Herald* understood the fraudulent nature of the American claims. They explained to their readers that the Korean government's attitude had not changed, the *Herald* adding that at least one village was looted and burned.[33] Van Buskirk was aghast at the entire affair. He tipped a printed copy of Admiral Rogers's panegyric into his diary between the entries for June 20 and 22. He then proceeded to annotate it, pointing out that the two-day expedition hardly demonstrated the mens' "endurance" that was commended in the order. He also wrote that three or four of the captured forts had no guns and were untenanted when the Marines and sailors arrived to capture them. He denounced several other aspects of Rogers's account, but his most scathing commentary dealt with events after the engagement. He recorded how, after the battle was over, the Americans carried out a horrendous massacre of the defeated troops. Obviously no word of the wanton slaughter was included in the official reports of the action by naval officers intent on proclaiming their triumph over Asian savagery. In fact, the only known record of the bloody acts of extermination against the defeated and defenseless Korean soldiers is that made by Philip C. Van Buskirk:

> There is an ugly feature more in our affair which for Truth's sake I must note. Near a hundred of the enemy's wounded crept under the shelter of a hamlet near by, and this hamlet, when resistance had ceased, was fired and burning, literally roasted alive many of these wounded Koreans. General Orders never record such things.[34]

Van Buskirk's setting down the massacre of wounded Koreans was not the only unique record he entered into diary during the years from 1870 to 1873 when he served on the *Palos*. With far more time than his duties required, he often passed idle hours making notes on the dining table conversations of his fellow officers. When American naval officers met in their ships' wardrooms for meals, recreation, and chit-chat, it is unlikely that any of them ever imagined that their words would be preserved by any of their associates. Conversation, after all, is an ephemeral thing. Most of it is gone and forgotten within minutes, hours or days after it occurs.

Afterword

Such would have been the case in the tiny *Palos* wardroom if Philip Van Buskirk had not found a large segment of his brother officers' talk so offensive that he was moved by boredom, exasperation and disgust to preserve it. To be sure, a good portion of what was spoken in the wardroom did not offend him. His associates talked of their ship, its men, the navy, and other professional matters. They discussed sports, reading, family, and homes thousands of miles away. None of this chatter bothered the mate. He found much of the time he spent in the wardroom pleasant enough. It was only when talk of debauchery dominated the conversation that he became outraged. The rule among officers was that there be no mention of politics, religion, or women, but Van Buskirk's *Palos* diary makes clear the last provision of the rule applied only to the white American ladies these men had left behind. Indeed, a sizeable segment of their talk consisted of tales of wild sexual escapades in ports their ships visited everywhere around the world.[35]

In his commentary on his colleagues' tales of sexual adventure, he claimed that they talked largely of trivia, "drinking, eating, whoring and 'pleasure.'" These are "the never-ending themes," he grumbled.[36] Officers speak of nothing but prostitutes, he fumed with a measure of exaggeration, and they continuously reiterate their exploits with them.[37] The conversation over wine and cigars is only of

> Woman–woman–woman–whores–whores–whoring.... We all know of these amours. They are recounted not once but daily, joked upon not seldom but hourly. And the language of these recitals! ... I have not yet hardihood enough to write verbatim any part of the amatory recitals which make up the conversation of our officers and their friends."[38]

Despite his protests about lacking the "hardihood" to preserve sexually explicit tales in his diary, Van Buskirk managed to record at least a few of them from the *Palos* wardroom, including the one by Ensign James Franklin about how he and one of his United States Naval Academy classmates spent a night in Malaga with several girls. The companion "screwed his girl twelve times, and went at her a thirteenth time, when they [?] pulled him off. The girl yelled like blazes."[39] Franklin was not the only one who reveled in describing the sexual adventures of others. The stroke oarsman of the Harvard crew in their famous race against Oxford on August 27, 1869, used to "scrouge" his sister according to a story Van Buskirk heard from Robert P. Pauling, paymaster of the *Palos*. The Harvard oarsman told Pauling about it so that he, too, could be put "in the way of enjoying 'man-and-wife' sport with the little sister."[40] A navy friend identified only as "Burd" regaled him with information on a party for the U.S.S. *Monongahela* attended by most of the ship's officers. The venue for the valedictory gathering: Yokohama's "Brothel No. 9." And all of it went into Philip Van Buskirk's diary. Such stories continued page after page — the captain having sex on board ship with a Chinese washerwomen, humorous tales of multiple doses of venereal disease, hours spent poring over each others' collections of pornography, and telling jokes of "sailors' knives and whores' snatches."[41] Unfortunately, the mate recorded none of the many jokes he heard (and probably told) in his diary. Similarly, he did not describe any of the pornography he examined during his *Palos* years, but characterized it by saying that "for filthy ingenuity of design [it surpassed] anything that [had] yet come out of France."[42] The only supposition on its precise nature that can be made from examining some of the crude, sexually explicit drawings that he occasionally drew on his diary pages is that at this stage in his life, in his mid to late thirties, his sexual longings and fantasies were by this time entirely heterosexual.

While Van Buskirk railed against the constant reiteration of the debauched practices of his fellow officers, he was not above participating in occasional debauch himself. Group sexual experiences, whether involving physical contact or merely being a member of an audience, were part of the bonding process among the community of American naval officers in the Pacific during the latter years of the nineteenth century, and although the mate preferred to visit brothels on his own, he was occasionally present for communal activities.[43] He wrote of attending an orgy on May 11, 1871, with over a dozen of his brother officers, where each man was provided a woman, and a child was brutally raped, "cracked" as it was described by officers Van Buskirk characterized sarcastically as "Christian gentlemen."

Van Buskirk's hostility to accounts of the unrestrained and uninhibited sexual adventures of his associates probably did not result from any residual homoerotic preferences. Once he donned the uniform of a mate in the United States Navy, his interest in boys was rapidly replaced by an enthusiastic and aggressive pursuit of females. The ample freedom and the new financial security he enjoyed may have contributed in some measure to his expanding attraction to the opposite sex. Although over the next years he remained interested in young, handsome boys, his sexual energies were expended almost exclusively with members of the opposite sex. This is not entirely surprising. He had in earlier years evinced an occasional interest in females. During the war, he recorded his unsatisfactory encounter with the filthy, wild-haired Julie at a sugar camp in the spring of 1864, and the following year he wrote of fondling the five-year-old Harriet Welsh.[44] As early as 1869 he regularly fantasized about marriage. The ideal wife, he decided at one point, might be a Gypsy woman. This was not a transitory notion. He was serious enough about the idea to investigate it in some detail. His research on the subject included a visit to the *American Cyclopedia*, reading a book identified only as *Gypsies of Spain*, and dipping into Alexander Walker's *Intermarriage, or the Natural Laws by Which Beauty, Health and Intellect Result from Certain Unions, and Deformity, Disease and Insanity from Others*. Most of Van Buskirk's connubial fantasies ranged far beyond Gypsies. Throughout 1869 and into the early 1870s he considered marriage to many women whose paths crossed his, but there was always an excuse not to approach them. He was too poor to marry Mary Jane Branzel. The pretty and loveable Sarah James chewed tobacco, drank strong coffee, slept late, and was illiterate. The compact, little Emma Gates was wonderful in all respects, but, alas, Sergeant Scanlon was courting her. And so it went with the lot of them, including "wellfavored" Helen Johnson, the fifteen-year-old Alvina, who needed to learn to cook, a scullery maid at Mont Alto, one Alice Blake, Mae, who was otherwise unidentified, Mary, the illegitimate daughter of a seamstress, and fourteen-year-olds Eugenie Duvall and Mary Snow who lived at 114 3rd Street, Washington, D.C. And there were several others, including a nameless Baltimore prostitute he thought he could induce to mend her ways. At the same time that his thoughts ranged across a bevy of girls and women he knew, he also considered marrying a Japanese lady, but never acted on the notion. His only semi-overt effort to find a bride came after reading an article in the July 31, 1869, issue of *Harper's Weekly*. The story was about Ida Lewis of Rhode Island, whose picture graced the magazine's cover. She was a lighthouse keeper's daughter who had saved a number of people from drowning, and the account of her in the magazine indicated she possessed domestic talents equal to her courage. He also learned from a crewman of the U.S.S. *Constitution* she was a wild girl with an illegitimate child. That piqued his interest, and he wrote her under a *nom de plume* proposing marriage. Not surprisingly, she did not reply to his offer.[45]

One of the geographical areas where Van Buskirk gloried in his lately-acquired, exuberant and unconstrained heterosexuality was in the Bonin Islands.[46] He had actually visited the small, volcanic outcroppings in the western Pacific years earlier when he was on board the *Plymouth*. The ship, after participating in the first of Commodore Matthew C. Perry's epic-making voyages to Japan in 1853, had been detached from his fleet and sent southward some six hundred miles to claim the islands for the United States. While anchored in the Bonins, at Peel Island's Port Lloyd harbor, he had few opportunities to go ashore and had almost no contact with the town's residents. Most of his time on land was spent searching for the wreckage or survivors from one of the *Plymouth*'s cutters that disappeared in a squall while on a fishing excursion. No trace of the boat or its crew of eighteen men was ever found. He returned to Port Lloyd in 1880 and 1881. As an officer by then, his duties involved superintending coal supplies for the United States navy's ships and assessing the potential for agricultural development on the islands. When he returned to Japan from the Bonins in 1881 on board the U.S.S. *Alert*, he brought with him seven of the local children. It is not entirely clear why the youngsters were being transported from their homes, but it appears that their journey was connected in one way or another to Christian missionary efforts. After arriving at Shimonoseki, he had dinner with two of the "larger" boys, then he put the entire contingent on a train for Tokyo, where they were to meet an otherwise-unidentified Mr. Shaw. There is no indication in the diary why he expended ninety-five yen taking the two boys to dinner, nor is there any commentary about them. Perhaps his failure to expound on their beauty and virtue as he would have done in previous times indicates his earlier fixations with handsome lads had diminished or disappeared. In any case, at the time he was involved in arranging transport for the seven youngsters to Tokyo, he and a friend visited a brothel to drink sake and to watch "pretty gaysios [*sic*] sing and play for us."[47] Like the ladies in Japan, those of the Bonins also caught Van Buskirk's eye and his pen in 1880. He noted down that across Peel Island from Port Lloyd was a Japanese settlement with a sake shop and two prostitutes. One of the women was kept by a "sleek-looking scoundrel," the other spoke some English, but was without a permanent home. He recorded no dalliances with either of them. On the 1881 visit he contemplated marriage to a local woman, Lisa Webb. He asked one of her relatives, George Bravo, for her hand, and said he would wait several days for an answer. Neither Miss Webb nor any nuptials are mentioned again in the diary, and there is no indication a union ever took place.[48]

Afterword

Philip Van Buskirk's final sojourn in the Bonin Islands came in 1898, when he spent three months there. In this final visit, there was nothing to perturb his tranquility. He was by then retired from the navy with a comfortable pension, there were no official duties to occupy his days, and he had plenty of time to keep his diary and assist in organizing the papers of the Savorys, a leading island family. Entries were made on almost every day of his stay, and he appended several dozen notes dealing with an assortment of topics. Most of the material dealt with immediate concerns — his table, his daily activities, the state of his bowel movements and nocturnal emissions, and disputes with local businessmen over money. Notes on the islanders were frequent. He commented on the books they read, their family feuds, the widespread alcoholism he observed, suicide, a suspected poisoning, a divorce, and a murder. Then there were the children. As in earlier decades, he made considerable effort to befriend young boys, but by the 1870s his interest in them appeared entirely aesthetic. Young Norman and Daniel accompanied him on his wanderings about Peel Island, where he had rented a cabin, and spent nights with him. Van Buskirk neither cataloged their beauties in his diary nor did he try to educate and improve them as he had done with his boy favorites in earlier decades. The little girls of the island interested him most. At least four of them became attached to the by then aging, half-toothless, and overweight former naval officer. They visited him regularly, tidied up his cabin, ran errands for him, and brought him his morning coffee.[49]

He called Agnes Grace Savory his "little Stony Beach Sweetheart." In mid-March, he wrote, they sunbathed and skinny dipped together with "no shame, no sense of decency." Mornings found the two in bed together where four-year-old Agnes took "to wanton sport as naturally and with as much vim [as] a young duck takes to the water."[50] Another of his diminutive "great chums" was Alice, who brought the mail and helped keep his cabin in order. He regularly hugged and kissed her, and she kissed him in return when he asked her to do so. His interest went beyond kissing and hugging, but the child was not as uninhibited as Agnes Savory.[51] "She draws a line at my scratching her pubes," Van Buskirk noted seemingly with a chuckle, "she struggles and laughs. Altogether she is a most loveable child, a picture of health and brimming over with good spirit."[52] In due course Alice quit visiting the cabin. The diary contains no speculation on the possible reason for her absence. There are only the penman's wistful comments that she no longer came by and that he rarely saw her anymore.[53] Another of his favorites, "best friend" Emily, accompanied him to town, to church, and went along with him to visit his island acquaintances. She also received instruction from him in her ABCs. Van Buskirk did not record her age, but he did once refer to her as "little Emily." Susanna also received instruction from the island's American visitor. He read to her from the Bible on several occasions, but there is no indication their relationship was anything more than didactic. Then, too, she was older than the other girls, certainly post-pubescent. She was pregnant at the time Van Buskirk assisted with her spiritual development. Edith, a youngster of unspecified age, who at least once carried a package to the cabin, was in no hurry to leave after the delivery. According to a diary note for April 30, 1898, the girl and her host indulged in "wanton sport upon the bed." She did not abandon him as little Alice had done. When he departed the Bonin Islands in early May, she gave him a bon voyage present, a little platter made of "axe-handle wood."[54] The diary entries that preserve Van Buskirk's "wanton" sports with prepubescent girls show no signs of contrition. Instead, they seem almost to have been penned by a schoolboy flaunting his childish wickedness. Still, he knew that some degree of circumspection might be useful in case the diary might someday be read by others. In his notes following the daily entries for March and April, where he arranged chronologically the encounters with Agnes, Emily, and Edith, he made some effort at concealment. He opened both lists that included the three girls' names with cryptic headings smacking of abbreviated Latin. The identical lines read: "Em. dal. con puella."[55]

When Van Buskirk visited the Bonin Islands in 1898, he was already two years into retirement. After leaving the navy he had purchased a farm in northwestern Washington with the intent of residing there permanently, but he found rural life less stimulating than he had imagined it would be. He then rented out his farm and traveled widely, visiting friends and relatives, and living for a time in Japan where, not surprisingly, he acquired a young girl as his companion. True to form, he spent considerable money and effort on her education while they were together. Occasionally a handsome boy caught his eye, and once, while home in Washington, he reached down the trousers of one such lad. Much to his embarrassment, the youngster told his mother of the incident, and the enraged woman confronted him. She denounced his conduct directly, but her harsh words hardly ruffled the retired ex-seafarer. Only one portion of her tirade affected him. He was deeply wounded when she told him pointedly that he was not a gentleman.

Afterword

In all, from the time he became a naval officer, Van Buskirk's shift in preference from boys to females became relatively complete. He recorded sexual encounters with over three hundred girls and women in the diary volumes he compiled after 1870. All of his partners were female, most were prostitutes, and from time to time he developed long-term relationships with some of the younger and more attractive of them. In a manner similar to that he adopted with Lewis Price and other lads, he often strove to educate and uplift his favorites. The intrusive, helpful and open-handed Van Buskirk was, of course, exploited as shamelessly by the professional girls he sought to improve as he had earlier been exploited by the boys he loved. They accepted money and favors, and humored him when necessary, but few developed genuine affection for their benefactor. One, in fact, lodged a paternity suit against him. The case was covered by San Francisco newspapers, and he copied their stories about him and his accuser into his diary, along with a verbatim reproduction of the entire court record of the trial. He was acquitted of the charge, but he lamented the substantial fee he was forced to pay to his lawyer.

As he grew older, the problems of farm management frequently became the subjects of diary entries. His careful records mentioned fields washed out by floods, disagreements with tenants, prices, and scores of additional vexations. On the personal level, he continued cataloging his bodily activities, though he was no longer concerned with masturbation, nocturnal emission, or the form and texture of his excrement. Instead, he wrote of diminishing ardor, an expanding waistline, dental problems, and an assortment of crotchets associated with maturity. By the first years of the new century he was considerably overweight and nearing toothlessness, but he was free from the devils of his youth. Diary entries reveal him to be financially secure, pleased with himself, and approving of the world. He died peacefully at Bemerton, Washington, on June 22, 1903.

Notes

Preface

1. "The Diary of Philip C. Van Buskirk," Philip C. Van Buskirk Papers, Manuscripts and University Archives, Special Collections Division, Acc3621-001 Allen Library, University of Washington, Seattle Washington [hereafter cited as VBD].

2. Nellie Heffner, Letter of Donation, October 18, 1905, Philip C. Van Buskirk Papers, Manuscripts and University Archives, Special Collections Division, Acc-3621-001 Allen Library, University of Washington, Seattle Washington.

3. The volume containing entries for the years from 1858 to 1860, in which Van Buskirk reconstructed the vaguely remembered entries for 1861 and 1862 on the final blank pages, had been stored with an acquaintance for some years. Van Buskirk wrote of retrieving it in his entry of December 3, 1864.

4. After 1890, Van Buskirk recopied almost all of his diaries dating from 1863 onward. He then had the copies professionally bound into annual volumes. The sequence of bound volumes ends in 1902. The diary he was keeping in 1903, the year of his death, cannot now be located.

5. Three articles he copied with almost absolute accuracy from the *San Francisco Examiner* are "A Young Woman's Woe," January 4, 1896; "Criminal Charge," March 29, 1896; and "Damages for Arrest," March 12, 1897. The copies are located in Volume 28 of the diary in notes 1 and 13 immediately following the entries for 1896 and in Volume 29, note 40, immediately following the entries for 1897.

Introduction

1. Portions of the material contained in the introduction were previously published in the *Lincoln Herald* ("Behind the Lines in the West: The Civil War Diary of a Confederate Deserter, 1861–1865," 103 [Winter 2001]: 194–203).

2. VBD, 4: October 7, 1858.

3. VBD, 4: October 7, 1858; Personal communication with Dorothy Rapp, United States Military Academy Archive, West Point, N.Y., to B. R. Burg, September 22, 1987.

4. VBD, 1: 293, inside back cover; VBD, 4: October 7, 1858; VBD, 5: preliminary page for 1864, July 18, August 28, September 2–4, 1864; VBD, 7: notes following entries for 1868; VBD, 35: June 9, 1901. For Van Buskirk's career at Georgetown, see "Memorandum Book," 215, "Classical Register," "Georgetown Alumni Directory," "Ledger G," 107 and "Ledger H," 28, 207–208, University Archives, Georgetown University Library, Washington, D.C.; Joseph T. Durkin, *Georgetown University: The Middle Years (1840–1900)* (Washington, D.C.: Georgetown University Press, 1963), 2, 4–5, 9–12; John M. Daley, *Georgetown University: Origin and Early Years* (Washington, D.C.: Georgetown University Press, 1957), 221–222. Dr. Samuel Semmes may have been Samuel Middleton Semmes, the brother of Raphael Semmes, the Confederate admiral who commanded the commerce raiders C.S.S. *Sumter* and C.S.S. *Alabama*. If so, he was very likely connected with Philip's father, through their common profession of the

law, their membership in the Maryland legislature, and by their Catholicism ("Rafael Semmes," http://www.newadvent.org/cathen/13712b.htm; "Rose Hill Cemetery, Samuel and Eleanora Semmes," http://www.rootsweb.com/~mdallegh/Cemetery/semmes.htm). Van Buskirk seems to indicate that the man who paid his charges was indeed Samuel Middleton Semmes in his diary entry for July 18, 1864. There is no apparent explanation for the medical prefix before Semmes's name in the Georgetown College records, if in fact the Semmes who paid Van Buskirk's charges was actually the admiral's brother.

5. VBD, 1:293, 295, 296–298, October 13, 1852, February 3, 1853, November 11, 1854; VBD, 3: March 20, June 15, September 28, 1855; VBD, 18: March 27, 1884. Over a half century later, Van Buskirk recalled his father's suicide in a notation made in 1901. He called 1845 "that fatal twelfth year of my life." In a note the following year he drew a rectangular box on a diary sheet and wrote in it the information that at 4:00 P.M. On Monday, June 9, his father died (ibid., 35: June 9, 1901, 36: June 9, 1902). Comments on the suicide were also penned elsewhere in the diary (VBD, 3: March 20, 1855; VBD, 22: June 9, 1887; VBD, 32: June 9, 1899). Marshall T. Polk, the student who put the paper in his shoes to make himself taller than Van Buskirk, later graduated from West Point, served in the United States Army, the Confederate Army, lost a leg at the Battle of Shiloh in 1862, and later was treasurer of the state of Tennessee. As treasurer, he diverted $400,000 of the public money to personal use, was convicted of the crime and sentenced to prison. He died in February of 1884 (VBD, 18: March 27, 1884; "Polk Still a Fugitive," New York Times, January 7, 1883; "Death of Ex-Treasurer Polk," New York Times, March 1, 1884).

6. "Size Roll of Marines Enlisted in the Service of the United States Marine Corps," Records of the United States Marine Corps, Bureau of Naval Personnel, record group 127, National Archives, Washington, D.C. See also the duplicate "Size Roll" entries interleaved between VBD, 1: 283–284. Boys between thirteen and eighteen years of age could be enlisted by their parents until they reached their majority (J. F. Callan and A. W. Russell, comps., Laws of the United States Relating to the Navy and Marine Corps from the Formation of the Government to 1859 [Baltimore: J. Murphy, 1859], 301; Harold D. Langley, Social Reform in the United States Navy, 1798–1862 [Urbana: University of Illinois Press, 1967], 106–107). John Betts lists the pay for boys at from six to eight dollars per month ("The U.S. Navy in the Mexican War" [Ph. D. Diss., University of Chicago, 1954], 72).

7. Burg, "Nocturnal Emission and Masturbatory Frequency Relationships: A Nineteenth-Century Account," Journal of Sex Research 24 (1988): 216–220; S[eth] Pancoast, Boyhood's Perils and Manhood's Curse: A Handbook for the Mother, Son and Daughter (Philadelphia: s.n., ca. 1860; reprint, Philadelphia: Potter, 1873), 266; Elizabeth Stephens, "Pathologizing Leaky Male Bodies: Spermatorrhea in Nineteenth-Century British Medicine and Popular Anatomical Museums," Journal of the History of Sexuality 17 (September 2008): 422, 424, 425, 426, 429; Ellen Bayuk Rosenman, "Body Doubles: The Spermatorrhea Panic," Journal of the History of Sexuality 12 (July 2003): 365–366. By the end of the nineteenth century, the fearsome ailment was no longer considered a disease (ibid., n. 8). Neither spermatorrhea nor nocturnal emissions are included in the first edition of the Merck manual published in 1899 as a reference for physicians (Merck's Manual of the Materia Medica: Together with a Summary of Therapeutic Indications and a Classification of Medicaments (New York: Merck and Co., 1899).

8. VBD, 1:293–298, September 25, October 20, 23, November 12, 1852, February 15, March 26, 27, page preceding entries for April 1853, April 1, September 2, October 31, November 20, 23 1853, March 21, November 14, 17, December 7, 11, 12, 21, 22, 31, 1854; VBD, 3: August 11, 1855; Alfred Stillé, Elements of General Pathology (Philadelphia: Lindsay and Blakiston, 1848), 247; A[nthelme Balthasar] Richerand, Elements of Physiology, trans. G. J. M. De Lys (Philadelphia: Thomas Dobson, 1818), 41–42; William Young, Pocket Aes-

culapius, or Every One His Own Physician: Being Observations on Marriage, Medically and Philosophically Considered, as Manhood's Early Decline, With Directions for Its Perfect Cure, Etc., 156th ed. (Philadelphia: s.n., 1848); L. D. Fleming, *Self-Pollution: The Cause of Youthful Decay Showing the Dangers and Remedy of Venereal Excesses* (New York: Wellman, 1846), 33; Leopold Deslandes, *Manhood: The Cause and Cure for Premature Decline with Directions for Its Perfect Restoration*, trans. "A Physician" (Boston: Otis Broaders, 1852). The tract on self-help was very likely Samuel La'mert's *Self-Preservation: A Medical Treatise on Nervous and Physical Disability, Spermatorrhoea, Impotence, and Sterility* (London: by the author, 1847).

9. VBD, 1: 294–298, March 1–2, 1853, inside back cover; VBD, 19: "Periods of My Life," item 1, following correspondence for 1885, note 37, following entries for 1885; Muster Roll of the United States Marine Corps, Naval Records Collection, T-1118, roll 17, January-December, 1849, National Archives, Washington, D.C.; *Plymouth* Log, Bureau of Naval Personnel, Deck Logs, record group 24, National Archives, Washington, D.C., June 18, 1851.

10. VBD, 1: September 26, October 4, 31, December 13, 1852, January 9, February 11, 1853, January 28, February 2, 6, 15, 16, March 15, 25, 28–29, April 2, 23, 24, 27, May 7, 28, June 4, 9, 10, 12, 13, July 23, 1854; *Plymouth* Log, April 9, 1853, *et passim*; Robert E. Johnson, *Far China Station: The U.S. Navy in Asian Waters* (Annapolis: United States Naval Institute Press, 1979), 44, 47, 62; Earl Cranston, "Shanghai in the Taiping Period," *Pacific Historical Review* 5 (May 1936): 152; Samuel E. Morison, "*Old Bruin,*" *Commodore Matthew C. Perry, 1794–1858* (Boston: Little, Brown, 1967), 297–299.

11. VBD, 1: *passim.*

12. VBD, 1: September 12, 1852.

13. VBD, 1: January 14, February 4, 1854; VBD, 18: March 27, 1884.

14. VBD, 1: February 9, November 21, July 30–31, October 30–31, entry preceding December 1, 1853, December 8, 11–30, 1853, January 14, 21–22, 24, 31, February 4, 7, 1854.

15. VBD, 1: May 28–30, June 2–4, 1854.

16. VBD, 1: September 8, 17, October 12, 20, November 19, 1852, January 16, 1853, entry preceding March 1, 1853, June 14, 18, 19, 1853, entry preceding July 1, 1853, entry preceding August 1, 1853, September 23, 1853.

17. VBD, 1: September 22, 1852.

18. VBD, 1: November 13, 1853, January 14, June 17–30, November 7, 30, 1854.

19. VBD, 1: September 21, October 2–3, 18, 1852.

20. VBD, 1: October 11, 1852.

21. VBD, 1: October 11, 17, November 15, 1852, January 1, February 1, 4, 1853, June 11–16, 1854.

22. VBD, 1: February 6, 11–13, 25–28, March 15–16, 19–20, 23, 28, April 24, 27–28, May 5, 8, 12, 15, 17, 31, August 14, 15, 27, entry preceding September 1, 1853, September 24, entry preceding October 1, 1853, October 25, December 13, 23–25, 1853, February 16, 19, March 10, May 1, 5, 7, 13, 15, 16, June 5, 1854.

23. VBD, 1: August 4, 1855.

24. VBD, 1: April 3–6, 17, 1854; *Plymouth* Log, July 13, 1854; Howard I. Chapelle, *The American Sailing Navy: The Ships and Their Development* (New York: Bonanza, 1949), 440; George E. Paulsen, " Under the Starry Banner on Muddy Flat Shanghai: 1854," *American Neptune* 30 (July 1970):155–166.

25. VBD, 1: September 1, 6, 13, 16–17, 26, December 9, 10, 11, 12, 14–18, 1852, January 9, February 11, June 19, 26–30, July 1, 12, 19, 1853, January 28, February 1, 2, 10, 18, 19–24, 28, March 12, 14, 15, 17, 18, 24, 25, 28, preliminary page for April 1854, April 20, 24, 27, 28, May 7, 12, 14, 17, 18, 21, 23–24, 26, 27, 29, June 2–5, 8, 9, 15, 16, 25–26, July 23, 24, 31, November 25, December 17, 23, 31, 1854, *et passim*; Walter Colton, *Deck and Port, or Incidents of a Cruise in the Frigate* Congress *to California* (New York: A. S. Barnes, 1850), 19; Harry K. Skallerup, *Books Afloat and Ashore: A History of Books, Libraries, and Reading among Seamen during the Age of Sail* (Hamden, CT: Shoe String Press, 1974, 96–97; [J. S. Henshaw], *Around the World: A Narrative of a Voyage in the East India Squadron under Commodore George C. Read* (New

York: Charles S. Francis, 1840), 1: 170–171, 190–191; Lars G. Sellstedt, *From Forecastle to Academy* (Buffalo: Matthews Northrop, 1904), 168–169; A Civilian [George Jones], *Sketches of Naval Life with Notices of Men, Manners, and Scenery on the Shores of the Mediterranean in a Series of Letters from the* Brandywine *and* Constitution *Frigates* (New Haven: Hezekiah Howe, 1829), 2: 242; J. Ross Browne, *Etchings of a Whaling Cruise* (New York: Harper, 1846), 110–111. Favorite works of American mariners were James Fenimore Cooper's *History of the United States of America* and Richard Henry Dana's *Two Years Before the Mast* (A Foretop-man [Henry J. Mercier], *Life in a Man-of-War, or Scenes in* Old Ironsides *during Her Cruise in the Pacific* [Philadelphia: L. R. Bailey, 1841; reprint, Boston: Houghton Mifflin, 1927], 108.

26. [George Lillie Craik], *Pursuit of Knowledge Under Difficulties: Illustrated by Anecdotes* (London: C. Knight, 1830); Horace Mann, *A Few Thoughts for a Young Man: A Lecture Delivered before the Boston Mercantile Library Assn. On Its Twenty-ninth Anniversary* (Boston: Ticknor, Reed, and Fields, 1850).

27. *The Art of Good Behavior* (New York: C. P. Huestis, 1846).

28. The French work from which *Silas Shovewell* was adapted and translated is entitled *L'Historie of Dom B.... Portier des Chartreux*. It is attributed to Jean-Charles Gervaise Latouche, and was first published in 1745, or earlier. The earliest English translation appeared in 1801. Over the course of the nineteenth century there were several more editions, the last two coming in 1896 and 1907 under the title *The Life and Adventures of Father Silas* (Thomas Rodd, *Elegant Literature. Part IV of a Catalogue of a Collection of Books: Consisting of Language, Poetry, Romances, Novels, Facetae, Prose, Miscellanies, Poligraphy, Philology, Literary History, and Bibliography* [London: Thomas Rodd, 1845], 219, entry 6688; http://eroticabibliophile.com/publishers_dugdale_year.php, item 20).

29. Archibald Alexander, *Brief Compendium of Biblical Truth* (Philadelphia: Presbyterian Board of Publications, 1846).

30. VBD, 1: April 8, 1853.

31. VBD, 1: April 8, 1853.

32. VBD, Monroe Transcript of Volume 2 (1853), 116–117. The volume of Van Buskirk's diary containing entries made during his sojourn to Japan with Commodore Perry has been lost. It was deposited at the University of Washington library with the other Van Buskirk materials in 1905, but cannot now be located. The citation is to a partial typescript of the volume made by Robert Monroe, a former librarian at the University of Washington. The typescript is held with the other diary volumes by the Allen Library at the University of Washington, Seattle, Washington.

33. VBD, 3: March–May, June–July, October–November, December 1856, *passim*, January–December, 1857, *passim*, concluding note, 1857; VBD, 4: January–August preliminary pages preceding August 24, 1858, September summary pages included between September 10 and 11, 1858, monthly summary pages preceding October, November, December 1858, January–December, summary pages preceding January 1859, pages 608–624 located immediately before March 1859 entries. The chart of abbreviations is included on preliminary pages for August–September 1859, monthly summary pages for 1860 preceding January 1860, January 27, September 10, 1860. See also William H. Macomb, "Journal of William Macomb Kept Aboard the USS *Portsmouth*," Naval Records Collection, record group 45, National Archives, Washington, D.C.

34. VBD, 4: summary pages for May–August, December 1858.

35. VBD, 4: summary pages for May–August preceding August 1858, August 24, September 11, 22, 1858, April 1, 1859.

36. VBD, 4: September 11, 1858.

37. VBD, 4: monthly summary page preceding August 1858, summary page included between September 10 and 11, 1858, September 6, 12–13, 17, 1858; Letter 8, Philip C. Van Buskirk, Navy Yard, Washington, D.C., to Senator James A. Mason, Washington, D.C., December 18, 1858, located immediately before entries beginning 1859; Philip C. Van Buskirk, United States Naval Academy, to Secretary of the Navy Isaac Toucey, Washington, D.C.; VBD, 4:

Notes (Introduction)

October 24, 1860; John S. Devlin, *The Case of Lieutenant Devlin* (s. l., s.n., 1842); Devlin, ed., *The Marine Corps in Mexico; Setting Forth Its Conduct As Established by Testimony before a General Court Martial Convened at Brooklyn, N.Y. September, 1852; for the Trial of First Lieut. John S. Devlin of the U.S. Marine Corps* (Washington, D.C.: Lemuel Towers, 1852). Charles James Faulkner was born in 1806, attended Georgetown University and served in the United States House of Representatives from Virginia. He died in 1884 (*Biographical Directory of the American Congress, 1774–1961* [Washington, D.C.: United States Government Printing Office, 1961], 877–878).

38. United States Pension Records, T-316, Filed February 9, 1859, Invalid Pension No. 1564, National Archives, Washington, D.C.; VBD, 4: summary page preceding August 1858, August 28, September 2–4, 1858, monthly summary pages for January–November preceding January 1859, item 5 preceding March 1859.

39. VBD, 4: March 28, 29, April 9, 13, 16, 27, May 1859.

40. VBD, 4: May, June 5, 10–12, 27, July 6, 1859.

41. VBD, 4: summary pages for July–September preceding January 1859, June–August 1859, *passim*, May 7, 1859, summary pages for April, May, August, September, December preceding January 1860.

42. VBD, 4: summary pages for October–December preceding January 1859, September–December 1859, *passim*, summary pages for April, June, August, September preceding January 1860, entry following December summary page for 1860 and immediately preceding entries for January 1860.

43. VBD, 4: July, *passim*, summary pages for August, September, October 1860, September 10, November 5, 1860; Richard S. West, *The Second Admiral: A Life of David Dixon Porter, 1813–1891* (New York: Coward McCann, 1937).

44. VBD, 4: October summary page preceding January 1859, September 14–23, October, August, November 5, 1859, summary page for December 1860, preceding January 1860, January 27, February 8, 1860.

45. VBD, 4: November 7, 1860.

46. VBD, 4: April 1860.

47. VBD, 4: September 25, 1860.

48. VBD, 4: October 12, 1860.

49. Jones's resignation was actually dated October 22, 1860 (Edward W. Callahan, *List of Officers of the Navy and of the United States Marine Corps from 1775 to 1900* [New York: Hamersly, 1901; reprint, New York: Haskell House, 1969], 689).

50. VBD, 4: note following dated entries for 1860.

51. VBD, November 9, 1860.

52. VBD, November 13, 1860.

53. VBD, November 15, 1860.

54. VBD, November 6, 1860.

55. VBD, note on summary page for December preceding entries for 1860.

56. VBD, 4: January 4, 1860; William H. Parker, *Recollections of a Naval Officer, 1841–1865* (New York: Scribner's, 1883), 201.

57. VBD, 4: April 15, 1861.

58. VBD, 4: April 22, 1861.

59. VBD, 4: April–May 1861.

60. VBD, 4: July 1861; David F. Riggs, *13th Virginia Infantry*, 2nd ed. (Lynchburg: H. E. Howard, 1988), 145.

61. VBD, 1–11, 145; Samuel D. Buck, *With the Old Confeds: Actual Experiences of a Captain of the Line* (Baltimore: H. E. Houck, 1925), 26–27.

62. *Ibid.* In the first winter of the war, both Union and Confederate forces took care to see to the comfort of their men. Major Theodore F. Lang, of the 6th West Virginia Cavalry, commented on his comfortable winter quarters near the Gauley Bridge area in western Virginia during the winter of 1861 and 1862 (Theodore F. Lang, *Loyal West Virginia from 1861–1865* [Baltimore: Deutsche, 1895; reprint, Huntington, WV: Blue Acorn, 1998], 47). Another Union officer, Lieutenant Jacob G. Beaver of the 51st Pennsylvania, wrote to his mother and sister describing his pleasant situation at Camp Curtin in Pennsylvania and at Camp Union, a few miles from Annapolis. He also wrote home about living well on Roanoke Island in North Carolina. The Confederate installation on the island, named Camp Georgia, had been captured in February of 1862 by Union forces, who

first renamed it Camp Burnside, then set about enjoying the amenities originally provided for its southern garrison. It contained, according to Beaver, excellent barracks, cots, thick mattresses, rockers, and easy chairs (Tim McKinney, *West Virginia Civil War Almanac* [Charleston, WV: Quarrier Press, 2000], 2: 568, 569, 572). Boredom seems to have been a standard feature of camp life everywhere in western Virginia. Confederate George P. Morgan wrote in his diary for August 25, 1861, "Pocahontas County.... The monotony of camp life scarcely justifies writing every day, because every day is the same" (George E. Moore, ed., "A Confederate Journal," *West Virginia History* 22 [July 1961]: 206).

63. VBD, 4: April 18, 1862; "Monthly Report of Prisoners of War, Deserters, Etc., Received at Headquarters, Forces West of Piedmont, Department of West Virginia, for July 10–20, 1864," Confederate Compiled Service Records, microfilm 324, reel 543, National Archives, Washington, D.C.

64. Mark A. Weitz, *More Damning than Slaughter: Desertion in the Confederate Army* (Lincoln: University of Nebraska Press, 2005), 93; Brian Reid and John White, "A Mob of Stragglers and Cowards: Desertion from the Union and Confederate Armies, 1861–1865," *Journal of Strategic Studies* 8 (March 1985): 66, 68–69, 70, 71; William Blair, *Virginia's Private War* (New York: Oxford University Press, 1998), 60–61, 64, 89–90, 92; Richard E. Beringer, "Identity and the Will to Fight," in *On the Road to Total War: The American Civil War and the German Wars of Unification, 1861–1871*, eds. Stig Förster and Jörg Nagler (Washington, D.C.: German Historical Institute and Cambridge: Cambridge University Press, 1997), 92–93, 94. For a sympathetic account of a deserter who fled Confederate ranks because of concern for his starving family, see Joel Chandler Harris's semi-autobiographical, partly fictional tale *On the Plantation: A Story of a Georgia Boy's Adventures during the War* (New York: Appleton, 1892; reprint Athens: University of Georgia Press, 1980), 138–140, 160, 164–181, 196–222.

65. VBD, 18: note 1 following entries for 1884; 19: note 1 following entries for 1885.

This was a difficult time for the 13th Virginia, according to Samuel D. Buck. The first year of the war was over, enlistments were expiring, and many men objected to being retained in the Confederate army past the period they had agreed to serve. This caused several desertions (*With the Old Confeds*, 27). See also Ella Lonn's classic, though now dated, study of desertion (*Desertion during the Civil War* [New York: Appleton, 1928; reprint, Gloucester, MA: Peter Smith, 1966], 17–19, 29, 31, 52–55, 96–99).

66. "Monthly Report of Prisoners of War, Deserters, Etc.," Confederate Compiled Service Records, microfilm 324, reel 453, National Archives, Washington, D.C.; Blair, *Virginia's Private War*, 64, 89–90.

67. Captain George H. Bragonier, Camp Jesse, New Creek, VA, to Major R. M. Cotwine, Wheeling, VA, May 26, 1862. Unfiled papers and slips belonging in Confederate Compiled Service Records, microfilm 347, reel 402, National Archives, Washington, D.C.; The Union forces did not begin keeping careful records of Confederate prisoners of war or deserters who took the loyalty oath until the summer of 1863 (Weitz, *More Damning than Slaughter*, 130, 131, 135, 250). The possibility that Van Buskirk might have been accused of spying, as indicated in Captain Bragonier's letter to Major Cotwine, is less ominous that it sounds. It did not mean he was likely to be tried, condemned, and executed even though he carried a diary that excited considerable interest and suspicion among several levels of his captors. Standard policy was to treat all deserters who had not surrendered to Union officers shortly after bolting from their units as spies until they could receive status reassignments (Lonn, *Desertion during the Civil War*, 93).

68. John H. King, *Three Hundred Days in a Yankee Prison: Reminiscence of War Life, Captivity, Imprisonment at Camp Chase, Ohio* (Atlanta: J. A. Daves, 1904; reprint, Kennesaw: Continental Book Co., 1959), 76, 94–96. An extended description of Camp Chase is provided by Lieutenant R. M. Collins of the 15th Texas Regiment. He arrived at the prison in the winter of 1863, and found the accommodations comfort-

able and the diet quite adequate (*Chapters from the Unwritten History of the War Between the States* [St. Louis: Nixon-Jones, 1893], 67, 87–92). Other prisoners housed at Camp Chase late in the war judged the facilities comfortable and healthy, but logged occasional complaints about the food (Henry C. Mettam, "Civil War Memoirs of the First Maryland Cavalry, C. S. A.," *Maryland Historical Magazine* 58 [June 1963]:164; Jonathan Will Dyer, *Four Years in the Confederate Army: A History of the Experiences of the Private Soldier in Camp, Hospital, Prison, on the March, and on the Battlefield, 1861–1865* [Evansville: Amelia W. Dyer, 1898], 36–43). These cordial accounts are contradicted by other residents of the prison. One characterized it as "stoutly built ... forbidding in aspect and anything but comfortable." This disaffected captive also complained of scant rations and the lack of blankets, although he noted officers were issued tents (John Watson Morton, *The Artillery of Nathan Bedford Forrest's Cavalry* [Nashville: Methodist Episcopal Church, 1909], 37). A second disgruntled Confederate described the prison as overcrowded and unpleasant, filled with filth and vermin (J. P. Austin, *The Blue and the Gray: Sketches of a Portion of the Unwritten History of the Great American Civil War* [Atlanta: Franklin Printing, 1899], 34). There is some indication that rations at Camp Chase were adequate early in the war, but the quantities served prisoners decreased as the conflict wore on (William H. Knauss, "The Story of Camp Chase," *The Ohio Magazine* [September 1906], 1: 233–236). Letters describing conditions at Camp Chase are available in "Civil War Materials," microfilm collection 17, roll 2, Ohio Historical Society, Columbus, Ohio (Personal communication with Thomas Rieder, Reference Archivist, Ohio Historical Society, Columbus, Ohio, January 19, 1999).

69. Philip C. Van Buskirk, Camp Chase, OH, to Colonel [unnamed commandant of Camp Chase], Camp Chase, OH, June 5, 1862. Unfiled papers and slips belonging in Confederate Compiled Service Records, microfilm 347, reel 402, National Archives, Washington, D.C.

70. Philip C. Van Buskirk, Camp Chase, OH, to Captain E. [W.] Over, Camp Chase, OH, June 28, 1862. Unfiled papers and slips belonging in Confederate Compiled Service Records, microfilm 347, reel 402, National Archives, Washington, D.C.

71. The "new" state to which Van Buskirk refers was the "Restored Government of Virginia" created at Wheeling in 1861 (Boyd B. Stutler, *West Virginia in the Civil War* [Charleston: Educational Foundation, Inc., 1966], 6; Stutler, "The Civil War in West Virginia," *West Virginia History*, 22 [January 1961]: 6). Two years later the "Restored Government" officially became the state of West Virginia. Contrast Van Buskirk's willingness to take the oath with northerner-turned-Confederate Edmund DeWitt Patterson's categorical refusal to do the same while a prisoner of war (Edmund DeWitt Patterson, *Yankee Rebel*, ed. John G. Barrett [Chapel Hill: University of North Carolina Press, 1966], 128–130).

72. Joseph Darr was, among other assignments, the superintendent of volunteer reenlistment for West Virginia (G. Wayne Smith, "Nathan Goff, Jr. in the Civil War," *West Virginia History*, 14 [January 1953], 124, note 73).

73. Philip C. Van Buskirk, Camp Chase, OH, to Captain Ed. [W.] Over, Camp Chase, OH, July 15, 1862. Unfiled papers and slips belonging in Confederate Compiled Service Records, microfilm 347, reel 402, National Archives, Washington, D.C.

74. Prisoner exchange programs began in the spring of 1862 and continued on until late 1863 (Weitz, *More Damning than Slaughter*, xiii, 53, 137, 164).

75. VBD, 4: August 26, 27, 28, September 9, 1862, September–December 1862, *passim*. For a grim account of the river voyage written by one of Van Buskirk's fellow prisoners, see Indiana W. Logan, ed., *Kelion Franklin Peddicord of Quirk's Scouts* (New York: Neale Publishing, 1908), 44–45. Jonathan Dyer, who made the trip from Camp Chase to Vicksburg, told of a much more pleasant journey, although he may have been on a later exchange than the one that included Van Buskirk and Peddicord (Dyer, *Four Years in the Confederate Army*, 45–52). Confederate records indicate Van

– 149 –

Buskirk was received on September 11, though he was not officially entered as "exchanged" until November ("Monthly Report of Prisoners of War, Deserters, Etc.," Confederate Compiled Service Records, microfilm 324, reel 453, National Archives, Washington, D.C.). See also Knauss, "The Story of Camp Chase," 127. The repatriation of prisoners from Camp Chase usually took about two weeks. One returned Confederate officer complained that the trip took seventeen days because the steamboat from Cairo to Vicksburg did not travel at night. Under ordinary circumstances, he claimed, the journey would have required only ten or twelve days (Austin, *The Blue and the Gray*, 42–44).

76. Stephen V. Ash, *When the Yankees Came: Conflict and Chaos in the Occupied South, 1861–1865* (Chapel Hill: University of North Carolina Press, 1995), 28–31, 53–55, 65–70, 81–83, 90–92, 131–137, 140, 144–145.

77. Mary Elizabeth Massey, *Refugee Life in the Confederacy* (Baton Rouge: Louisiana State University Press, 1964), 3, 163–164.

78. Blair, *Virginia's Private War*, 68–69, 71, 92.

79. West Virginia was formally admitted to the United States on June 30, 1863. John Mead Gould, *History of the First- Tenth- Twenty-ninth Maine Regiment* (Portland: Berry, 1871), 110. It is unclear how many West Virginians favored the Union side and how many supported the Confederacy. The maximum number of men from western Virginia and West Virginia who served in the Union armies has been estimated at approximately 30,000. There are no firm estimates of the total who served in the southern forces (McKinney, *West Virginia Civil War Almanac*, 2:1). One former Union officer, writing thirty years after the war, maintained that the Confederacy had significant recruiting problems in western Virginia early in the war (Lang, *Loyal West Virginia*, 59).

80. Richard Orr Curry, *A House Divided: A Study of Statehood, Politics, and the Copperhead Movement in West Virginia* (Pittsburgh: University of Pittsburgh Press, 1964), 7–8, 56–57, 65; Curry and Gerald F. Ham, "The Bushwhacker's War: Insur-

gency and Counter-insurgency in West Virginia," *Civil War History* 10 (December 1964): 416; James Carter Linger, *Confederate Military Units of West Virginia* (Tulsa: pub. by author, 1989), 17; McKinney, *The Civil War in Fayette County, West Virginia* (Charleston: Pictorial Histories Publishing Co., 1988), 191; Stutler, "Civil War in West Virginia," 79–80. See also Frank Klement, "General John B. Floyd and the West Virginia Campaigns of 1861," *West Virginia History* 7 (April 1947): 319–333 and Edward C. Smith, *The Borderland in the Civil War* (New York: Macmillan, 1937), 207–209, 362, 366. One Union officer, commenting on the character of bushwhackers, claimed they were improvident, cruel, murderous, fiendish, and uneducated (Lang, *Loyal West Virginia*, 8–9). On occasion, captured bushwhackers were known to have fatal "accidents" before they reached the military prisons to which they were headed (McKinney, *The Civil War in Greenbrier County, West Virginia* [Charleston: Pictoral Histories Publishing Co., 1988], 167).

81. Both armies regularly looted cattle and horses as they moved through the areas Van Buskirk frequented. The thefts began in the war's earliest days and continued until the cessation of hostilities in 1865 (Ash, *When the Yankees Came*, 100–101; Richard R. Duncan, *Lee's Endangered Left: The Civil War in Western Virginia, Spring of 1864* [Baton Rouge: Louisiana State University Press, 1998], 74–75, 105–107; Kenneth W. Noe, "Exterminating Savages: The Union Army and Mountain Guerillas in Southern West Virginia, 1861–1862," in *The Civil War in Appalachia: Collected Essays*, eds. Kenneth W. Noe and Shannon H. Wilson [Knoxville: University of Tennessee Press, 1997], 105–109, 116.

82. VBD, 7: note 7 following entries for 1868. Samuel Price was born in 1805, studied law, and settled at Lewisburg, in Greenbrier County, Virginia, around 1838. He held numerous local offices over the years, and in 1863 he was elected lieutenant governor of Virginia. He served in that capacity throughout the war. Later, in 1876, he was selected to complete the unexpired term of a U.S. senator from West Virginia

Notes (Introduction)

who died while in office. Price was an unsuccessful candidate for the seat when elections were held later that year. He died in 1884 (Curry, *House Divided*, 177; *Biographical Directory of the American Congress*, 1482). Francis Thomas, a Marylander, was born in 1799. He attended St. John's College at Annapolis, studied law, and was admitted to the bar in 1820. After serving in his state's legislature, in the U.S. Congress, and as president of the Chesapeake and Ohio Canal Company, he was elected to the governorship of Maryland and held the office from 1841 to 1844. From 1861 to 1869 he again represented his district in the U.S. House of Representatives. After the war, he was a collector of internal revenue and later the U.S. minister to Peru. He was killed by a locomotive while walking along railroad tracks near Frankville, Maryland, in 1876 (*ibid.*, 1704).

83. A native of New Hampton, New Hampshire, Kelley was born in 1807. He later migrated to western Virginia, probably in the 1840s. He grew wealthy as a merchant and railroad freight agent, and was recognized as one of the area's leading citizens. When the war came, he organized the First Virginia Regiment and served as its colonel. He was severely wounded at the Battle of Philippi, but after his recovery rose rapidly to the rank of brigadier general and was later promoted to major general. By 1864 he commanded areas in West Virginia and Maryland. After the war he held several government posts. He died at Oakland, Maryland in 1891 ("General Kelley," *Harper's Weekly*, November 16, 1861, 732; "Domestic Intelligence," *Harper's Weekly*, January 9, 1864, 19; Stutler, *West Virginia in the Civil War*, 258, 274; Genevieve Brown, "A History of the 6th Regiment, West Virginia Vols.," *West Virginia History* 9 [July 1948]: 331, 339; Duncan, *Lee's Endangered Left*, 11 ff.; John W. Shaffer, *Clash of Loyalties: A Border County in the Civil War* [Morgantown: West Virginia University Press, 2003], 101; G. Wayne Smith, "Nathan Goff, Jr. in the Civil War," 123).

84. For more on attitudes toward freed slaves held by northerners, southerners, and by freed slaves, themselves, see Duncan, *Lee's Endangered Left*, 227–228.

85. VBD, 4: June 5, 1859.

86. Spencer Tucker, *Brigadier General John D. Imboden: Confederate Commander in the Shenandoah* (Lexington: University Press of Kentucky, 2002), 111–112, 119–121; Desertion was not severely punished in the Army of Northern Virginia for most of the war's duration. Lee, in fact, referred to his former soldiers who served with Imboden as "absentees" rather than deserters (Weitz, *More Damning than Slaughter*, 96–101,149, 151, 155, 158, 161–162, 199; Reid and White, "Mob of Stragglers," 70–71).

87. Another soldier on the expedition, James E. Hall of the 31st Virginia Infantry, was also forced by adverse conditions to abbreviate his journal keeping during Imboden's raid (Ruth Woods Dayton, ed., *The Diary of a Confederate Soldier, James E. Hall* [s. l.: privately printed, 1961], 72–77). See also Stutler, *West Virginia in the Civil War*, 210–214; Festus P. Summers, ed., *A Borderland Confederate* (Pittsburgh: University of Pittsburgh Press, 1962), 58–65. Henry C. Mettam, a member of the cavalry brigade under the command of General William E. Jones was operating in the same area during the month that Van Buskirk served with Imboden. He, too, wrote of rain beginning about April 22 and lasting for a week (Mettam, "Civil War Memoirs," 147). Another source indicates the rain lasted twice that long (Virgil Carrington Jones, *Gray Ghosts and Rebel Raiders* [New York; Holt, 1956], 164), while still another wrote of both rain and snow ([Henry Corbin?], "Diary of a Virginian Cavalryman, 1863–4," *The Historical Magazine* 2 [October 1873]: 210). See also McKinney, *Civil War in Greenbrier County*, 252–253. Although the Confederacy had lost control of strategic salt works in the area, their recapture was evidently not part of Imboden's mission (Lonn, *Salt as a Factor in the Confederacy* [New York: Walter Neale, 1933], 192.

88. [Illeg.] Col. Commanding, Piedmont [illeg.]burg, WV, to Lieutenant C. A. Freeman, Cumberland, MD, July 15, 1864, Unfiled papers and slips belonging in Confederate Compiled Service Records, microfilm 347, reel 402, National Archives, Washington, D.C.; Duncan, *Lee's Endangered Left*, 158; Barbara J. Howe, "The Civil

War at Bulltown," *West Virginia History* 44 (October 1982): 14, 22; William M. Lamers, *The Edge of Glory: A Biography of General William S. Rosecrans, U.S.A.* (New York: Harcourt, 1961), 27, 63–64; G. Wayne Smith, "Nathan Goff, Jr., in the Civil War," 120–121; Shaffer, *Clash of Loyalties*, 97–98, 100; Summers, "The Jones-Imboden Raid," *West Virginia History* 1 (October 1939), 20–21; Tucker, *John D. Imboden*, 119, 123–126, 128–129, 132, 134–136.

89. [Illeg.] Col. Commanding, Piedmont, [illeg.]burg, WV, to Lieutenant C. A. Freeman, Cumberland, MD, July 15, 1864, Unfiled papers and slips belonging in Confederate Compiled Service Records, microfilm 347, reel 402.

90. VBD, 5: July 18, 1864.

91. VBD, October 2, 1865.

The Civil War Diary of Philip C. Van Buskirk

1. It is not possible to discover which battle Van Buskirk anticipated in December. During the winter of 1861 and 1862, there were many skirmishes in Virginia, and he could have been anticipating any one of them. The Centerville to which he refers was a heavily-fortified segment of the Confederate defensive complex at Manassas in Northern Virginia (George B. McClellan, Report on the Organization and Campaigns of the Army of the Potomac: To Which Is Added an Account of the Campaign in Western Virginia [New York: Sheldon and Co., 1864], 122–123).

2. Elijah Van Buskirk is probably an uncle to Philip.

3. When Van Buskirk arrived in Lewisburg it was in Federal hands, having been taken by northern forces in April of 1862. The population was approximately 800, and the town boasted a courthouse, a carpenter's shop, six stores, one hotel, three churches, one academy, Frazier's Star Tavern, and the first red brick building west of the Alleghenies. The Battle of Lewisburg, a Confederate attempt to retake the town on May 23, 1862, was the only engagement actually fought within the town itself (J. W. Benjamin, "Gray Forces Defeated in Battle of Lewisburg," *West Virginia History*, 20 [October 1959], 28, 29; William Childers, "Virginian's Dilemma: The Civil War Diary of Isaac Noyes Smith," *West Virginia History* 27 (April 1865): 199; Val Husley, "'Men of Virginia — Men of Kanawha — To Arms!' A History of the 22nd Virginia Volunteer Infantry Regiment," *West Virginia History* 35 (1973): 224; McKinney, *Civil War in Greenbrier County*, 29–30, 169–196).

4. This was the first of the schools Van Buskirk would establish during the war years. None of the schools were successful. It is clear from his journal entries, he could not attract enough pupils or generate enough tuition to make teaching a paying profession. Some young men, even though underage, had gone off to war, reducing the potential pool of students. Then, too, the impoverished rural folk whose children he proposed to teach simply could not afford to send their youngsters to school. Additionally, parents may have been unimpressed with his performance as a teacher and chose not to patronize his institutions. Unfortunately, he left no commentary on what he taught, but it seems unlikely that he tried to politicize his pupils, as was commonly done by teachers in the period (Peter W. Bardiglio, "On the Border: White Children and the Politics of War in Maryland," in *The War Was You and Me: Civilians in the American Civil War*, ed. Joan E. Cashin [Princeton: Princeton University Press, 2002], 318, 323; Emmy E. Werner, *Reluctant Witnesses: Childrens' Voices from the Civil War* [Boulder, CO: Westview, 1998], 9–12). General A. W. G. Davis was a substantial Greenbrier County landowner, and was related to Lieutenant Governor Samuel Price by marriage. He had been a general in the pre-war Virginia militia, and in 1861 superintended the operation of a saltpeter works that supplied the Confederate war effort (McKinney, *Civil War in Greenbrier County*, 2, 7; "Mini Bios of People of Scots Descent: Biography of John Stuart," http://www.electricscotland.com/history/world/bios/stuart_john.htm; "Charles L. Davis, Bi-

Notes (The Diary)

ographies, Greenbrier County, West Virginia, D," http://www.rootsweb.com/~wv
greenb/bios-d.htm). James Lucius Davis
served as a cavalry commander for the Confederacy (McKinney, *Civil War in Greenbrier County*, 32–33).

5. Price owned a house in town and at
Richlands, the family farm a few miles away
in the countryside. Van Buskirk traveled
between the two properties frequently.

6. Van Buskirk's school closed on March
20. The 22nd had been posted in the
Lewisburg area since late fall of 1861
(McKinney, *Civil War in Fayette County*, 111,
123).

7. Samuel Lewis Price, called Lewis
throughout the diary, was the thirteen-
year-old son of Governor Samuel Price. He
was born on July 10, 1850, according to Van
Buskirk's opening remarks immediately
preceding the first diary entry for January,
1864.

8. Peyton was a major landowner in
Greenbrier County. Five of his sons fought
for the Confederacy. He was related by
marriage to Lieutenant Governor Price
("Mini Bios ... Biography of John Stuart";
"Charles L. Peyton," http://homepages.
rootsweb.com/~vfcrook/greenbrier/bios/
charleslpeyton.txt).

9. The "expedition" was the Jones-Imboden Raid, planned to destroy a large section of the Baltimore and Ohio Railroad,
overthrow the Union-organized government, and gather recruits and supplies for
Confederate forces. Van Buskirk's failure
to record any details of the operation was due
to both inclement weather and to the fact
that his unit was almost continuously on
the move while trying to carry out its mission. The raid was a failure in many respects. Although substantial amounts of
supplies were captured, the railroad was not
severely damaged, the number of recruits
obtained was below expectations, and Imboden discovered that support for the Confederacy in western Virginia was far less enthusiastic than southern leaders had
expected. He expressed his disappointment
in a final report to General R. H. Chilton,
the adjutant and inspector of the Army of
Northern Virginia. He partially excused his
failure by explaining that "the people of the

northwest are to all intents and purposes, a
conquered people. Their spirit is broken by
tyranny where they are true to our cause,
and those who are against us are the blackest hearted, most despicable villains upon
the continent" (Haviland Harris Abbot,
"General John D. Imboden," *West Virginia
History*, 21 [January 1960]: 101–102). The
General's assessment of the situation might
also explain the lack of hostility Van
Buskirk encountered as a Confederate deserter in western Virginia. It seems likely
Imboden's report was disingenuous at best.
He wrote that his troops engaged in no illegal foraging and claimed locals freely accepted Confederate currency at a time
when its value in the area had probably
plummeted (Roy Bird Cook, *Lewis County
in the Civil War* [Charleston: Jarret, 1924],
64, 74–75, 78). See also Summers, "Jones-Imboden Raid," 127.

10. According to one source, the 22nd
did not join Imboden until April 20 (Terry
Lowry, *22nd Virginia Infantry*, 2d ed.
[Lynchburg: H. E. Howard, 1988], 39).

11. The reference is probably to William
Renick Kincaid, a substantial landowner
in the Lewisburg area. He was at his plantation, "The Meadows," in June of 1863.
He did not join the Confederate 4th Virginia Cavalry until November 25 of that
year ("The Ancient and Historic Kincaid
Family of Virginia," http://www.geocities.
com/heartland/meadows/4756/?20061).
The Dietzs, like the Kincaids, were among
Greenbrier County's affluent residents,
owning a substantial two-story house that
was used as both a military headquarters
and a hospital during the early years of the
war (McKinney, *Civil War in Greenbrier
County*, 67).

12. This was the 1st Brigade of Major
General Samuel Jones's force in the Confederate army's Western Department of Virginia (Stutler, *West Virginia*, 242–244;
Mark M. Boatner, *The Civil War* Dictionary [New York: McKay, 1959], 235, 443,
903–904). When the forces under the command of General John Echols, including
the 22nd Regiment, were ordered to support Lee in northern Virginia after Gettysburg, Edgar's battalion remained in West
Virginia (Husley, "Men of Virginia," 228).

13. This was the Battle of Rocky Gap, known also as the Battle of Dry Creek, Howard's Creek, or White Sulphur Springs (Stutler, *West Virginia*, 242). Major General Samuel Jones, the Confederate commander at the battle, concurred with Van Buskirk that it was a "warm" affair (Lang, *Loyal West Virginia*, 361). Union forces were defeated in the battle and forced to retreat, but their foray was successful in that it destroyed over $5,000,000 in Confederate supplies (William Woods Averell, *Ten Years in the Saddle: The Memoir of William Woods Averell*, eds. Edward K. Eckert and Nicholas J. Amato [San Raphael: Presidio Press, 1978], 390–391. See also Frederick W. B. Hassler, "The Military View of Passing Events, From Inside the Confederacy, No II. The Campaign in West Virginia, 1861 and 1862," *Historical Magazine* [December 1869]: 356).

14. The boy may have been the nephew of Matthew Arbuckle, who owned a large farm with a comfortable log house five miles north of Lewisburg on some of the best land in Greenbrier County ("Arbuckle Family," in "Biographies, Greenbrier County, WV — 'A,'" http://www.wvgenweb.org/greenbrier/bios/bios-a.htm; Childers, "Virginian's Dilemma," 199–200).

15. The Kanawha Valley had long been the tentative preserve of Union forces. Residents in northwest Virginia were culturally distinct from those in other parts of the state, and anti-secessionist sentiment was relatively strong there, particularly after the Confederate defeats at the Battle of Philippi on June 3 and the Battle of Rich Mountain on July 11, 1861 (Blair, *Virginia's Private War*, 19, 35, 39).

16. Van Buskirk had never mentioned the 23rd in any of his earlier diary entries, but the battalion was part of Echols' Brigade, with which he had previously served. The 22nd Virginia Infantry was also part of Echols' Brigade (McKinney, *Civil War in Greenbrier County*, 272).

17. Captain Runnels Davis, C. S. A., was the son of General A. W. G. Davis. He was killed at the Battle of Cedar Creek, October 19, 1864 ("Charles L. Davis," *Biographies, Greenbrier County, West Virginia*, "D"

[http://www.rootsweb.com/~wvgreenb/bios-d.htm]).

18. This was the Battle of Droop Mountain. The defeated Confederates were allowed to retreat from the battle unmolested. General William W. Averell explained in his report that he "hoped that by letting the enemy alone during the night, [they] might loiter on the route and be caught the next day between my command and the force expected from the Kanawha Valley" (Lang, *Loyal West Virginia*, 363). His failure to capitalize on his victory created severe doubts about his abilities as a commander, doubts already held by a number of senior Union officers (Duncan, *Lee's Endangered Left*, 73; Averell, *Ten Years in the Saddle*, 389). See also *History of Pocahontas County, West Virginia, 1981, Birthplace of Rivers* (Marlinton: Pocahontas County Historical Society, 1982), 47–48.

19. Van Buskirk probably should have accepted the Arbuckles' invitation. Another ex–Confederate who stayed with them, Isaac Noyes Smith, reported in late 1861 that the family's table included milk, honey, and butter. He also wrote they had many books, a good fireplace, and linen sheets (Childers, "Virginian's Dilemma," 199–200).

20. Memoranda 1, 3, 4, 5, and 6 consist entirely of lists containing names of people Van Buskirk met, places he stayed, money borrowed from friends or relatives, and records of nocturnal emissions. They have been deleted.

21. George Schultz, as noted earlier, was a friend Van Buskirk from the 1850s when they served together as Marine Corps musicians.

22. Major Joseph Darr served as provost marshal at the headquarters of the 1st Virginia Cavalry early in the war (Ellen Wilkins Tompkins, ed., "'The Colonel's Lady': Some Letters of Ellen Wilkins Tompkins, July–December 1861," *The Virginia Magazine of History and Biography*, 69 [October 1961], 411). He is correctly identified by Van Buskirk as Joseph Darr later in the diary (VBD, 5: July 18, 1864).

23. Van Buskirk left no clue to the meaning of the initials or what is apparently a Chinese character or symbol.

24. Lilburn Peyton was the son of Charles L. Peyton ("Charles L. Peyton," http://homepages.rootsweb.com/~vfcrook/greenbrier/bios/charleslpeyton.txt).

25. Van Buskirk's sin was probably that of the biblical Onan. In earlier volumes of the diary he is regularly wracked by guilt over masturbation.

26. Passes to cross the lines were apparently issued in an arbitrary and irregular fashion by both armies in the area. See Tompkins, "The Colonel's Lady," 388, 394, 397–399, 402, 403, 409, 410–411.

27. Rumors were a constant feature of life between the lines. Often they were wrong, but the tendency among those who heard them was to believe those that brought word of what they hoped to hear. Secessionists welcomed rumors of Confederate victories. Unionists were cheered to hear of United States' triumphs (Stephen Cresswell, ed., "Civil War Diary from French Creek: Collections from the Diary of Sirene Bunten," *West Virginia History* 48 [1989], 131, 134, 136–140).

28. Houses of prostitution were often found in garrison towns throughout the Civil War (Ash, *When the Yankees Came*, 85–86).

29. Possibly A. R. Barbee of the 22nd Virginia Infantry (McKinney, *Civil War in Greenbrier County*, 158).

30. Bungers Mill, or Bungers Mills, as it was sometimes spelled during the period, was about four miles west of Lewisburg (McKinney, *Civil War in Greenbrier County*, 26, 83; "Place Names in West Virginia, 'B,'" http://www.wvculture.org/history/placenamb.html, 19).

31. Colonel Abia A. Tomlinson served under the command of Colonel Rutherford B. Hayes in both the 5th West Virginia Volunteer Infantry and the 13th West Virginia Volunteer Infantry (Kimberly Ball Hieronimus Brownlee, "History of the 13th West Virginia Volunteer Infantry," http://www.wvcivilwar.com/13thinf.shtml; "E-History, Operations in N. Va., W. Va, Md., and Pa.," http://ehistory.osu.edu/uscw/library/or/090/0982/cfm).

32. On the matter of horses, friend and enemy were flexible terms. Union and Confederate forces both freely appropriated horses and wagons from persons they identified as enemies, and often did the same to those who shared their sympathies. Sometimes owners were compensated, other times they were not (Charles Lieb, *Nine Months in the Quartermaster Department* [Cincinnati: Moore, Wilsatch, Keys, 1862], 53–58, 93, 130; Gould, *History of the First- Tenth- Twenty-ninth Regiment*, 127).

33. Joel Chandler Harris also reported in his semi-autobiographical, part fictional account of the war that in his one experience with Yankee foragers in Georgia he found them to be "good-humored," with the exception of one German whose rapaciousness was reigned in by the flat of an officer's sword (Harris, *On the Plantation*, 226).

34. A similar judgment was made by the wife of Confederate colonel Christopher Q. Tompkins, of the 22nd Regiment of Virginia Volunteers. She described Union soldiers she encountered as "cut throat" and "villainous looking" (Tompkins, "The Colonel's Lady," 392), but she regularly praised their officers for protecting her and her family from looting as well as inconvenience (*Ibid.*, 393, 395, 397, 403, 406, 408, 412, 418). All in the area were not so fortunate, and Union soldiers frequently made off with food and livestock whenever possible (Jesse Sellers Colton, ed., *The Civil War Journal and Correspondence of Matthias B. Colton* [New York: Macrae-Smith, 1931], 100–101; George A. Wood, *The Seventh Regiment: A Record* [New York: James Miller, 1865], 76; Gould, *History of the First- Tenth- Twenty-ninth Maine Regiment*, 127).

35. The reports were more or less correct. The indecisive outcome of the Battle of the Wilderness (May 5–7) was construed by southerners as a Confederate victory because Grant's forces were compelled to give up some ground (Robert G. Scott, *Into the Wilderness with the Army of the Potomac* [Bloomington: Indiana University Press, 1985], 178–182). The other engagements Van Buskirk mentioned were indisputably Federal defeats. They included Breckenridge's May 15 defeat of Major General Franz Sigel, not Crook, at New Market (H. A. DuPont, *The Campaign of 1864 in the Valley of Virginia and the Expedition to*

Lynchburg [New York: National Americana Society, 1925], 13–34), the failure of the Union army's April expedition to take Camden, Arkansas — although Major General Frederick Steele only retreated from the town, he did not surrender to General Sterling Price as Van Buskirk reported (Ludwell H. Johnson, *Red River Campaign: Politics and Cotton in the Civil War* [Baltimore: Johns Hopkins University Press, 1958], 40, 177, 193–195), and the capture of Plymouth, North Carolina (April 17–20) by southern forces (Richard N. Current, *Lincoln's Loyalists: Union Soldiers from the Confederacy* [Boston: Northeastern University Press, 1992], 166–167).

36. Probably Captain Richard Blazer of Blazer's Scouts. The unit was in Greenbrier County at this time along with Tomlinson's 5th West Virginia Infantry (McKinney, *Civil War in Greenbrier County*, 280).

37. Brigadier General Duffié was a Parisian graduate of St. Cyr, the French national military college. He moved to the United States in 1859. When the Civil War began, he accepted a commission as a captain in the 2nd New York Cavalry, and was promoted to brigadier general in June of 1863 (Duncan, *Lee's Endangered Left*, 229).

38. Van Buskirk's own footnote provides the information that the doctor's initials are "L. L."

39. There is at least one report that General Averell ordered his men to confiscate and butcher sheep belonging to local residents. After the Battle of Droop Mountain, early in November of 1863, he may have directed that three men from each company slaughter enough sheep to feed his hungry troops (William Davis Slease, *The Fourteenth Pennsylvania Cavalry in the Civil War* [Pittsburgh: Art Engraving and Printing, 1915], 109).

40. Union forces in the area were unforgiving when locals who killed their men were apprehended. Two men were executed at Sutton, West Virginia, for using a scythe to decapitate a young soldier. Evidence of their crime was provided by the wife of one of the men (Michael Egan, *The Flying Gray-haired Yank: Or, the Adventures of a Volunteer, a Personal Narrative of Thrilling*

Experiences as an Army Courier, a Volunteer Captain, a Prisoner of War, a Fugitive from Southern Dungeons, a Guest Among the Contrabands and Unionists ... A True Narrative of the Civil War [Philadelphia: Hubbard Brothers, 1888], 85–88). See also Wood, *Seventh Regiment*, 65–67. For an account of a southern sympathizer who almost met the same fate, see Daniel S. DeWees, *Recollections of a Lifetime* (Eden: s.n., 1904), 34–35. The David Creigh case became a *cause célèbre* in Greenbrier County. He was no ordinary citizen, but a prosperous merchant who owned a Georgian-style mansion, served as an elder of the Presbyterian church, sympathized with the southern cause, sent three sons to fight for the Confederacy, and had connections to the leading families in the area. After a trial at Bungers Mills characterized by dubious procedures, he was convicted and executed. His body was left hanging from a tree as a warning to others against killing Union soldiers (McKinney, *The Civil War in Greenbrier County*, 297–326; David L. Phillips, "David Creigh and the Burning of Chambersburg, Pennsylvania," http://www.wv civilwar.com/creigh.shtml).

41. The reference is to Thurmond's Rangers, a unit that was part of Echols' Brigade along with the 22nd Virginia Volunteer Infantry (McKinney, *Civil War in Greenbrier County*, 272).

42. The Union forces were retreating after their failure (June 17–18) to hold Lynchburg, a strategic rail center. For an eye-witness account of events, see DuPont, *Campaign of 1864*, 75–97.

43. John Letcher was the secessionist governor of Virginia from 1860 to 1864 (*Biographical Directory of the American Congress*, 1213). General David Hunter ordered Letcher's house and its expensive furnishings in Lexington burned on June 12, 1864, in retaliation for a proclamation the governor issued encouraging Virginians to resist advancing Union armies and denouncing the invaders in intemperate and abusive terminology (F. N. Boney, *John Letcher of Virginia: The Story of Virginia's Civil War Governor* [Tuscaloosa: University of Alabama Press, 1966], 206–208; DuPont, *Campaign of 1864*, 69; Margaret Letcher Showell, "Ex-

governor Letcher's Home," *Southern Historical Society Papers*, 18 [1890]: 394).

44. Contrary to the opinion of Union officers and Union soldiers who wrote in their letters, diaries, and other later accounts of the war, bushwackers were not drawn from the lowest, poorest, and least educated of the social order. In general they tended to be of a middling sort. They often owned and livestock, the members of their bands were often relatives, and they ranged in age from teenagers to men in their forties and fifties. For information on bushwackers and who they were in Van Buskirk's area, see Kenneth W. Noe, "Who Were the Bushwhackers? Age, Class, Kin, and Western Virginia's Confederate Guerrillas, 1861–1862," *Civil War History* 49 (March 2003): 5–31. Information on how Union forces in other theaters of war dealt with bushwhackers or irregular forces who killed their soldiers can be found in Robert Mackey's "Bushwackers, Provosts, and Tories: The Guerrilla War in Arkansas," in *Guerrillas, Unionists, and Violence on the Confederate Homefront*, ed. Donald Sutherland (Fayettville: University of Arkansas Press, 1999), 171–185, and Kenneth C. Barnes, "The Williams Clan's Civil War: How an Arkansas Farm Family became a Guerrilla Band" in *Enemies of the Country: New Perspectives on Unionists in the Civil War South*, eds. John C. Inscoe and Robert C. Kenzer (Athens: University of Georgia Press, 2001), 188–207. Atrocities by Union forced were relatively rare during the course of the war. Partisan bands made up of Confederate deserters were far more likely to commit atrocities against civilians living in areas controlled by Southern armies (Weitz, *More Damning than Slaughter*, 109). On the subject of civil war atrocities, see the splendid essays by Michael Fellman, "Inside Wars: The Cultural Crisis of Warfare and the Values of Ordinary People," in *Guerrillas, Unionists, and Violence on the Confederate Homefront*, ed. Daniel Sutherland (Fayetteville: University of Arkansas Press, 1999), 187–199, and Fellman, "At the Nihilist Edge: Reflections on Guerrilla Warfare During the American Civil War," in *On the Road to Total War*, 519–540.

45. The men of the 15th New York as-signed to foraging duties were not likely to have been impressed by weeping women at this stage of the war. They had been badly pummeled at Lynchburg on June 17 and 18, and during their retreat to Lewisburg over the next week they had little rest and scant rations. They subsisted almost entirely on roots and berries. Over the previous months of campaigning, foragers from the 15th regularly encountered wailing women claiming to have no food. Information garnered from Blacks and searches conducted by the soldiers often revealed the women were lying (Chauncy S. Norton, *The Red Neck Ties, or History of the Fifteenth New York Volunteer Cavalry* [Ithaca: Journal Book and Job Printing House, 1891], 25–26, 41–43, 150). See also DuPont, *Campaign of 1864*, 90.

46. Charlie is probably Charles W. Peyton, the son of Charles L. Peyton.

47. Horse rustling was a serious problem for residents of the area. It was practiced by soldiers of both armies, irregular troops, and marauding bands (DeWees, *Reflections of a Lifetime*, 36–39; Gould, *History of the First- Tenth- Twenty-ninth Maine Regiment*, 127; Genevieve Brown, "A History of the Sixth Regiment, West Virginia Infantry Volunteers," M. A. thesis [West Virginia University, 1936], 35).

48. This was not Van Buskirk's first visit to Weston or Bulltown. He had been at the strategically located towns when he marched with Imboden's raiders in the spring of 1863. Bulltown remained a focal point for troop movements and a haven for bushwhackers throughout the war. A minor battle was fought there in October of 1863 (Cook, *Lewis County*, 5, 70–71; Howe, "Civil War at Bullhorn," 6–7, 10–11, 14–16, 34; McKinney, *The Civil War in Greenbrier County*, 167).

49. This must have been a list of battles in which Van Buskirk had fought. His baptism of fire was in an attack on a Chinese fort at Shanghai on April 4, 1854, in a minor engagement known as the Battle of Muddy Flat. See Paulsen, "Under the Starry Banner on Muddy Flat."

50. Yahrling was one of the 6th West Virginia Volunteers (Brown, "History of the Sixth Regiment," 340).

51. Van Buskirk must have told this to

many others. Some years later, in 1870, G. A. Parrée was named to be a federal judge, and was evidently concerned about the effect the story might have on his nomination. He spent considerable effort first locating Van Buskirk and then bringing him to Martinsburg, West Virginia, to sign a statement saying that he had never induced him to join the Confederate army. The two men met in Martinsburg, and after chatting for a time, Van Buskirk decided that it must have been a Thomas Perry rather than G. A. Parrée who gave him the advice. He signed the paper. Parrée then paid his travel expenses and provided an extra $5.00 for his time. When Van Buskirk wrote of the recantation in his diary, he added the information that Governor Francis Thomas, with whom he was again residing in 1870, considered Parrée to be an "unmitigated rascal" (VBD, 8: January 4, 1870).

52. This is the Boyd who was married to one of Van Buskirk's aunts and who, in 1858, assisted him in his failed efforts to obtain a lieutenancy in the Marine Corps by introducing him to Congressman James Faulkner of Virginia.

53. The full title of an earlier edition of the book by E. S. Drieude indicates why Van Buskirk so wished he could give a copy to Lewis. It is *Lorenzo: or the Empire of Religion. By a Non-Conformist, a Convert to the Catholic Faith* (Baltimore: J. Murphy, 1844).

54. There are no complete files of the *Cumberland Union* extant. Van Buskirk's piece cannot be located among the surviving issues.

55. Not further identified in the diary.

56. The governor's calculations as well as Van Buskirk's first "fumbling" calculations made in his presence have been omitted.

57. The inability to identify the sympathies of roving bands or even large contingents of men was not unusual in areas where loyalties were often uncertain. Both Union and Confederate forces not only wore each others' uniforms as disguises from time to time in such places, and roving bands of partisans and deserters favoring both northern and southern causes often impersonated the enemy to gain in-

formation or the element of surprise. See Fellman, *Inside War: The Guerrilla Conflict in Missouri During the American Civil War* (New York: Oxford University Press, 1989), 28–29, 31–32, 121–122, 168–171 and Fellman, "Inside Wars: The Cultural Crisis of Warfare."

58. *Easy Lessons in Chinese, or Progressive Exercises to Facilitate the Study of that Language Especially Adapted to the Study of the Cantonese Dialect* (Macao: Chinese Repository, 1842) by S. Wells Williams was the book Van Buskirk used in his occasional efforts to master the Chinese language when he served in the Far East during the 1850s.

59. This appears to signal the end of Van Buskirk's school, but he gave no intimation in his Civil War diary or any of the diary volumes that followed of the cause for its termination.

60. Van Buskirk's friendship with both Schultz and McFarland dated back to his service on board the *Plymouth* in the early 1850s.

61. Van Buskirk evidently left the Browning family when his school closed and moved back in with Francis Thomas.

62. Matt. 6:34.

63. "Hawthorne" is not further identified.

64. This was the Washington, D.C., home of George Schultz and his family, near the headquarters barracks. The number, 150, is the designation Van Buskirk used as a reference for the Schultz family home on assorted domicile lists he included in the diary. The actual address was 724 9th Street, S. E., Washington, D.C.

65. This is a reference to the Schultz family and their house.

66. Joe is not further identified in this or subsequent diary volumes. He is perhaps Joseph Schultz, the brother of George Schultz, Van Buskirk's former idol.

67. President Andrew Johnson's Thanksgiving Day proclamation in 1865 placed the holiday on the first Thursday in December. The next year it was returned to the day chosen by Lincoln in 1863, the last Thursday of November. It remained there, with some exceptions, until 1941 when it was fixed on the fourth Thursday in November

by a joint resolution of Congress (Jane M. Hatch, ed., *The American Book of Days* [New York: W. W. Wilson, 1978], 1055–1056).

Afterword

1. VBD, 5: November 20, 1865, note at end of entries for 1865, January 9, 10, 15, 16, 18, 1866, introductory note to March 1866, notes 2 and 8 following entries for 1866; Frank M. Bennett, *The Steam Navy of the United States; A History of the Growth of the Steam Vessel of War in the U.S. Navy and of the Naval Engineer Corps* (Pittsburgh: W. T. Nicholson, 1896), 447; Donald L. Canney lists the *Swatara* as a single-screw vessel (*Frigates, Sloops, and Gunboats, 1815–1865*, vol. 1, *The Old Steam Navy* [Annapolis: United States Naval Institute Press, 1990], 121–125; Chapelle, *American Sailing Navy*, 536, 549; Paul H. Silverstone, *Warships of the Civil War Navies* (Annapolis: United States Naval Institute Press, 1989), 56; Bernard Brodie, *Sea Power in the Machine Age* (Princeton: Princeton University Press, 1943; reprint, New York: Greenwood, 1969), 150–151; James Russell Soley, *The Blockade and the Cruisers* (New York: Scribner's, 1883), 245. Canney and Silverstone list the *Swatara*'s maximum speed as twelve knots (125, 56, respectively).

2. VBD, 5: November 15, 1865, January 5, March 25, May 21, 28, June 24, July 10, 12, August 2, 1866.

3. VBD, 5: December 1–2, 4, 28, 29, 1866; VBD, 6: April 17, 1867, April 1867, *passim*.

4. VBD, 6: preliminary page for January, 1867, January 20, preliminary page for February 1867, February 23, 27, preliminary page for March 1867, March 17, preliminary page for April 1867, April 1, 3, 11, 12, 17, 19–25, May 12, 23, 24, 1867; Silverstone, *Warships of the Civil War Navies,* 109.

5. VBD, 6: January 31, notes 145, 146, 153, 158, included as entries for November 1867.

6. VBD, 5: January 31, 1867, notes 144–145, 148, 149, 152, 156, included as entries for November 1867.

7. VBD, 6: note 11, included as an entry for February 1867.

8. *Ibid.*

9. VBD, 6: note 144, included as an entry for October 1867.

10. VBD, 6: note 148, 152, included as entries for November 1867.

11. VBD, 6: May, August, December 1867; VBD, 7: March 2, May 22, 26, October 7, 1868, January, 6, 13–14, 27, March 25, April 8, June 17, 24, August 3, 25, 1869; VBD, 8: May 21, June 1, July 6, 8, 16, 17, 18, 20, 30, September 22, October 1, November 28, 1870; VBD, 9: February 24, March 11, July 31, 1871; VBD, 10: introductory page to March 1872, April 2, 1872, introductory page to April 1873, undated second page after entries for July 1, 1873, September 24, 26, 1873, September 4, 30, October 2, 14, 20, 1874.

12. VBD, 10: October 2, 1874.

13. VBD, 8: August 13, 1870; VBD, 9: September 1, 1871.

14. VBD, 9: March 20, 1871.

15. By this time, Van Buskirk had completely rationalized his wartime service. On January 15, 1870, while he was anxiously waiting to find out if his stint with the 13th Virginia Infantry would disqualify him from any federal employment, he wrote in volume 8 of his diary that "my service in the rebel army was in reality a thing of compulsion. My connection with the Confederacy was from beginning to end involuntary." The comment obviously reflects his situation when he wrote it. It is disingenuous at best, and more accurately described as dishonest. Still, Van Buskirk's "southern identity" never ran deep. His lack of commitment reflected a general feeling throughout the ranks of men who fought for the Confederacy according to many academic and popular historians writing since the 1980s. They have argued that a combination of insufficient will and lack of commitment to the newly-created slave nation were basic causes for the defeat in 1865. The myths of Confederate solidarity, singleness of purpose, and dedication were manufactured after the war, along with the notion of the "Lost Cause" (Gary W. Gallagher, *The Confederate War* [Cambridge: Harvard University Press, 1997], 4–5).

16. Frank Thomas was the son of Lemuel Durbin Williams and Sarah O'-Donald, both of Washington, D.C. Lemuel died on August 1, 1865, leaving his wife with five children. Frank was the youngest, born in 1862. It is unlikely Governor Thomas actually adopted the boy. More likely he simply took him in. An older brother, Eugene Judge Williams, apparently did not become part of the Thomas family (personal communication with Williams descendant, June 17, 2006).

17. VBD, 8: January 1, 1870.

18. VBD, 8: January 16, 1870.

19. VBD, 8: January 1, 9, 16, 1870.

20. Philip C. Van Buskirk, Washington, D.C., to Frank Thomas [Mont Alto, Maryland ?], February 28, 1870, private collection.

21. Philip C. Van Buskirk, on board the U.S.S. *Palos*, Boston, Massachusetts, to [Eugene] Judge [Williams], [Washington, D.C.?], March 15, 1870; Philip C. Van Buskirk, Yokohama, Japan, to Frank Thomas, Lima, Peru, July 7, 1873, Philip C. Van Buskirk, on board steamer *Japan*, at sea, July 28, 1873, private collection; *Biographical Directory of the American Congress*, 1704.

22. VBD, 8: preliminary page for March 1870, March 10, 1870.

23. Philip C. Van Buskirk, Hankow [China] to Francis Thomas [Lima, Peru], May 10, 1873, private collection.

24. In the text, quotations, and notes, the earlier spelling, "Corea," has been changed to "Korea" in line with modern usage. For comprehensive accounts of the 1871 Korean expedition and events surrounding it, see Robert E. Johnson, *Rear Admiral John Rodgers, 1812–1892* (Annapolis: United States Naval Institute Press, 1967), 304–333 and Robert E. Johnson, *Far China Station*, 154–169. An abbreviated account is contained in David F. Long, *Gold Braid and Foreign Relations: Diplomatic Activities of U.S. Naval Officers, 1798–1883* (Annapolis: United States Naval Institute Press, 1988), 374–380. For a more complete account of events leading directly to the massacre, see Burg, "Dissenter's Diary: Philip C. Van Buskirk, the US Navy, and the Han River Massacre of 1871," *International Journal of Maritime History* 12 (December 2000): 53–67.

25. Philip C. Van Buskirk, Boisée Bay, Korea, to Francis Thomas, [Mont Alto, MD ?], June 3, 1871, private collection.

26. For a comprehensive examination of the context of the American military action and the details of its execution, see Gordon H. Chang, "Whose 'Barbarism'? Whose 'Treachery'? Race and Civilization in the Unknown United States-Korean War of 1871," *Journal of American History* 89 (March 2003): 1331–1365.

27. The fleet assembled off the Korean coast in 1871 was sent to intimidate residents of the Hermit Kingdom. The flagship, the *Colorado*, was one of the largest warships in the United States Navy. She was 264 feet long at the waterline, mounted forty-seven guns, and carried a compliment of forty-seven officers and 571 men. Three other ships in the fleet were over 250 feet in length. At the time, Korea was a tributary state of China, hence the involvement of American diplomatic representatives to China in the expedition (Chang, "Whose 'Barbarism?'" 1339, 1343); *American Diplomatic and Public Papers: The United States and China*, Series II: *The United States, China, and Imperial Rivalries, 1861–1893*, ed. Jule Davids [Wilmington: Scholarly Resources, 1979], 119. [Hereafter referred to as *ADPP*]).

28. John P. Cowles, Jr., on board *Colorado*, Boisée Bay, Korea, to Frederick F. Low, on board *Colorado*, Boisée Bay, Korea, June 2, 1871, *ADPP*, 123.

29. VBD, 9: June 1, 1871.

30. Chang, "Whose 'Barbarism?'"1338; Frederick F. Low, on board *Colorado*, Boisée Bay, Korea, to Secretary of State Hamilton Fish, Washington, D.C., June 2, 1871, *ADPP*, 121; Peter Karsten, *The Naval Aristocracy: The Golden Age of Annapolis and the Emergence of Modern American Navalism* (New York: Free Press, 1972), 199.

31. *A Narrative of the French Expedition to Korea in 1866, the U.S. Expedition in 1871, and the Expedition of the H.M.S.* Ringdove *in 1871* (Shanghai: reprinted from the *North-China Herald*, 1871), 11–17. The commander of the marine detachment that was part of the fleet anchored off the Korean

coast was Van Buskirk's old nemesis from his days as a musician at the United States Naval Academy, Captain McLane Tilton (Chang, "Whose 'Barbarism?'" 1344). For pictures of the invasion by the expedition's official photographer, Felice Beato, see Terry Bennett, *Korea Caught in Time* (Reading, UK: Garnet, 2009).

32. "General Order by Admiral Rogers, U.S. Flag Ship the *Colorado*, Boisée Anchorage, Korea," in *Narrative of the ... U.S. Expedition*, 17–18. The order also appeared in the *New York Times*, August 22, 1871.

33. Chang, "Whose 'Barbarism?'" 1354.

34. The quotation is appended to the printed copy of General Order No. 32 issued by Admiral John Rogers which Van Buskirk tipped into his diary and is dated June 29, 1871. The mate's ultimate evaluation of the entire expedition was absolutely negative. He wrote that the Americans killed over 400 Koreans and did not get the hoped-for treaty. The destroyed forts were rebuilt within a matter of days, he added, and he was undoubtedly correct in claiming that a second American incursion would be resisted with the same courage and dogged determination as the first (VBD, 9: June 22, 1871). Some days later he provided an accurate summation of what had occurred. "We came in great force, tried intimidation, blundered into wholesale butchery, and depart today with the curses of a whole people ... but give me Captains and Admirals for dressing up even such a thing as this, so as [to] cover themselves with a sort of glory as growing out if it. Instead of halters they will ask and receive from their countrymen laurels" (*ibid.*, July 3, 1871). The U.S. fleet sailed from Korea shortly after their amphibious operation. Almost a dozen years later, a treaty of amity and commerce was negotiated peacefully between the United States and Korea. The American casualties in the ill-considered action against the forts included three dead and nine wounded. Van Buskirk was correct in predicting that participants in the affair would receive "laurels." Six who participated in the assault were awarded the Medal of Honor, and a plaque dedicated to the officer who died in the fray was installed at the United States Naval Academy (Chang, "Whose 'Barbarism?'" 1355).

35. VBD, 9: September 9, 1871. For a fuller account of Van Buskirk's wardroom conversations, naval officers' pornography, and a sampling of the scurrilous adventures he and his associates had ashore, see Burg, "Officers, Gentlemen, 'Man Talk,' and Group Sex in the 'Old Navy,' 1870–1873," *Journal of the History of Sexuality* 11 (July 2002): 439–456. Naval historian Peter Karsten describes some of the adventures of America's officers ashore as "wild and woolly" affairs (*Naval Aristocracy*, 101).

36. VBD, 8: March 15, 20, 1870, 9: March 13, 1871.

37. VBD, 8: September 1, 1870.

38. VBD, 9: August 25, 1871.

39. VBD, 9: September 9, 1871. Franklin was an 1869 graduate of the academy (*Register of Alumni Historical Reference, Classes of 1846–1919* [Annapolis: United States Naval Academy Alumni Association, Inc., 1999], 34; Callahan, *List of the Officers of the Navy*, 203, 639).

40. VBD, 9: March 10, 1871.

41. VBD, 9: concluding note following entries for 1870, July 1, August 25, 1871, April 16, 18, 1872; VBD, 16: June 15, November 10, 22, 1881.

42. VBD, 9: August 25, 1871.

43. VBD, 8: November 28, December 6, 9, 1870; VBD, 9: April introductory page, 1871, April 30, May 11, 1871; VBD, 16: June 15, November 22, 1881. One such group event was described by naval surgeon Samuel P. Boyer, surgeon of the U.S.S. *Iroquois*, a steam-powered sloop of war. As his account of the festival indicates, a good time was had by all:

> October 16, 1868. This P.M., commencing at 8 P.M. And winding up towards the small hours of the night, the medical officers and paymasters of the American men-of-war had a grand "John Nugie," or ... a "Johnnie Nookee." ... eighteen or twenty officers constituted the party ... the girls are about half full of saki; the gentlemen drink enough to make them feel their oats. As soon as the girls are naked, why so soon do they commence to perform all manners of tricks, dancing in the

most voluptuous manner, placing themselves in all the different kinds of attitudes that one might imagine men and women would take whilst having carnal communication with each other.... Our old Admiral and all the Captains had a "Johnnie Nookee" a few days ago [Samuel. P. Boyer, *Naval Surgeon: Revolt in Japan 1868–1869, the Diary of Samuel Pellman Boyer*, eds. Elinor Barnes and James A. Barnes (Bloomington: University of Indiana Press, 1963), 102–103].

44. VBD, 5: March 9–10, 1864, July 5, 1865.

45. VBD, 7: January 30, February 6, 8, April 2, 17, 18, 26, May 11, July 30, preliminary page for August 1869, August 5, 21, 1869, note at the end of entries for 1869 containing a marriage proposal for Sarah James that was probably never sent because she could not read. Monthly abstracts for January, February, April, May, June, August, October, November December 1969; VBD, 8: January 9, 31, February 6, 1870; VBD, 10: August 29, September 8, 21, 1873. Alexander Walker, *Intermarriage, or the Natural Laws by Which Beauty, Health and Intellect Result from Certain Unions, and Deformity, Disease and Insanity from Others* (London: John Churchill, 1841). The book on Gypsies was probably George Henry Borrow's *The Zincali; or an Account of the Gypsies of Spain* (London: John Murray, 1841). Van Buskirk could have used one of any number of editions the *American Cyclopedia* issued between 1857 and 1866 under the full title *New American Cyclopedia: A Popular Dictionary of General Knowledge*, eds. George Ripley and Charles A. Dana (New York: Appleton, 1857–1866). See also "Ida Lewis, the Newport Heroine," *Harper's Weekly* 13 (July 31, 1869): cover, 484.

46. For data on Van Buskirk's visits to the Bonin Islands, see Burg, "Information on Everyday Life from Historical Documents," in *Refereed Papers from the 1st International Small Island Cultures Conference*, ed. Mike Evans (Sidney, AU: Small Island Cultures Research Initiative, 2005), 14–28.

47. VBD, 16: November 22, 1881, note 50, following entries for 1881.

48. VBD, 15: June 29, 1880; VBD, 16: May 17, 1881.

49. VBD, 31: February 5, notes following entries for February, March 11, 12, 1898; Van Buskirk's presence in the Bonins is mentioned briefly, along with a note on an island child attending a mission school in Japan during the 1870s in a curious history of the Bonins by Lionel B. Cholmondeley, a British missionary. Whether the child is one of the seven Buskirk earlier accompanied to Japan is not clear (*A History of the Bonin Islands from the Year 1827 to the Year 1876 and of Nathaniel Savory, One of the Original Settlers to Which Is Added a Short Supplement Dealing with the Islands After Their Occupation by the Japanese* [London: Constable, 1915], vii, 160).

50. VBD, 31: March 12, 14, 15, 24, 1898, notes following entries for March 1898.

51. VBD, 31: note following entries for February 1898, March 26, April 5, April 20, 1898.

52. VBD, 31: March 22, 1898.

53. VBD, 31: March 22, note following entries for March 1898, April 18, notes following entries for April 1898.

54. VBD, 31: March 24, notes at the end of entries for March 1898, April 2, 3, 14, 15, 17, 23, 24, 27, 30, note following entries for April 1898, May 3, 1898.

55. VBD, 31: notes "SE" [for "Self Examination"] following entries for March and April 1898.

Bibliography

Unpublished Sources

Betts, John. "The U.S. Navy in the Mexican War." Ph. D. Diss., University of Chicago, 1954.

Bragonier, Captain George H., Camp Jesse, New Creek, VA, to Major R. M. Cotwine, Wheeling, VA, May 26, 1862. Unfiled papers and slips belonging in Confederate Compiled Service Records, microfilm 347, reel 402, National Archives, Washington, D.C.

Brown, Genevieve. "A History of the Sixth Regiment, West Virginia Infantry Volunteers." M. A. Thesis, West Virginia University, 1936.

"Civil War Materials." Microfilm Collection 17, roll 2. Ohio Historical Society, Columbus, Ohio.

"Classical Register." University Archives, Georgetown University Library, Washington, D.C.

[Illeg.], Colonel. Commanding Piedmont, [Illeg.]burg, WV to Lieutenant C. A. Freeman, Cumberland, MD, July 15, 1864. Unfiled papers and slips belonging in Confederate Compiled Service Records, microfilm 347, reel 402, National Archives, Washington, D.C.

Heffner, Nellie. Letter of Donation, October 18, 1905. Philip C. Van Buskirk Papers. Manuscripts and University Archives, Special Collections Division, Acc3621-001 Allen Library, University of Washington, Seattle, Washington.

"Ledger G." University Archives, Georgetown University Library, Washington, D.C.

"Ledger H." University Archives, Georgetown University Library, Washington, D.C.

Macomb, William H. "Journal of William Macomb Kept Aboard the USS *Portsmouth*." Naval Records Collection, record group 45, National Archives, Washington, D.C.

"Memorandum Book." University Archives, Georgetown University Library, Washington, D.C.

"Monthly Report of Prisoners of War, Deserters, Etc., Received at Headquarters, Forces West of Piedmont, Department of West Virginia for July 10–20, 1864." Confederate Compiled Service Records, microfilm 324, reel 543, National Archives, Washington, D.C.

Muster Roll of the United States Marine Corps. Naval Records Collection, T-1118, rolls 17, 18, National Archives, Washington, D.C.

Plymouth Log. Bureau of Naval Personnel, Deck Logs, record group 24, National Archives, Washington, D.C.

Bibliography

Rapp, Dorothy. United States Military Academy Archive, West Point, New York, to B. R. Burg, September 22, 1987.

Rieder, Thomas. Ohio Historical Society, Columbus, OH, to B. R. Burg, January 19, 1999.

"Size Roll of Marines Enlisted in the Service of the United States Marine Corps." Records of the United States Marine Corps, Bureau of Naval Personnel, record group 127, National Archives, Washington, D.C.

United States Pension Records, T-316, Filed February 9, 1859. Invalid Pension No. 1564, National Archives, Washington, D.C.

Van Buskirk, Philip C. Boisée Bay (Lat. 37° 30'), West Coast of Korea, to Francis Thomas, [Mont Alto, MD ?], June 3, 1871, private collection.

_____. Camp Chase, OH, to Captain E. [W.] Over, Camp Chase, OH, June 28, July 15, 1862. Unfiled papers and slips belonging in Confederate Compiled Service Records, microfilm 347, reel 402, National Archives, Washington, D.C.

_____. Camp Chase, OH, to Colonel [unnamed commandant of Camp Chase], Camp Chase, OH, June 5, 1862. Unfiled papers and slips belonging in Confederate Compiled Service Records, microfilm 347, reel 402, National Archives, Washington, D.C.

_____. "Diary of _____." Philip C. Van Buskirk Papers. Manuscripts and University Archives, Special Collections Division, Acc3621-001 Allen Library, University of Washington, Seattle, Washington.

_____. Hankow, [China], to Francis Thomas, [Lima, Peru], May 10, 1873, private collection.

_____. Monroe Transcript of Volume 2 (1853). "Diary of Philip C. Van Buskirk." Philip C. Van Buskirk Papers. Manuscripts and University Archives, Special Collections Division, Acc3621-001 Allen Library, University of Washington, Seattle, Washington.

_____. On board steamer _Japan_ at sea, July 28, 1873, private collection.

_____. On board the U.S.S. _Palos_, Boston, MA, to [Eugene] Judge [Williams], Washington, D.C.[?], March 15, 1870, private collection.

_____. Yokohama, Japan, to Frank Thomas, Lima, Peru, July 7, 1873, private collection.

_____. Washington, D.C., to Frank Thomas, [Mt. Alto, MD?], February 28, 1870, private collection.

Electronic Sources

"Ancient and Historic Kincaid Family of Virginia." http://www.geocities.com/ heart land/meadows/4756/?20061.

"Arbuckle Family." In "Biographies, Greenbrier County, WV — 'A.'" http://www. wv genweb.org/greenbrier/bios/bios-a.htm.

Brownlee, Kimberly Ball Hieronimus. "History of the 13th West Virginia Volunteer Infantry." http://www.wvcivilwar.com/13thginf.shtml.

"Charles L. Davis." In "Biographies, Greenbrier County, WV — "D." http://www. rootsweb.com/~wvgreen/bios/bios-d.htm.

"Charles L. Peyton." http://homepages.rootsweb.com/~vfcrook/greenbrier/ bios/charles lpeyton.txt.

Bibliography

"E-History, Operations in N. Va., W. Va, Md., and Pa." http://ehistory.osu. edu/uscw/library/or/090/0982/cfm.

"Erotica Bibliophile." http://eroticabibliophile.com/publishers_dugdale_year.php.

"Mini Bios of People of Scots Descent: Biography of John Stuart." http://www. elec tricscotland.com/history/world/bios/stuart_john.htm.

Phillips, David L. "David Creigh and the Burning of Chambersburg, Pennsylvania." http://www.wvcivilwar.com/creigh/shtml.

"Place Names in West Virginia, 'B.'" http://www.wvculture.org/history/placnamb. html.

"Rafael Semmes." http://www.newadvent.org/cathen/13712b.htm.

"Rose Hill Cemetery, Samuel and Eleanora Semmes." http://www.rootsweb.com/~ mdallegh/Cemetery/semmes.htm.

Published Sources

Abbott, Haviland Harris. "General John D. Imboden." *West Virginia History* 21 (6 January 1960): 88–122.

Alexander, Archibald. *Brief Compendium of Biblical Truth*. Philadelphia: Presbyterian Board of Publications, 1846.

American Diplomatic and Public Papers: The United States and China, Series II: *The United States, China, and Imperial Rivalries, 1861–1893*. Edited by Jule Davids. Wilmington, DE: Scholarly Resources, 1979.

The Art of Good Behavior; and Letter Writer on Love, Courtship, and Marriage: A Complete Guide for Ladies and Gentlemen, Particularly Those Who Have Not Enjoyed the Advantages of Fashionable Life. New York: C. P. Huestis, 1846.

Ash, Stephen V. *When the Yankees Came: Conflict and Chaos in the Occupied South, 1861–1865*. Chapel Hill: University of North Carolina Press, 1995.

Austin, J. P. *The Blue and the Gray; Sketches of a Portion of the Unwritten History of the Great American Civil War*. Atlanta: Franklin Printing, 1899.

Averell, William Woods. *Ten Years in the Saddle: The Memoir of William Woods Averell*. Edited by Edward K. Eckert and Nicholas J. Amato. San Raphael: Presidio Press, 1978.

Bardiglio, Peter W. "On the Border: White Children and the Politics of War in Maryland." In *The War Was You and Me: Civilians in the American Civil War*. Edited by Joan E. Cashin. Princeton: Princeton University Press, 2002.

Barnes, Kenneth C. "The Williams Clan's Civil War: How an Arkansas Farm Family became a Guerrilla Band." In *Enemies of the Country: New Perspectives on Unionists in the Civil War South*. Edited by John C. Inscoe and Robert C. Kenzer. Athens: University of Georgia Press, 2001.

Benjamin, J. W. "Gray Forces Defeated in Battle of Lewisburg." *West Virginia History* 20 (October 1959): 24–35.

Bennett, Frank M. *The Steam Navy of the United States; A History of the Growth of the Steam Vessel of War in the U.S. Navy and of the Naval Engineer Corps*. Pittsburgh: W. T. Nicholson, 1896.

Bennett, Terry. *Korea Caught in Time*. Reading, UK: Garnet, 2009.

Beringer, Richard E. "Identity and the Will to Fight." In *On the Road to Total War:*

Bibliography

The American Civil War and the German Wars of Unification, 1861–1871. Edited by Stig Förster and Jörg Nagler, 75–100. Washington, D.C.: German Historical Institute and Cambridge: Cambridge University Press, 1997.

Biographical Directory of the American Congress, 1774–1961. Washington, D.C.: United States Government Printing Office, 1961.

Blair, William. *Virginia's Private War.* New York: Oxford University Press, 1998.

Boatner, Mark M. *The Civil War Dictionary.* New York: McKay, 1959.

Boney, F. N. *John Letcher of Virginia: The Story of Virginia's Civil War Governor.* Tuscaloosa: University of Alabama Press, 1966.

Borrow, George Henry. *The Zincali; or an Account of the Gypsies of Spain.* London: John Murray, 1841.

Boyer, Samuel P. *Naval Surgeon: Revolt in Japan 1868–1869, the Diary of Samuel Pellman Boyer.* Edited by Elinor Barnes and James A. Barnes. Bloomington: University of Indiana Press, 1963.

Brodie, Bernard. *Sea Power in the Machine Age.* Princeton: Princeton University Press, 1943. Reprint, New York: Greenwood, 1969.

Brown, Genevieve. "A History of the 6th Regiment, West Virginia Vols." *West Virginia History* 9 (July 1948): 315–368.

Browne, J. Ross. *Etchings of a Whaling Cruise.* New York: Harper, 1846.

Buck, Samuel D. *With the Old Confeds: Actual Experiences of a Captain of the Line.* Baltimore: H. E. Houck, 1925.

Burg, B. R. *An American Seafarer in the Age of Sail: The Erotic Diaries of Philip C. Van Buskirk.* New Haven: Yale University Press, 1994.

_____. "Behind the Lines in the West: The Civil War Diary of a Confederate Deserter, 1861–1865." *Lincoln Herald* 103 (Winter 2001): 194–203.

_____. "Dissenter's Diary: Philip C. Van Buskirk, the US Navy, and the Han River Massacre of 1871." *International Journal of Maritime History* 12 (December 2000): 53–67.

_____. "Information on Everyday Life from Historical Documents." In *Refereed Papers from the 1st International Small Islands Cultures Conference.* Edited by Mike Evans. Sidney, AU: Small Island Cultures Research Initiative, 2005.

_____. "Nocturnal Emission and Masturbatory Frequency Relationships: A Nineteenth-Century Account." *The Journal of Sex Research* 24 (1988): 216–220.

_____. "Officers, Gentlemen, 'Man Talk,' and Group Sex in the 'Old Navy,' 1870–1873." *Journal of the History of Sexuality* 11 (July 2002): 439–456.

Callahan, Edward W. *List of Officers of the Navy and of the United States Marine Corps from 1775 to 1890.* New York: L. R. Hamersly, 1901. Reprint, New York: Haskell House, 1969.

Callan, J. F., and A. W. Russell, comps. *Laws of the United States Relating to the Navy and Marine Corps from the Formation of the Government to 1859.* Baltimore: J. Murphy, 1859.

Canney, Donald L. *Frigates, Sloops, and Gunboats, 1815–1865.* Vol. 1, *The Old Steam Navy.* Annapolis: United States Naval Institute Press, 1990.

Chang, Gordon H. "Whose 'Barbarism'? Whose 'Treachery'? Race and Civilization in the Unknown United States-Korean War of 1871." *Journal of American History* 89 (March 2003): 1331–1365.

Chapelle, Howard I. *The American Sailing Navy: The Ships and their Development.* New York, Bonanza, 1949.

Bibliography

Childers, William. "A Virginian's Dilemma: The Civil War Diary of Isaac Noyes Smith." *West Virginia History* 27 (April 1965): 173–200.

Cholmondeley, Lionel B. *A History of the Bonin Islands from the Year 1827 to the Year 1876 and of Nathaniel Savory, One of the Original Settlers to Which Is Added a Short Supplement Dealing with the Islands After Their Occupation by the Japanese.* London: Constable, 1915.

A Civilian. [Jones, George]. *Sketches of Naval Life, with Notices of Men, Manners, and Scenery on the Shores of the Mediterranean in a Series of Letters from the* Brandywine *and* Constitution *Frigates.* 2 vols. New Haven: Hezekiah Howe, 1829.

Cohen, Stan. "Col. George S. Patton and the 22nd Infantry Regiment." *West Virginia History* 26 (April 1965): 178–190.

Collins, R. M. *Chapters from the Unwritten History of the War Between the States.* St. Louis: Nixon-Jones, 1893.

Colton, Jesse Sellers, ed. *The Civil War Journal and Correspondence of Matthias B. Colton.* Philadelphia: Macrae-Smith, 1931.

Colton, Walter. *Deck and Port, or Incidents of a Cruise in the Frigate* Congress *to California.* New York: A. S. Barnes, 1850.

Cook, Roy Bird. *Lewis County in the Civil War.* Charleston: Jarret, 1924.

[Corbin, Henry?]. "Diary of a Virginian Cavalryman, 1863–4." *The Historical Magazine* 2 (October 1873): 210–215.

Cowles, John P. Jr., on board *Colorado,* Boisée Bay, Korea, to Frederick F. Low, on board *Colorado,* Isle Boisée, Korea, June 2, 1871. In *American Diplomatic and Public Papers: The United States and China,* Series II, *The United States, China, and Imperial Rivalries, 1861–1893.* Edited by Jule Davids. Wilmington: Scholarly Resources, 1979.

[Craik, George Lillie]. *Pursuit of Knowledge Under Difficulties: Illustrated by Anecdotes.* London: C. Knight, 1830.

Cranston, Earl. "Shanghai in the Taiping Period." *Pacific Historical Review* 5 (May 1936): 147–160.

Cresswell, Stephen, ed. "Civil War Diary from French Creek: Selections from the Diary of Sirene Bunten." *West Virginia History* 48 (1989): 131–141.

"Criminal Charge." *San Francisco Examiner,* March 29, 1896.

Current, Richard N. *Lincoln's Loyalists: Union Soldiers from the Confederacy.* Boston: Northeastern University Press, 1992.

Curry, Richard Orr, and Gerald F. Ham, "The Bushwhacker's War: Insurgency and Counter-insurgency in West Virginia." *Civil War History* 10 (December 1964): 416–433.

_____. *A House Divided: A Study of Statehood, Politics, and the Copperhead Movement in West Virginia.* Pittsburgh: University of Pittsburgh Press, 1964.

Daley, John M. *Georgetown University: Origin and Early Years.* Washington, D.C.: Georgetown University Press, 1957.

"Damages for Arrest." *San Francisco Examiner,* March 12, 1897.

Dayton, Ruth Woods, ed. *The Diary of a Confederate Soldier, James E. Hall.* S. l.: privately printed, 1961.

"Death of Ex-Treasurer Polk." *New York Times,* March 1, 1884.

Deslandes, Leopold. *Manhood: The Causes of Its Premature Decline with Directions for Its Perfect Restoration.* Trans. by "A Physician." Boston: Otis, Broaders, 1842.

Devlin, John S. *The Case of Lieutenant Devlin.* S. l.: s n., 1842.

Bibliography

_____. ed. *The Marine Corps in Mexico; Setting Forth Its Conduct as Established by Testimony Before a General Court Martial Convened at Brooklyn, N.Y. September, 1852; for the Trial of First Lieut. John S. Devlin of the U.S. Marine Corps.* Washington, D.C.: Lemuel Towers, 1852.

DeWees, Daniel S. *Reflections of a Lifetime.* Eden: s.n., 1904.

"Domestic Intelligence." *Harper's Weekly*, January 9, 1864.

Drieude, E. S. *Lorenzo: or the Empire of Religion. By a Scotch Non-Conformist, A Convert to the Catholic Faith.* Baltimore: J. Murphy, 1844.

Duncan, Richard R. *Lee's Endangered Left: The Civil War in Western Virginia, Spring of 1864.* Baton Rouge: Louisiana State University Press, 1998.

DuPont, H. A. *The Campaign of 1864 in the Valley of Virginia and the Expedition to Lynchburg.* New York: National Americana Society, 1925.

Durkin, Joseph T. *Georgetown University: The Middle Years (1840–1900).* Washington, D.C.: Georgetown University Press, 1963.

Dyer, Jonathan Will. *Four Years in the Confederate Army: A History of the Experiences of the Private Soldier in Camp, Hospital, Prison, on the March, and on the Battlefield, 1861–1865.* Evansville: Amelia W. Dyer, 1898.

Egan, Michael. *The Flying Gray-haired Yank: Or, the Adventures of a Volunteer, a Personal Narrative of Thrilling Experiences as an Army Courier, a Volunteer Captain, a Prisoner of War, a Fugitive from Southern Dungeons, a Guest Among the Contrabands and Unionists ... A True Narrative of the Civil War.* Philadelphia: Hubbard Brothers, 1888.

Fellman, Michael. "At the Nihilist Edge: Reflections on Guerrilla Warfare During the American Civil War." In *On the Road to Total War: The American Civil War and the German Wars of Unification, 1861–1871.* Edited by Stig Förster and Jörg Nagler. Washington, D.C.: German Historical Institute and Cambridge: Cambridge University Press, 1977.

_____. "Inside Wars: The Cultural Crisis of Warfare and the Values of Ordinary People." In *Guerrillas, Unionists, and Violence on the Confederate Homefront.* Edited by Daniel Sutherland. Fayetteville: University of Arkansas Press, 1999. 519–540.

_____. *Inside War: The Guerrilla Conflict in Missouri During the American Civil War.* New York: Oxford University Press, 1989.

Fleming, L. D. *Self-Pollution: The Cause of Youthful Decay Showing the Dangers and Remedy of Venereal Excesses.* New York: Wellman, 1846.

A Fore-top-man. [Mercier, Henry J.]. *Life in a Man-of-War, or Scenes in* Old Ironsides *During Her Cruise in the Pacific.* Philadelphia: L. R. Bailey, 1841. Reprint, Boston: Houghton Mifflin, 1927.

Förster, Stig and Jörg Nagler, eds. *On the Road to Total War: The American Civil War and the German Wars of Unification, 1861–1871.* Washington, D.C.: German Historical Institute and Cambridge: Cambridge University Press, 1997.

Gallagher, Gary W. *The Confederate War.* Cambridge: Harvard University Press, 1997.

"General Kelley." *Harper's Weekly*, November 16, 1861.

Gould, John Mead. *History of the First- Tenth- Twenty-ninth Maine Regiment.* Portland, ME: Berry, 1871.

Harper's Weekly. November 16, 1861, 732, January 9, 1864, 19.

Harris, Joel Chandler. *On the Plantation: A Story of a Georgia Boy's Adventures During*

Bibliography

the War. New York: Appleton, 1892. Reprint Athens: University of Georgia Press, 1980.

Hassler, Frederick W. B. "The Military View of Passing Events, from Inside the Confederacy, No II. The Campaign in West Virginia, 1861 and 1862." *Historical Magazine* (December 1869): 355–358.

Hatch, Jane M., ed. *The American Book of Days*. New York: W. W. Wilson, 1978.

[Henshaw, J. S.]. *Around the World: A Narrative of a Voyage in the East India Squadron Under Commodore George C. Read*. 2 vols. New York: Charles S. Francis, 1840.

History of Pocahontas County, West Virginia, 1981, Birthplace of Rivers. Marlinton: Pocahontas County Historical Society, 1982.

Howe, Barbara J. "The Civil War at Bullhorn." *West Virginia History* 44 (October 1982): 1–40.

Husley, Val. "'Men of Virginia — Men of Kanawha — To Arms!' A History of the 22nd Virginia Volunteer Infantry Regiment." *West Virginia History* 35 (1973): 220–236.

"Ida Lewis, the Newport Heroine." *Harper's Weekly*, July 31, 1869.

Johnson, Ludwell H. *Red River Campaign: Politics and Cotton in the Civil War*. Baltimore: Johns Hopkins University Press, 1958.

Johnson, Robert E. *Far China Station: The U.S. Navy in Asian Waters*. Annapolis: United States Naval Institute Press, 1979.

_____. *Rear Admiral John Rodgers, 1812–1892*. Annapolis: United States Naval Institute Press, 1967.

Jones, Virgil Carrington. *Gray Ghosts and Rebel Raiders*. New York: Holt, 1956.

Karsten, Peter. *The Naval Aristocracy: The Golden Age of Annapolis and the Emergence of Modern American Navalism*. New York: Free Press, 1972.

King, John H. *Three Hundred Days in a Yankee Prison: Reminiscence of War Life, Captivity, Imprisonment at Camp Chase, Ohio*. Atlanta: J. A. Davis, 1904. Reprint, Kennesaw: Continental Book Co., 1959.

Klement, Frank. "General John B. Floyd and the West Virginia Campaigns of 1861." *West Virginia History* 7 (April 1947): 319–333.

Knauss, William H. "The Story of Camp Chase." *The Ohio Magazine* 1 (September 1906): 233–240.

Lamers, William M. *The Edge of Glory: A Biography of General William S. Rosecrans, U.S.A.* New York: Harcourt, 1961.

La'mert, Samuel. *Self-Preservation: A Medical Treatise on Nervous and Physical Disability, Spermatorrhoea, Impotence, and Sterility*. London: Samuel La'mert, 1847.

Lang, Theodore F. *Loyal West Virginia from 1861–1865*. Baltimore: Deutsche, 1895. Reprint, Huntington: Blue Acorn, 1998.

Langley, Harold D. *Social Reform in the United States Navy, 1798–1862*. Urbana: University of Illinois Press, 1976.

Lieb, Charles. *Nine Months in the Quartermaster Department*. Cincinnati: Moore, Wilsatch, Keys, 1862.

Linger, James Carter. *Confederate Military Units of West Virginia*. Tulsa: James Carter Linger, 1989.

Logan, Indiana W., ed. *Kelion Franklin Peddicord of Quirk's Scouts*. New York: Neale, 1908.

Long, David F. *Gold Braid and Foreign Relations: Diplomatic Activities of U.S. Naval Officers, 1798–1883*. Annapolis: United States Naval Institute Press, 1988.

Bibliography

Lonn, Ella. *Desertion During the Civil War.* New York: Appleton, 1928. Reprint, Gloucester, MA: Peter Smith, 1966.
_____. *Salt as a Factor in the Confederacy.* New York: Walter Neale, 1933.
Low, Frederick F., on board *Colorado,* Boisée Bay, Korea, to Secretary of State Hamilton Fish, Washington, D.C., June 2, 1871. In *American Diplomatic and Public Papers: The United States and China,* Series II: *The United States, China, and Imperial Rivalries, 1861–1893.* Edited by Jule Davids. Wilmington: Scholarly Resources, 1979, 121.
Lowry, Terry. *22nd Virginia Infantry,* 2nd ed. Lynchburg: H. E. Howard, 1988.
Mackey, Robert. "Bushwackers, Provosts, and Tories: The Guerrilla War in Arkansas." In *Guerrillas, Unionists, and Violence on the Confederate Homefront.* Edited by Daniel Sutherland. Fayetteville: University of Arkansas Press, 1999. 187–199.
Mann, Horace. *A Few Thoughts for a Young Man: A Lecture Delivered Before the Boston Mercantile Library Assn. On Its Twenty-ninth Anniversary.* Boston: Ticknor, Reed and Fields, 1850.
Massey, Mary Elizabeth. *Refugee Life in the Confederacy.* Baton Rouge: Louisiana State University Press, 1964.
McClellan, George B. *Report on the Organization and Campaigns of the Army of the Potomac: To Which Is Added an Account of the Campaign in Western Virginia.* New York: Sheldon, 1864.
McKinney, Tim. *The Civil War in Fayette County, West Virginia.* Charleston: Pictoral Histories Publishing, 1988.
_____. *The Civil War in Greenbrier County, West Virginia.* Charleston: Quarrier, 2004.
_____. *West Virginia Civil War Almanac.* Vol. 1. Charleston: Quarrier Press, 1998. Vol. 2. Charleston: Quarrier Press, 2000.
Merck's Manual of the Materia Medica: Together with a Summary of Therapeutic Indications and a Classification of Medicaments. New York: Merck, 1899.
Mettam, Henry C. "Civil War Memoirs of the First Maryland Cavalry, C. S. A." *Maryland Historical Magazine* 58 (June 1963): 137–169.
Moore, George E., ed. "A Confederate Journal." *West Virginia History* 22 (July 1961): 201–216.
Morison, Samuel E. *"Old Bruin," Commodore Matthew C. Perry, 1794–1858.* Boston: Little, Brown, 1967.
Morton, John Watson. *The Artillery of Nathan Bedford Forrest's Cavalry.* Nashville: Methodist Episcopal Church, 1909.
Narrative of the French Expedition to Korea in 1866, the U.S. Expedition in 1871, and the Expedition of the H.M.S. Ringdove in 1871. Shanghai: reprinted from the *North-China Herald,* 1871.
New American Cyclopedia: A Popular Dictionary of General Knowledge. Edited by George Ripley and Charles A. Dana. New York: Appleton, 1857–1866.
Noe, Kenneth W. "'Exterminating Savages': The Union Army and Mountain Guerillas in Southern West Virginia, 1861–1862." In *The Civil War in Appalachia: Collected Essays.* Edited by Kenneth W. Noe and Shannon H. Wilson. Knoxville: University of Tennessee Press, 1997.
_____. "Who Were the Bushwackers? Age, Class, Kin, and Western Virginia's Confederate Guerrillas, 1861–1862." *Civil War History* 49 (March 2003): 38–72.
Norton, Chauncy S. *The Red Neckties, or History of the Fifteenth New York Volunteer Cavalry.* Ithaca: Journal Book and Job Printing House, 1891.

Bibliography

Pancoast, S[eth]. *Boyhood's Perils and Manhood's Curse: A Handbook for the Mother, Son and Daughter*. Philadelphia: s.n., ca. 1860. Reprint, Philadelphia: Potter, 1873.

Parker, William H. *Recollections of a Naval Officer, 1841–1865*. New York: Scribner's, 1883.

Patterson, Edmund DeWitt. *Yankee Rebel*. Edited by John G. Barrett. Chapel Hill: University of North Carolina Press, 1966.

Paulsen, George E. "Under the Starry Banner on Muddy Flat Shanghai: 1854." *American Neptune* 30 (July 1970): 155–166.

"Polk Still a Fugitive." *New York Times*, January 7, 1883.

Register of Alumni Historical Reference, Classes of 1846–1919. Annapolis: United States Naval Academy Alumni Association, Inc., 1999.

Reid, Brian, and John White. "A Mob of Stragglers and Cowards: Desertion from the Union and Confederate Armies, 1861–1865." *Journal of Strategic Studies* 8 (March 1985): 64–77.

Richerand, A[nthelme Balthasar]. *Elements of Physiology*. Translated by G. J. M. De Lys. Philadelphia: Thomas Dobson, 1818.

Riggs, David F. *13th Virginia Infantry*, 2d ed. Lynchburg: H. E. Howard, 1988.

Rodd, Thomas. *Elegant Literature. Part IV of a Catalogue of a Collection of Books: Consisting of Language, Poetry, Romances, Novels, Facetae, Prose, Miscellanies, Poligraphy, Philology, Literary History, and Bibliography*. London: Thomas Rodd, 1845.

Rogers, John. "General Order by Admiral Rogers, U.S. Flag Ship the *Colorado*, Boisée Anchorage, Korea." In *Narrative of the French Expedition to Korea in 1866, the U.S. Expedition in 1871, and the Expedition of the H.M.S.* Ringdove *in 1871*. Shanghai: reprinted from the *North-China Herald*, 1871, 17–18.

_____. "General Order by Admiral Rogers, U.S. Flag Ship the *Colorado*, Boisée Anchorage, Korea." *New York Times*, August 22, 1871.

Rosenman, Ellen Bayuk. "Body Doubles: The Spermatorrhea Panic." *Journal of the History of Sexuality* 12 (July 2003): 365–399.

Scott, Robert G. *Into the Wilderness with the Army of the Potomac*. Bloomington: Indiana University Press, 1985.

Sellstedt, Lars G. *From Forecastle to Academy*. Buffalo: Matthews Northrop, 1904.

Shaffer, John W. *Clash of Loyalties: A Border County in the Civil War*. Morgantown: University of West Virginia Press, 2003.

Showell, Margaret Letcher. "Ex-governor Letcher's Home." *Southern Historical Society Papers* 18 (1890): 393–397.

Silverstone, Paul H. *Warships of the Civil War Navies*. Annapolis: United States Naval Institute Press, 1989.

Skallerup, Harry K. *Books Afloat and Ashore: A History of Books, Libraries, and Reading Among Seamen During the Age of Sail*. Hamden: Shoe String Press, 1974.

Slease, William Davis. *The Fourteenth Pennsylvania Cavalry in the Civil War*. Pittsburgh: Art Engraving and Printing, 1915.

Smith, Edward C. *The Borderland in the Civil War*. New York: Macmillan, 1937.

Smith, G. Wayne. "Nathan Goff, Jr. in the Civil War." *West Virginia History* 14 (January 1953): 108–135.

Soley, James Russell. *The Blockade and the Cruisers*. New York: Scribner's, 1883.

Stephens, Elizabeth. "Pathologizing Leaky Male Bodies: Spermatorrhea in Nineteenth-

Bibliography

Century British Medicine and Popular Anatomical Museums." *Journal of the History of Sexuality* 17 (September 2008): 421–438.

Stillé, Alfred. *Elements of General Pathology*. Philadelphia: Lindsey and Blakiston, 1848.

Stutler, Boyd B. "The Civil War in West Virginia." *West Virginia History* 22 (January 1961): 76–82.

_____. *West Virginia in the Civil War*. Charleston: Educational Foundation, Inc., 1966.

Summers, Festus P. "The Jones-Imboden Raid." *West Virginia History* 1 (October 1939): 15–29.

_____, ed. *A Borderland Confederate*. Pittsburgh: University of Pittsburgh Press, 1962.

Tompkins, Ellen Wilkins, ed. "The Colonel's Lady: Some Letters of Ellen Wilkins Tompkins, July-December 1861." *The Virginia Magazine of History and Biography*, 69 (October 1961): 387–419.

Tucker, Spencer C. *Brigadier General John D. Imboden: Confederate Commander in the Shenandoah*. Lexington: University Press of Kentucky, 2002.

Walker, Alexander. *Intermarriage, or the Natural Laws by Which Beauty, Health and Intellect Result from Certain Unions, and Deformity, Disease and Insanity from Others*. London: John Constable, 1841.

Weitz, Mark A. *More Damning than Slaughter: Desertion in the Confederate Army*. Lincoln: University of Nebraska Press, 2005.

Werner, Emmy E. *Reluctant Witnesses: Childrens' Voices from the Civil War*. Boulder: Westview, 1998.

West, Richard S. *The Second Admiral: A Life of David Dixon Porter, 1813–1891*. New York: Coward McCann, 1937.

Williams, S. Wells. *Easy Lessons in Chinese, or Progressive Exercises to Facilitate the Study of That Language Especially Adapted to the Study of the Cantonese Dialect*. Macao: Chinese Repository, 1842.

Wood, George A. *The Seventh Regiment: A Record*. New York: James Miller, 1865.

Young, William. *Pocket Aesculapius, or Every One His Own Physician: Being Observations on Marriage, Medically and Philosophically Considered, as Manhood's Early Decline, with Directions for Its Perfect Cure, Etc*. 156th ed. Philadelphia: s.n., 1848.

"A Young Woman's Woe." *San Francisco Examiner*, January 4, 1896.

Index

Index

Brothels 155*n*28
Brown, Anne 106
Brown, Betsy 106
Brown, Fanny 106
Brown, Gen. W.C. 105
Browning, Mr. 106
Browning family 99, 158*n*61
Buchanan, Pres. James 27
Buck, Samuel D. 148*n*65
"Bug-hunters" (WV home guard company) 83
Bull Run, Battle of *see* Battles
Bulltown, Battle of *see* Battles
Bulltown, WV 83, 157*n*48
Bungers Mills 66, 72, 75, 77, 155*n*30, 156*n*40
Bushwackers 40, 77, 156*n*40, 157*n*44, 157*n*48, 150*n*80

Cairo, IL 50, 150*n*75
Caldwell, Dr. 79–80
Callahan's Station, WV 54
Camden, AR 156*n*35
Camp Burnside *see* Camp Georgia
Camp Chase, OH 36, 37, 38, 40, 49, 50, 58, 80, 148*n*68, 149*n*75, 149*n*68, 150*n*75
Camp Curtin, PA 147*n*62
Camp Georgia, NC 147–148*n*62
Camp Jesse, VA 36
Camp Union, MD 147*n*62
Camp Walker, VA 35, 49
Canton, China 23, 128
Capron, Smith 57
Carter (former Price family slave) 68
Cathcart, Sgt. 118
Cedar Creek, Battle of *see* Battles
Centerville, VA 49, 152*n*1
Charles Town (Charlestown), Jefferson Co., WV 1, 5, 11, 60, 87, 101, 107, 112
"Chaw for Chaw" *see* Masturbation
Cherry Tree River (WV) 81
Chesapeake and Ohio Canal Co. 151*n*82
Chilton, Gen. R.H. 153*n*29
Chipley, Capt. John 52
Chipley, Capt. Tom 52
Clark, Adjutant General E.W. 68, 71, 72
Clarksburg, WV 79, 80, 82, 84, 87, 98, 110
Coffee, Mrs. Mary 88
Coffee, Matt 88
Coffee, Patrick 89
Cold Knob Mountain, WV 81

Coleman, George 15
Collins, Lt. R.M. 148*n*68
USS *Colorado see* Ships
Comfort for soldiers 147–148*n*62, 148*n*68, 149*n*68
Comstock, Dr. L.L. 69, 71, 76, 77, 78, 156*n*38
USS *Constitution see* Ships
Cordell, Dr. (father of George) 60
Cordell, George 60
Cotwine, Maj. R.M. 36, 148*n*67
Cowles, John P., Jr. 132
Crabtree Bridge 102
Craik, George *see Pursuit of Knowledge Under Difficulties*
Cranberry Summit, WV 92
Crawford, Mr. (Navy blacksmith) 121–122
Creigh, David 75, 79, 86, 156*n*40
Crook, Gen. George 67, 75, 76, 155*n*35
USS *Cumberland see* Ships
Cumberland, MD 5, 9, 44, 85, 86, 87, 88, 90, 92, 97, 98, 99, 100
Cumberland Union (newspaper) 95–96, 158*n*54

Dagenhart, William 13–14
Darr, Maj. Joseph 58, 87, 149*n*72, 154*n*22
Davis, Gen. A.W.G. 50, 55, 56, 57, 59, 61, 152*n*4, 155*n*17
Davis, Clinton 125, 126, 127
Davis, Col. James Lucius 50
Davis, Pres. Jefferson 87
Davis, Lewis Jefferson 50
Davis, Lochlin 55
Davis, Lt. 56
Davis, Capt. Runnels 55, 154*n*17
Davis family 80
Davis's sawmill 39, 94, 96
Depot Hotel (Oakland, MD) 95
Desertion, Army of Northern Virginia 151*n*86
Deslandes, Leopold *see Manhood: The Causes of Its Premature Decline with Directions for Its Perfect Restoration*
Devlin, Lt. John S. 26
DeWill, Mrs. 94
Dietz family 135*n*11
Dixon, John 106
Dodrill, Mr. 82
Doran, Purser Edward C. 21
Downey, Col. Stephen W. 97

Index

Index

Index

Index

Index

West, Richard 101
West Point *see* United States Military
  Academy
Westernport, MD 100, 108
Weston, WV 83–84, 98, 157n48
Wheeling, WV 36, 37, 49, 58
White, Mr. 97
White Sulphur Springs, WV 75, 76
White Sulphur Springs, Battle of *see*
  Battles
Wilderness, Battle of *see* Battles
Wilkinson, Capt. 84, 85
Williams, Eugene Judge 131, 160n16
Williams, Frank *see* Thomas, Frank
Williams, Lemuel 161n16
Williams, Lt. 115
Williams, S. Wells 158n58
Williams, Sarah O'Donald 160n16
Willis, C.H. 69, 71

Wills Creek Bridge 87
Wills Creek, MD 88
Wilson, Mrs. 98
Winchester, WV 107
Woodrum, J.J. 71, 74
Wunderlich, Mrs. 116
USS *Wyandank see* Ships

Yahrling, Lt. C.F.A. 84, 85, 157n50
Young, William *see* *Pocket Aesculapius, or
  Every One His Own Physician: Being
  Observations on Marriage, Medically
  and Philosophically Considered, as Man-
  hood's Early Decline, with Directions for
  Its Perfect Cure, Etc.*

*The Zincali; or an Account of the Gypsies of
  Spain* (George Henry Borrow) 137